## Section 5 — Home and Environment

## Section 6 — Education and Work

## Section 7 — Grammar

Published by CGP

Contributors:
Angela Billington
Esther Bond
Polly Cotterill
Charley Darbishire
Chris Dennett
Paul Jordin
Andy Park
Katherine Stewart
Claire Thompson
Hayley Thompson
Jennifer Underwood
Tim Wakeling
James Paul Wallis
Karen Wells

With thanks to Janice Eadington, Glenn Rogers,
Janet Sheldon and Markus Wagner for the proofreading.

This book was produced with stereotypical Teutonic efficiency.

ISBN: 978 1 84762 294 5

Groovy website: www.cgpbooks.co.uk
Jolly bits of clipart from CorelDRAW®
Printed by Elanders Ltd, Newcastle upon Tyne.

Based on the classic CGP style created by Richard Parsons.

# Numbers and Amounts

No two ways about it, you've got to know the numbers — so get cracking.

## Eins, zwei, drei — One, two, three...

| | |
|---|---|
| 0 | null |
| 1 | eins |
| 2 | zwei |
| 3 | drei |
| 4 | vier |
| 5 | fünf |
| 6 | sechs |
| 7 | sieben |
| 8 | acht |
| 9 | neun |
| 10 | zehn |
| 11 | elf |
| 12 | zwölf |

**1** It all starts off easy enough. Learn zero to twelve — no probs. Watch out though — you might hear people on the phone say 'zwo' instead of 'zwei'.

| | |
|---|---|
| 13 | dreizehn |
| 14 | vierzehn |
| 15 | fünfzehn |
| 16 | sechzehn |
| 17 | siebzehn |
| 18 | achtzehn |
| 19 | neunzehn |

**2** You can work out the teens using numbers one to ten — for example thirteen is just 'three' and 'ten' stuck together (drei+zehn). BUT 16 and 17 are different — they lose the '-s' and '-en' from the ends of 'sechs' and 'sieben'.

| | | | |
|---|---|---|---|
| 20 | zwanzig | 60 | sechzig |
| 30 | dreißig | 70 | siebzig |
| 40 | vierzig | 80 | achtzig |
| 50 | fünfzig | 90 | neunzig |

**3** After dreißig all the ten-type numbers are easy.

| | | | | | |
|---|---|---|---|---|---|
| 21 | einundzwanzig | 24 | vierundzwanzig | 27 | siebenundzwanzig |
| 22 | zweiundzwanzig | 25 | fünfundzwanzig | 28 | achtundzwanzig |
| 23 | dreiundzwanzig | 26 | sechsundzwanzig | 29 | neunundzwanzig |

| | |
|---|---|
| 100 | hundert |
| 1000 | tausend |
| 1,000,000 | eine Million |

**4** The in-between numbers are the tricky ones. For these you say the numbers backwards. Say 'two and thirty' instead of 'thirty-two'.

**zweiunddreißig** = Thirty-two

**5** When you get to hundreds and thousands it's simple again — thousands come before hundreds, and hundreds before the rest of the numbers.

**tausendfünfhundertzweiunddreißig**

1000    500    32    = 1532

## Erste, zweite, dritte — First, second, third...

| | | | |
|---|---|---|---|
| 1st | das erste | | |
| 2nd | das zweite | 8th | das achte |
| 3rd | das dritte | 9th | das neunte |
| 4th | das vierte | 10th | das zehnte |
| 5th | das fünfte | 20th | das zwanzigste |
| 6th | das sechste | 21st | das einundzwanzigste |
| 7th | das siebte | 100th | das hundertste |

In German, '1st' is written '1.'.

*Sometimes the endings change, see pages 84-85 for help.*

1) For numbers between 1 and 19, add '-te' to the number in German. The four exceptions are in purple.
2) From 20 onwards, just add '-ste' to the German number.

*The article won't always be 'das', e.g.*

**Nehmen Sie die erste Straße links.**

= Take the first street on the left.

## Wie viel? — How much?

Little words for 'how many' or 'how much' are really vital. There are a lot of them to learn down there, but don't skimp — write each one out in different sentences and make sure you don't miss any.

**Ich habe beide Äpfel.** = I have both apples.

| | | | |
|---|---|---|---|
| all: | alle | some: | manche |
| other: | andere | several: | mehrere |
| one and a half: | anderthalb | many: | viele |
| no: | keine | few: | wenige |

**Jeden Tag fahre ich Rad.**

= I go cycling every day.

*See page 92 for more on 'jeder'.*

**Ich weiß nichts darüber.**

= I know nothing about it.

*lots: viel    little: wenig*

## It's as easy as 1, 2, 3...

You might already know great chunks of this — that's great. Then you can spend more time checking that you know the rest of the page. Make sure you know all of those words about amounts. The best way to check is to cover up the page, and then try to write them down.

# Times and Dates

Knowing how to say the time is <u>vital</u> — examiners love it.

## Wie viel Uhr ist es? — What time is it?

There are loads of ways of saying the time in German — just like English.
You need to learn 'em all of course.

| Wie viel Uhr ist es? | ← | = What time is it? | → | Wie spät ist es? |

1) Something o'clock:

| It's 1 o'clock: | (Es ist) ein Uhr | ← ein Uhr, not eine Uhr. |
| It's two o'clock: | (Es ist) zwei Uhr |
| It's 8pm: | (Es ist) zwanzig Uhr |

Be <u>careful</u> with 'halb':
'<u>halb drei</u>' means 'half <u>to</u>
three' (i.e. <u>half past two</u>)
not half past three.

2) Quarter to and past, half past:

| quarter past two: | <u>Viertel nach</u> zwei |
| half past two: | <u>halb</u> drei |
| quarter to three: | <u>Viertel vor</u> drei |

3) '... past' and '... to':

| twenty past seven: | <u>zwanzig nach</u> sieben |
| twelve minutes past eight: | <u>zwölf nach</u> acht |
| ten to two: | <u>zehn vor</u> zwei |

Wie viel Uhr
ist es?

4) The <u>24-hour clock</u>:
They use it a lot in Germany
— and it's easier too.

| 03.14: | drei Uhr vierzehn |
| 20.32: | zwanzig Uhr zweiunddreißig |
| 19.55: | neunzehn Uhr fünfundfünfzig |

## Die Woche — The week

This is '<u>must-learn</u>' stuff — it'll gain you simple marks in your assessments.

Hmm... did I put
my 'Montag'
underpants on?

**DAYS OF THE WEEK**

| Monday: | Montag |
| Tuesday: | Dienstag |
| Wednesday: | Mittwoch |
| Thursday: | Donnerstag |
| Friday: | Freitag |
| Saturday: | Samstag/Sonnabend |
| Sunday: | Sonntag |

Days of the week are all <u>masculine</u>.
If you want to say '<u>on Monday</u>', it's
either '<u>Montag</u>' or '<u>am Montag</u>' —
but <u>not</u> 'an Montag'.

**SOME USEFUL WORDS ABOUT THE WEEK**

| today: | heute |
| tomorrow: | morgen |
| yesterday: | gestern |
| the day after tomorrow: | übermorgen |
| the day before yesterday: | vorgestern |
| week: | die Woche (-n) |
| weekend: | das Wochenende (-n) |
| on Mondays: | montags |

**Dienstags** gehe ich einkaufen.

= I go shopping on <u>Tuesdays</u> (every Tuesday).

**Dienstag** fahre ich weg.

= I'm going away
on <u>Tuesday</u>.

Remember, plurals are always 'die'.

## Wie viel Uhr ist es, Herr Wolf?

Time is <u>ultra-important</u>. In the mark schemes they specifically mention being able to say
<u>when</u> you do things — and you can't do that if you don't know how to say the <u>days of the</u>
<u>week</u> and things like '<u>tomorrow</u>' or '<u>weekend</u>'. So what are you waiting for... <u>Learn it</u>.

# Times and Dates

You're <u>bound</u> to get asked about something to do with dates. When you're going on holiday, when Billy went to the concert... that sort of thing. It's practically <u>guaranteed</u>.

## Januar, Februar, März, April...

German month names are blummin' similar to the English — make sure you learn what's different.

| | | | |
|---|---|---|---|
| January: | Januar | July: | Juli |
| February: | Februar | August: | August |
| March: | März | September: | September |
| April: | April | October: | Oktober |
| May: | Mai | November: | November |
| June: | Juni | December: | Dezember |

*Er fährt* Juli / im Juli *weg.*

= He's going away <u>in July</u>.

1 Like the days, the months are masculine. Say '<u>Januar</u>' or '<u>im Januar</u>', <u>not</u> 'in Januar'.

| season: | die Jahreszeit (-en) |
|---|---|
| spring: | Frühling |
| summer: | Sommer |
| autumn: | Herbst |
| winter: | Winter |

2 The seasons are masculine too.

## Im Jahre zweitausendelf — In the year 2011

See pages 10-11 for letters.

Write the date out like this for an informal letter... ...and like this for a formal letter.

*den 5. März* = 5th March

*den 12.11.2011* = 12th November, 2011

Here's how to <u>say</u> the date — it's a bit different because you have to pronounce all the numbers.

In German you <u>NEVER</u> say 'In 2011...' like we do in English, you say:

*Im Jahre* zweitausendelf *...* = In the year <u>2011</u>.

The special endings are because this is the <u>dative</u> case, <u>see page 85</u>.

*Ich komme am zwanzigsten Oktober.* = I am coming on the 20th of October.

Like in English, the year is '<u>neunzehnhundert...</u>' rather than '<u>tausendneunhundert...</u>'.

*Ich bin wurde am dritten März neunzehnhundertfünfundneunzig geboren.* = I was born on the 3rd of March 1995.

## Morgen — Tomorrow... Gestern — Yesterday

Use these with the <u>stuff</u> on the <u>page 2</u> — together they're <u>great</u> for sorting out your social life.

| | |
|---|---|
| tomorrow: | morgen |
| yesterday: | gestern |
| this morning: | heute Morgen |
| this afternoon: | heute Nachmittag |
| tonight: | heute Nacht |
| tomorrow morning: | morgen früh |
| this week: | diese Woche |
| next week: | nächste Woche |
| last week: | letzte Woche |
| every two weeks: | alle zwei Wochen |
| every day: | jeden Tag |
| at the weekend: | am Wochenende |
| recently: | neulich |

*Was machst du* heute Abend *?*

= What are you doing <u>this evening</u>?

i.e. <u>not</u> 'morgen Morgen' even though the word for tomorrow is 'morgen' as well.

| always: | immer |
|---|---|
| never: | nie |
| often: | oft, häufig |
| sometimes: | manchmal |

*Ich fahre* selten *Ski.* = I <u>seldom</u> go skiing.

# Dates — better at the cinema than in German...

This stuff is absolutely <u>crucial</u>. It's got to be worth making the effort to learn it — it'll get you loads more marks. And as an added bonus, it's not that hard. Hurrah. Make sure you learn all that <u>heute Abend / morgen früh</u> business too, cos it might well come in handy somewhere.

4

# Asking Questions

You've got to be able to understand questions. You might have to ask them too.

## Wann — when... warum — why... wo — where

| | |
|---|---|
| when?: | wann? |
| why?: | warum? |
| why?: | wieso? |
| where?: | wo? |
| where (to)?: | wohin? |
| where (from)?: | woher? |
| how?: | wie? |
| how much?: | wie viel? |
| how many?: | wie viele? |
| who/whom?: | wer/wen/wem? |
| what?: | was? |
| which (one)?: | welche/r/s? |

It's really important that you learn these question words.

**Wann** kommst du wieder nach Hause?

= **When** are you coming back home?

See page 98 for when to use wer/wen/wem and page 92 for more about 'welche'.

**Wie viele** Karotten möchten Sie?

= **How many** carrots would you like?

## Reverse word order to ask a question

In English you change 'I can go' to 'Can I go?' to make it into a question — you can in German too.

subject — verb

**Ich kann** mitkommen.  = I can come along.

Put the verb first and then the verb's subject to show it's a question:

**Kann ich** mitkommen?  = Can I come along?

Don't forget to stick a question mark on the end.

verb — subject

**Kommt dein Bruder** auch?  = Is your brother coming too?

## Learn how to say 'isn't it?'

The most common words used for this are 'nicht (wahr)?', 'ja?' and 'oder?'. Just stick them on the end of a statement with a comma first and bung a question mark on the end — lovely.

Gut, **nicht** ?  = Good, isn't it?

Du warst auch da, **oder** ?  = You were there too, weren't you?

Es ging gut, **ja** ?  = It went well, did it?

## Add 'wo' to a word to mean 'what'

See pages 95-96 for more prepositions.

Instead of saying 'mit was' or 'auf was' or anything else using a preposition and 'was' (what), you can make a handy little word to do the whole thing. Add 'wo(r)' to the preposition and use that.

| | |
|---|---|
| *What* are you writing *with*?: | Womit schreibst du? |
| What ... on?: | Worauf ... ? |
| What ... about?: | Worüber ... ? |
| What ... for?: | Wozu ... ? |

If the preposition starts with a vowel you need to add an 'r' between it and the 'wo'.

## Word order — I'll have 2 six-letter words please...

The secret to most of GCSE German is to learn a phrase, and learn the words you can change in it, and what you can change them to. Once you know how to ask 'How many carrots would you like?', it doesn't take much more to be able to ask 'How many apples would you like?'...

# Being Polite

This stuff is <u>dead important</u> — without it you'll lose marks and sound rude — 'nuff said.

## Wie geht's? — How are you?

You've <u>absolutely</u> got to know these phrases. You need to be able to <u>say</u> them, and to <u>understand</u> them. It's utterly crucial — so make sure you know these <u>inside out</u>.

> 'Wie geht es (dir)?' is often shortened to 'Wie geht's?'.

| | |
|---|---|
| *How are you?:* | Wie geht es dir? |
| *How are you? (formal):* | Wie geht es Ihnen? |
| *How are you? (informal plural):* | Wie geht es euch? |

These two aren't used as much — but they could still pop up in an exam:

| | |
|---|---|
| *Nice to meet you:* | Schön, Sie/dich kennen zu lernen |
| *I'm pleased to meet you:* | Es freut mich, Sie/dich kennen zu lernen |

Remember: Sie = formal, dich = informal

## Bitte — Please... Danke — Thank you

Easy stuff — probably the first German words you ever learnt. When someone says '<u>danke</u>' it is polite to say '<u>bitte</u>' or '<u>bitte schön</u>'.

| | | | |
|---|---|---|---|
| *please:* | bitte | *you're welcome:* | bitte schön/bitte sehr |
| *thank you:* | danke/danke schön | *it was nothing:* | nichts zu danken |

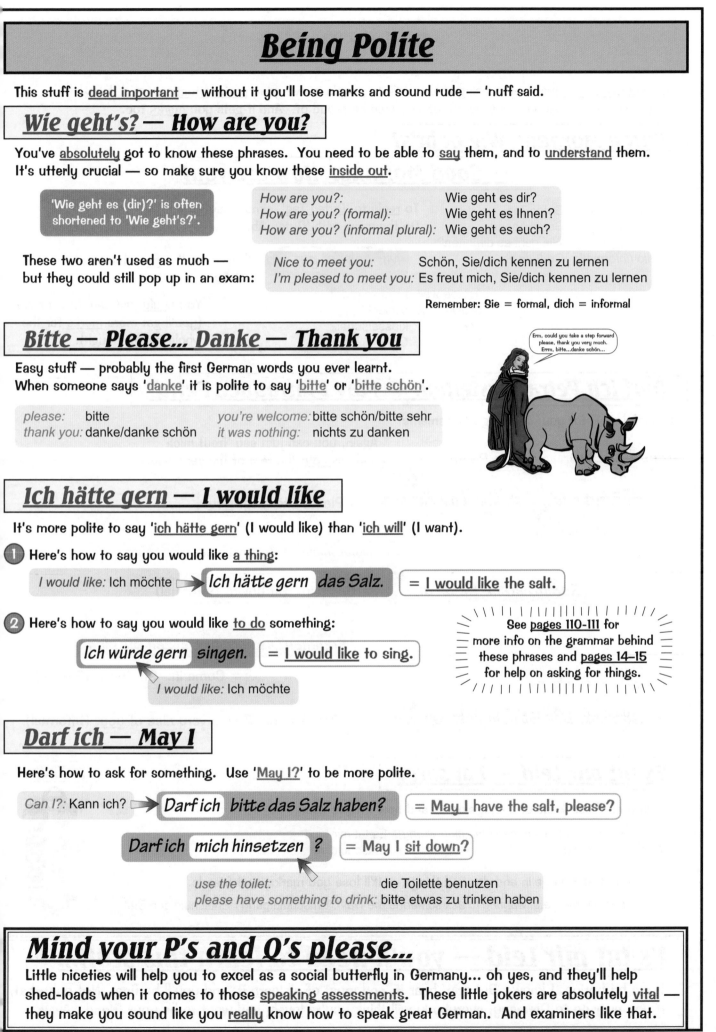

> Erm, could you take a step forward please, thank you very much. Erm, bitte...danke schön...

## Ich hätte gern — I would like

It's more polite to say '<u>ich hätte gern</u>' (I would like) than '<u>ich will</u>' (I want).

1 Here's how to say you would like <u>a thing</u>:

*I would like:* Ich möchte ➤ **Ich hätte gern** das Salz. = <u>I would like</u> the salt.

2 Here's how to say you would like <u>to do</u> something:

**Ich würde gern** singen. = <u>I would like</u> to sing.

*I would like:* Ich möchte

See <u>pages 110-111</u> for more info on the grammar behind these phrases and <u>pages 14–15</u> for help on asking for things.

## Darf ich — May I

Here's how to ask for something. Use '<u>May I?</u>' to be more polite.

*Can I?:* Kann ich? ➤ **Darf ich** bitte das Salz haben? = <u>May I</u> have the salt, please?

**Darf ich** mich hinsetzen ? = May I <u>sit down</u>?

| | |
|---|---|
| *use the toilet:* | die Toilette benutzen |
| *please have something to drink:* | bitte etwas zu trinken haben |

## Mind your P's and Q's please...

Little niceties will help you to excel as a social butterfly in Germany... oh yes, and they'll help shed-loads when it comes to those <u>speaking assessments</u>. These little jokers are absolutely <u>vital</u> — they make you sound like you <u>really</u> know how to speak great German. And examiners like that.

# Being Polite

Polite conversation just means being able to talk to people in everyday social situations, and doing it properly and politely in a way your mother would be proud of.  And it gets you marks too.

## Guten Morgen!  Wie geht's?
## — Good Morning!  How are you?

Good day / hello: Guten Tag
Good evening: Guten Abend
How are you?: Wie geht es dir/Ihnen?
Hello (informal): Grüß dich!

To reply to 'Guten Tag', simply say 'Guten Tag' back.
Do the same with 'Guten Abend'.

*Mir geht's gut, danke.*  = I'm fine thanks.

not too well: nicht so gut
badly/I'm ill: schlecht
great: klasse/super
OK: OK

You could just say 'Gut, danke' (you'll get more marks for the whole thing, though).

## Darf ich Petra vorstellen? — May I introduce Petra?

All useful stuff for your speaking assessments.

*Dies ist Petra.*  = This is Petra.

Again, you can just say 'freut mich' and miss out the rest of the sentence.

*Es freut mich, dich kennen zu lernen.*  = Pleased to meet you.

you (formal): Sie

you (plural, informal): Kommt herein.  Setzt euch.

*Komm herein.  Setz dich.*  = Come in.  Sit down. (Informal)

*Kommen Sie herein.  Setzen Sie sich.*  = Come in.  Sit down. (Formal)

you (singular & plural formal): Ihnen
you (plural, informal): euch

*Vielen Dank.  Das ist sehr nett von dir.*  = Thank you.  That is very nice of you. (Informal)

## Es tut mir Leid — I'm sorry

Learn both these ways of apologising — and how they're used.

I'm sorry (when you've done something wrong): Es tut mir Leid
Sorry! (to a friend): Entschuldige!

Don't just barge in and demand things — it'll lose you marks, and friends.

Excuse me! (e.g. wanting to ask someone the way): Entschuldigung / Entschuldigen Sie!

Entschuldigung! Erm... do you come here often?

## Es tut mir Leid — you'll need to learn this stuff...

It's a bit boring, I know.  But grin, bear it, and most of all learn it, and you'll be fine.  Not only that, if you ever go to Germany, everybody will think you're lovely and want to be your friend.  Aww.

# Opinions

To get a decent mark, you need to be able to say what you think about things.  So get <u>learning</u> this little lot...

## Magst du...? — Do you like...?

| Magst du | diese Band | ? | | = Do you like <u>this band</u>? |

This needs to be in the <u>accusative</u> case, see the grammar section <u>page 84</u>.

*this film:*         diesen Film
*this newspaper:*  diese Zeitung
*this book:*        dieses Buch

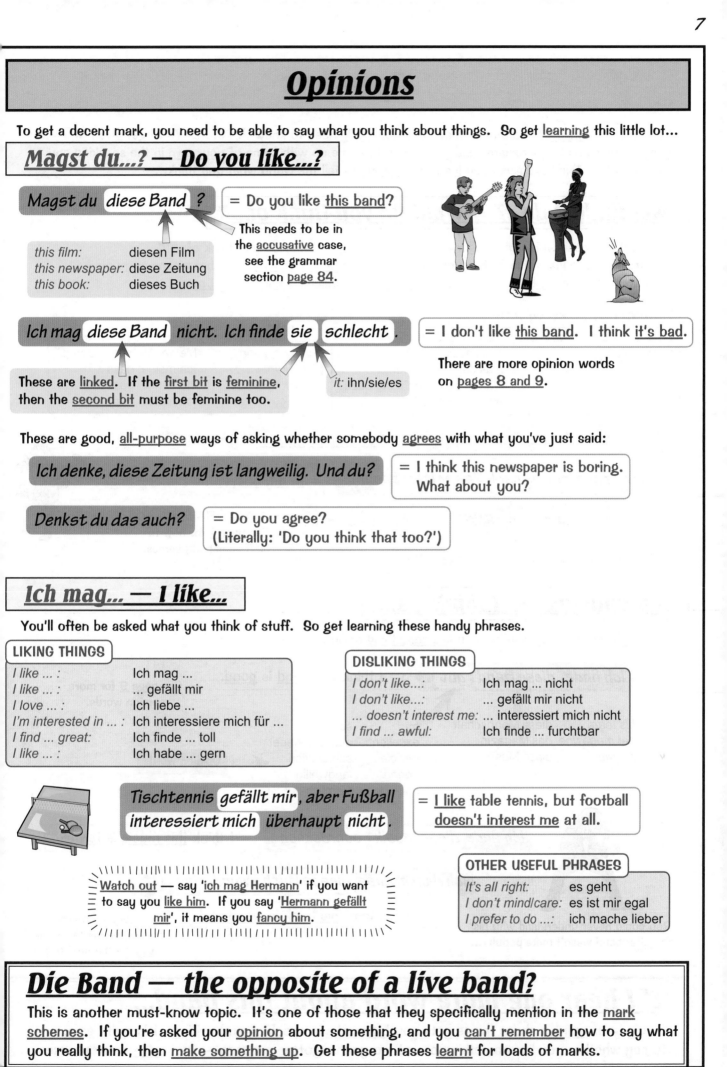

| Ich mag | diese Band | nicht. Ich finde | sie | schlecht | . | | = I don't like <u>this band</u>.  I think <u>it's bad</u>.

These are <u>linked</u>.  If the <u>first bit</u> is <u>feminine</u>, then the <u>second bit</u> must be feminine too.

*it:* ihn/sie/es

There are more opinion words on <u>pages 8 and 9</u>.

These are good, <u>all-purpose</u> ways of asking whether somebody <u>agrees</u> with what you've just said:

| Ich denke, diese Zeitung ist langweilig. Und du? | | = I think this newspaper is boring. What about you? |

| Denkst du das auch? | | = Do you agree? (Literally: 'Do you think that too?') |

## Ich mag... — I like...

You'll often be asked what you think of stuff.  So get learning these handy phrases.

**LIKING THINGS**

| *I like ... :* | Ich mag ... |
| *I like ... :* | ... gefällt mir |
| *I love ... :* | Ich liebe ... |
| *I'm interested in ... :* | Ich interessiere mich für ... |
| *I find ... great:* | Ich finde ... toll |
| *I like ... :* | Ich habe ... gern |

**DISLIKING THINGS**

| *I don't like...:* | Ich mag ... nicht |
| *I don't like...:* | ... gefällt mir nicht |
| *... doesn't interest me:* | ... interessiert mich nicht |
| *I find ... awful:* | Ich finde ... furchtbar |

| Tischtennis gefällt mir, aber Fußball interessiert mich überhaupt nicht. | | = <u>I like</u> table tennis, but football <u>doesn't interest me</u> at all. |

**OTHER USEFUL PHRASES**

| *It's all right:* | es geht |
| *I don't mind/care:* | es ist mir egal |
| *I prefer to do ...:* | ich mache lieber |

<u>Watch out</u> — say '<u>ich mag Hermann</u>' if you want to say you <u>like him</u>.  If you say '<u>Hermann gefällt mir</u>', it means you <u>fancy him</u>.

## Die Band — the opposite of a live band?

This is another must-know topic.  It's one of those that they specifically mention in the <u>mark schemes</u>.  If you're asked your <u>opinion</u> about something, and you <u>can't remember</u> how to say what you really think, then <u>make something up</u>.  Get these phrases <u>learnt</u> for loads of marks.

# Opinions

Yep, still on <u>opinions</u> I'm afraid — that's cos you <u>really</u> need to know this stuff. You'll get given <u>other people's</u> opinions in your exams and you'll need to come up with some of <u>your own</u> in the speaking and writing tasks. This page gives you <u>loads more ways</u> to tell the world what you think...

## Wie findest du...? — What do you think of...?

<u>Look out</u> for these words, they <u>all</u> mean the <u>same thing</u> — 'what do you think of ...?'.
If you can use loads of these then your German will be <u>dead interesting</u> — that means <u>more marks</u> of course. But be <u>really careful</u> about '<u>ich meine</u>' — it means '<u>I think</u>', not '<u>I mean</u>'.

**FINDING OUT SOMEONE'S OPINION**

| | |
|---|---|
| *What do you think of... ?:* | Was hältst du von...? |
| *What do you think of...?:* | Wie findest du...? |
| *What do you think of...?:* | Was denkst du über...? |
| *What's your opinion of that?:* | Was ist deine Meinung dazu? |
| *What do you think?:* | Was meinst du? |

**I THINK...**

| | |
|---|---|
| *In my opinion ... :* | Meiner Meinung nach ... |
| *I think that ... :* | Ich meine, dass ... |
| *I think that ... :* | Ich denke, dass ... |
| *I think ... is ... :* | Ich halte ... für ... |

**Wie findest du** meinen Freund? = <u>What do you think of</u> my boyfriend?

**Meiner Meinung nach** ist er interessant. = <u>In my opinion</u> he's interesting.

**Ich halte** ihn **für** verrückt. = <u>I think</u> he's mad.

This is in the <u>accusative case</u> — see page 84.

See page 7 for how to ask if somebody agrees.

## Ich finde es... — I think it's...

You might have to say whether you <u>like something</u> or not.

**Ich finde** diese Band gut. = I think <u>this band</u> is <u>good</u>.

See page 9 for more opinion words.

| | |
|---|---|
| *this team:* | diese Mannschaft |
| *that magazine:* | das Magazin |
| *this music:* | diese Musik |

| | |
|---|---|
| *bad:* | schlecht |
| *excellent:* | ausgezeichnet |
| *terrible:* | schrecklich |
| *boring:* | langweilig |
| *quite good:* | ziemlich gut |

Opinion words

**Ich finde** diese Musik schrecklich. = I think <u>this music</u> is <u>terrible</u>.

**Ich denke, dass** dieses Buch wunderbar ist. = I think that <u>this book</u> is <u>wonderful</u>.

'<u>Dass</u>' sends the verb to the end of the sentence (like '<u>weil</u>' on the next page).

Rob could never understand why his air guitar band wasn't more popular...

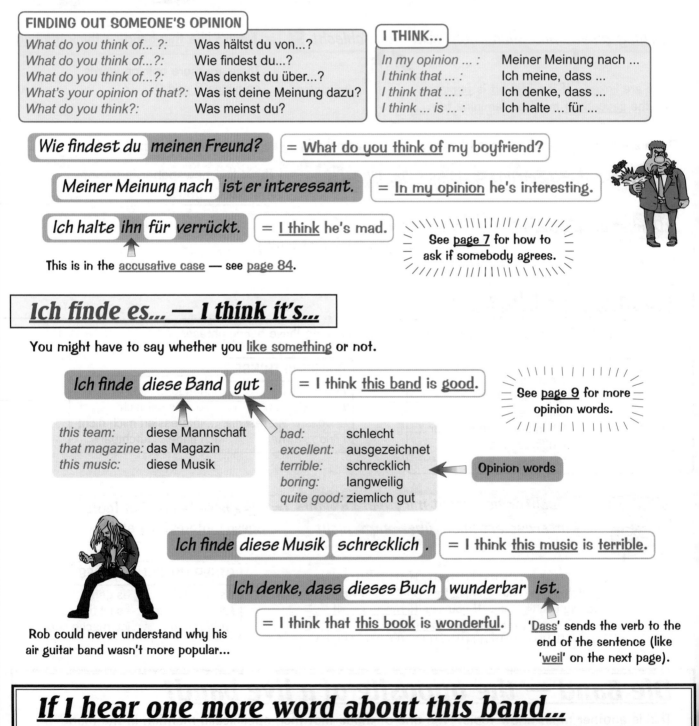

## If I hear one more word about this band...

Giving your <u>opinion</u> about things gets you <u>big marks</u> in speaking and writing. It's quite <u>easy</u> to say whether you like something or not, so you've got <u>no excuses</u> — just <u>learn</u> these phrases.

# Opinions

After you've <u>impressed</u> the examiners by saying you like or hate something, really <u>knock their socks off</u> by explaining <u>why</u>.

## Toll — Great... Furchtbar — Terrible

Here are some words you can use to <u>describe</u> things you <u>like</u> or <u>don't like</u>.
They're <u>really easy</u> to use, so it's worth <u>learning</u> them.

| | | | | | |
|---|---|---|---|---|---|
| *great:* | toll / prima<br>super / klasse | *excellent:* | ausgezeichnet | *not nice (person):* | unsympathisch |
| *good:* | gut | *fantastic:* | fantastisch | *bad:* | schlecht / schlimm |
| *lovely:* | schön | *fabulous:* | fabelhaft | *terrible:* | furchtbar / schlimm |
| *beautiful:* | wunderschön | *interesting:* | interessant | | fürchterlich |
| *friendly:* | freundlich | *nice (person):* | nett | *awful:* | mies |
| | | | sympathisch | *ugly:* | hässlich |

**Bob ist toll .** = <u>Bob</u> is <u>great</u>.

**Tennis ist furchtbar .** = <u>Tennis</u> is <u>terrible</u>.

## Weil — Because

'Weil' is <u>ultra-important</u> — it's the main German word for <u>because</u>.
When you use '<u>weil</u>' the <u>verb</u> in that part of the sentence gets shoved to the <u>end</u>.

Remember: a <u>verb</u> is a <u>doing</u> word.

This means that...

**Der Film gefällt mir. Er ist interessant.** = I like the film. It is interesting.

... becomes: *verb*

See <u>page 89</u> for other words like 'weil'.

**Der Film gefällt mir, weil er interessant ist.** = I like the film, because it is interesting.

**Ich finde sie sehr nett , weil sie freundlich ist.** = I think she's very <u>nice</u> because she is <u>friendly</u>.

There's always a comma before 'weil'.

**Ich mag ihn nicht, weil er langweilig ist.** = I don't like him because he is <u>boring</u>.

## Denn — Because

It's handy to know that '<u>denn</u>', like 'weil', means '<u>because</u>'.
'Denn' is <u>dead useful</u>, cos it <u>doesn't</u> change the word order.

Don't confuse '<u>denn</u>' with '<u>dann</u>', which means '<u>then</u>'.

**Ich mag ihn nicht, <u>denn er ist</u> langweilig.** = I don't like him because he is boring.

## Deutsch ist toll/fabelhaft/furchtbar...*

It's no good only knowing how to ask someone else's opinion, or how to say 'I think', without being able to say <u>what</u> you think. All these phrases are great, because you can just <u>stick them together</u> to get a sentence. Just make sure you don't say something <u>daft</u> like 'I like it because it's boring'.

* Delete as appropriate

# Writing Informal Letters

You might have to <u>write a letter</u> in German at some point.
So <u>learn</u> how to lay out a letter and how to say Dear Bill, and all the stuff like that.

## Lieber Hermann — Dear Hermann

You've got to be able to <u>start</u> and <u>end</u> a letter properly.
OK, this one's a bit short, but it shows you how to start and end it, and where to put the <u>date</u>.

Put where you live and the date up here. Check out <u>page 3</u> on dates.

This means Dear Hermann. If you're writing to a woman, you'd put <u>Liebe</u> instead of <u>Lieber</u>.

You <u>don't</u> need a capital letter here.

Many greetings.

If you're female, you put <u>deine</u> instead of <u>dein</u>.

This means: 'Many thanks for your letter.'

These two are really great phrases to use in letters.

This means: 'I was so pleased to hear from you again.'

Millom, den 5. März

Lieber Hermann,

vielen Dank für deinen Brief.
Ich habe mich so gefreut,
mal wieder von dir zu hören.

Viele Grüße,

dein Albert

"Lieber Hermann,
willkommen in Dumpsville..."

## Use these phrases in your letters

One thing that you can use for just about <u>every</u> informal letter is asking how the person is:

*Wie geht's?*   = How are you?

You can use this one to start a letter, just after Dear whoever.

And here are a couple of things that are good to put <u>just before</u> you <u>sign off</u>:

*Ich freue mich schon darauf, dich wieder zu sehen.*   = I'm already looking forward to seeing you again.

*Ich hoffe, bald wieder von dir zu hören.*   = I hope to hear from you again soon.

## German letters — keep them Brief...

This is pretty <u>easy</u> stuff, but it could well help with your writing assessment. Make sure you can use the German <u>stock phrases</u> — then your letter will sound <u>authentic</u>. There <u>aren't</u> any secrets to the <u>main part</u> of the letter — just stick to what you know and it'll all be tickety-boo.

# Writing Formal Letters

It might not be fair, but they expect you to be able to write a <u>formal</u> letter as well.
Most often they want you to write to <u>book</u> a <u>hotel room</u>. For more hotel vocab see <u>page 47</u>.

## Put your name and address at the top

Put <u>your</u> name and address up here.

The <u>name and address</u> of who you're writing to goes here.

You <u>don't</u> need a capital letter here.

This lot means:
If possible I would like to reserve three rooms with you for the 4th - 18th June, inclusive. We need a double room and two single rooms. I would be very grateful if you could inform me as soon as possible whether we can have the rooms and how much they'll cost.

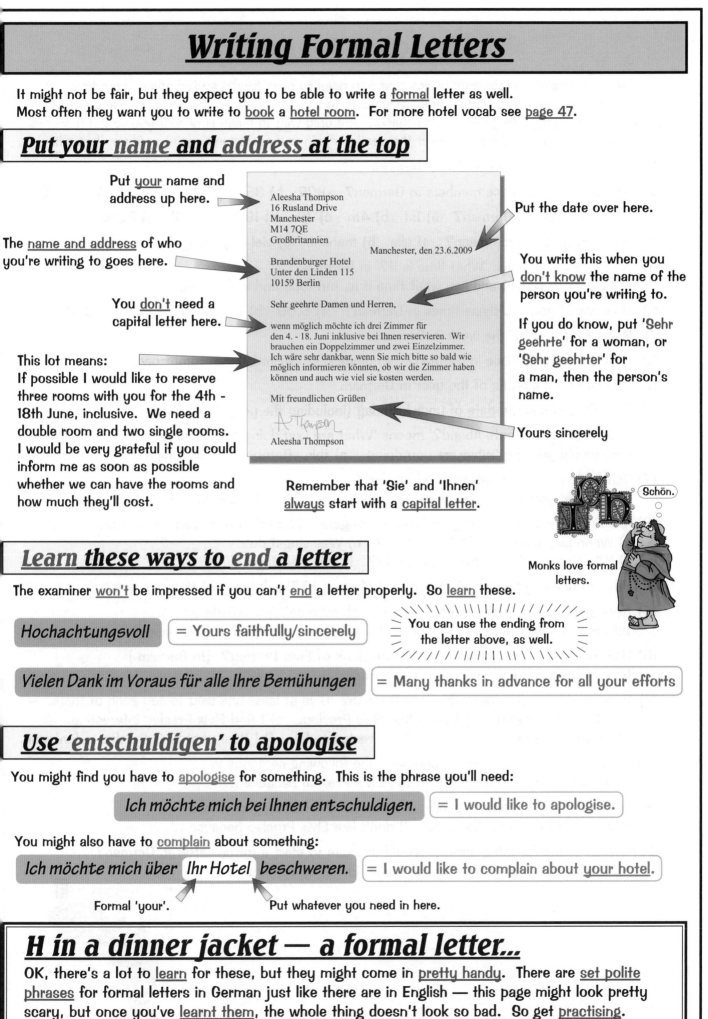

Aleesha Thompson
16 Rusland Drive
Manchester
M14 7QE
Großbritannien

Manchester, den 23.6.2009

Brandenburger Hotel
Unter den Linden 115
10159 Berlin

Sehr geehrte Damen und Herren,

wenn möglich möchte ich drei Zimmer für den 4. - 18. Juni inklusive bei Ihnen reservieren. Wir brauchen ein Doppelzimmer und zwei Einzelzimmer. Ich wäre sehr dankbar, wenn Sie mich bitte so bald wie möglich informieren könnten, ob wir die Zimmer haben können und auch wie viel sie kosten werden.

Mit freundlichen Grüßen

Aleesha Thompson

Put the date over here.

You write this when you <u>don't know</u> the name of the person you're writing to.

If you do know, put 'Sehr geehrte' for a woman, or 'Sehr geehrter' for a man, then the person's name.

Yours sincerely

Remember that 'Sie' and 'Ihnen' <u>always</u> start with a <u>capital letter</u>.

Monks love formal letters. (Schön.)

## Learn these ways to end a letter

The examiner <u>won't</u> be impressed if you can't <u>end</u> a letter properly. So <u>learn</u> these.

**Hochachtungsvoll** = Yours faithfully/sincerely

You can use the ending from the letter above, as well.

**Vielen Dank im Voraus für alle Ihre Bemühungen** = Many thanks in advance for all your efforts

## Use 'entschuldigen' to apologise

You might find you have to <u>apologise</u> for something. This is the phrase you'll need:

**Ich möchte mich bei Ihnen entschuldigen.** = I would like to apologise.

You might also have to <u>complain</u> about something:

**Ich möchte mich über Ihr Hotel beschweren.** = I would like to complain about <u>your hotel</u>.

Formal 'your'.    Put whatever you need in here.

## H in a dinner jacket — a formal letter...

OK, there's a lot to <u>learn</u> for these, but they might come in <u>pretty handy</u>. There are <u>set polite phrases</u> for formal letters in German just like there are in English — this page might look pretty scary, but once you've <u>learnt them</u>, the whole thing doesn't look so bad. So get <u>practising</u>.

# Revision Summary

This section contains the absolute basics that you need to have <u>totally sorted</u> come exam time. The stuff on your <u>opinions</u>, and on <u>times</u> (including today, tomorrow, every week, on Mondays etc.), can make a really <u>big difference</u> to your marks. The only way to make sure that you've got it sorted is to do <u>all</u> of these questions. Go over the section again and again (and again) until you know it.

1) Count out loud from 1 to 20 in German.

2) How do you say these numbers in German? a) 22  b) 35  c) 58  d) 71  e) 112  f) 2101

3) What are these in German?  a) 1st  b) 4th  c) 7th  d) 19th  e) 25th  f) 52nd

4) What do these words mean?  a) alle  b) manche  c) viel  d) wenig

5) Give two ways to ask 'What time is it?' in German.
   Look at your watch, and say what time it is, out loud and in German.

6) How would you say these times in German?  a) 5.00  b) 10.30  c) 13.22  d) 16.45

7) Say all the days of the week in German.

8) How do you say these in German?  a) yesterday  b) today  c) tomorrow

9) Say all of the months of the year in German.

10) How do you say the <u>date</u> of your birthday (including the <u>year</u>) in German?

11) 'Was machst du heute Abend?' means 'What are you doing this evening?'
    How would you say 'What are you doing  a) this afternoon?'  b) tonight?'  c) next week?'

12) 'Ich fahre selten Ski' means 'I seldom ski.'
    How would you say:  a) 'I never ski.'  b) 'I often ski.'  c) 'I sometimes ski.'

13) 'Du singst' means 'You sing' or 'You are singing'.  What do these questions mean?
    a) Wann singst du?  b) Wo singst du?  c) Was singst du?
    d) Wie singst du?  e) Warum singst du?  f) Wie viel singst du?

14) How do you say these in German?  a) Please  b) Thank you  c) How are you?

15) Here are some phrases: 'ich hätte gern', 'ich möchte', 'ich würde gern'.
    Which two could you use to say you'd like  a) some coffee?  b) to dance?

16) How would you ask someone what they think of Elvis Presley?  (In German.)
    Give as many ways of asking it as you can.

17) How would you say these things in German?  Give at least one way to say each of them.
    a) I like Elvis Presley.  b) I don't like Elvis Presley.  c) I find Elvis Presley interesting.
    d) I love Elvis Presley.  e) I find Elvis Presley awful.  f) I think that Elvis Presley is fantastic.

18) To win this week's star prize, complete the following sentence in
    10 words or less (in German):  'I like Elvis Presley because...'

19) To win last week's potato peelings, complete the following sentence
    in 10 words or less (in German):  'I don't like Elvis Presley because...'

20) Which of the following phrases would you use to start a <u>formal</u> letter in German?
    a) Sehr geehrter Herr Presley,  b) Lieber Elvis,  c) Yo Elvis.

You need 'General Stuff' to do well in the exam.

General 1. Stuff

Leave me alone.

# Food

The <u>more</u> of this lot you learn, the <u>better</u>.  Luckily, a lot of these are <u>similar</u> to the English words.

## Gemüsehändler und Metzger — Greengrocer and butcher

This is basic, <u>meat and two veg</u> vocab.  You really do need to know it.

Remember, plurals are always 'die'.

**VEGETABLES: DAS GEMÜSE**

| | |
|---|---|
| potato: | die Kartoffel (-n) |
| carrot: | die Möhre (-n), |
| | die Karotte (-n) |
| tomato: | die Tomate (-n) |
| cucumber: | die Gurke (-n) |
| onion: | die Zwiebel (-n) |
| cauliflower: | der Blumenkohl (-) |
| cabbage: | der Kohl (-e) |
| lettuce: | der Kopfsalat (-e) |
| pea: | die Erbse (-n) |

**FRUIT: DAS OBST**

| | |
|---|---|
| apple: | der Apfel (die Äpfel) |
| banana: | die Banane (-n) |
| strawberry: | die Erdbeere (-n) |
| lemon: | die Zitrone (-n) |
| orange: | die Orange (-n) |
| | die Apfelsine (-n) |
| raspberry: | die Himbeere (-n) |
| peach: | der Pfirsich (-e) |
| pear: | die Birne (-n) |

**MEAT: DAS FLEISCH**

| | |
|---|---|
| beef: | das Rindfleisch |
| pork: | das Schweinefleisch |
| chicken: | das Hähnchen |
| roast chicken: | das Brathähnchen |
| sausage: | die Wurst (die Würste) |
| lamb: | das Lamm(fleisch) |
| steak: | das Steak (-s) |

## Getränke und Süßigkeiten — Drinks and sweets

You'll need to know these — you can't describe a meal without mentioning <u>dessert</u> and a <u>drink</u>.

**SWEET THINGS: DIE SÜßIGKEITEN**

| | |
|---|---|
| cake: | der Kuchen (-) |
| biscuit: | der Keks (-e) |
| ice cream: | das Eis (-) |
| chocolate: | die Schokolade |
| sugar: | der Zucker |
| jam / marmalade: | die Marmelade |
| cream: | die Sahne |
| gateau: | die Torte (-n) |

**DRINKS: DIE GETRÄNKE**

| | |
|---|---|
| beer: | das Bier |
| red wine: | der Rotwein |
| white wine: | der Weißwein |
| tea: | der Tee |
| coffee: | der Kaffee |
| orange juice: | der Orangensaft |
| | / der Apfelsinensaft |
| apple juice: | der Apfelsaft |
| mineral water: | das Mineralwasser |

I'm on a seafood diet. I see food and I eat it.

Sergeant Stern, dodgy old joke squad. You're nicked, sunshine.

## Andere Lebensmittel — Other foods

You'll need to know <u>lots</u> of other foods too.  Learn <u>as many</u> of these as you can.

**OTHER FOODS: ANDERE LEBENSMITTEL**

| | |
|---|---|
| bread: | das Brot (-e) |
| bread roll: | das Brötchen (-) |
| milk: | die Milch |
| butter: | die Butter |
| cheese: | der Käse (-) |
| egg: | das Ei (-er) |
| salt: | das Salz |
| pepper: | der Pfeffer |
| rice: | der Reis |
| pasta (plural): | die Nudeln |
| yogurt: | der Joghurt (-s) |
| muesli: | das Müsli |

**GERMAN SPECIALITIES: DEUTSCHE SPEZIALITÄTEN**

| | |
|---|---|
| pickled cabbage: | das Sauerkraut |
| boiled sausage: | die Bockwurst (die Bockwürste) |
| fried sausage: | die Bratwurst (die Bratwürste) |
| sausage with curry sauce: | die Currywurst (die Currywürste) |
| veal slice fried in breadcrumbs: | das Schnitzel (-) |
| dumpling: | der Knödel (-n) |
| German noodles (plural): | die Spätzle |
| sweet fruit juice drink: | der Nektar |
| German Christmas cake: | die Stolle (-n) |

# What's Kuchen...

Phew — that's made me hungry.  Now, you might need to talk or write about <u>healthy and unhealthy</u> <u>foods</u> or say what your <u>favourite meal</u> is — so make sure you're properly prepared.  <u>Learn</u> these.

# Mealtimes

This page is full of stuff that you can use all the time — not just at mealtimes. Use it to say <u>what you like</u>, and to ask people <u>politely</u> for things. You've just <u>got</u> to know it.

## Ich mag... — I like...

These expressions <u>aren't</u> just for food — use them to talk about <u>anything</u> you <u>like</u> or <u>dislike</u>.

Ich mag **Äpfel** .  = I like <u>apples</u>.

bananas: *Bananen*   cream: *Sahne*

Ich mag **kein Gemüse** .  = I <u>don't</u> like <u>vegetables</u>.

apples: *keine Äpfel*   coffee: *keinen Kaffee*

Ich bin **Vegetarier(in)** .  = I'm a <u>vegetarian</u>.

vegan: *Veganer(in)*

<u>Remember:</u> Add the '<u>-in</u>' to the end of '<u>Vegetarier</u>' for women and girls.

## Ja bitte — Yes please

It doesn't come any <u>easier</u> than this.

**Ja bitte.**  = Yes please.

**Nein danke.**  = No thanks.

Important:
Always say 'Ja bitte',
not 'Ja danke'.

## Könnten Sie...? — Could you...?

Two <u>mega-important</u> phrases that you've got to <u>learn</u> and be able to use <u>properly</u>.

Könnten Sie mir bitte **den Pfeffer** reichen?

a napkin: eine Serviette
the sugar: den Zucker
the cream: die Sahne
the milk: die Milch

= Could you pass me <u>the pepper</u>, please?

Darf ich bitte **das Salz** haben?  = May I have <u>the salt</u>, please?

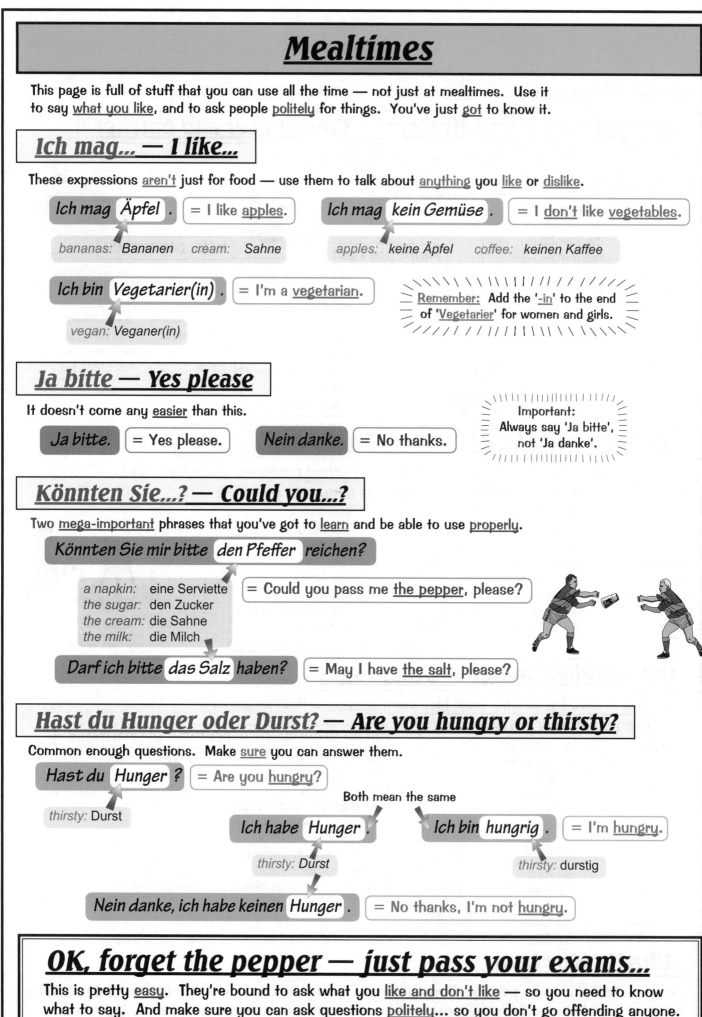

## Hast du Hunger oder Durst? — Are you hungry or thirsty?

Common enough questions. Make <u>sure</u> you can answer them.

Hast du **Hunger** ?  = Are you <u>hungry</u>?

thirsty: Durst

Both mean the same

Ich habe **Hunger** .

thirsty: Durst

Ich bin **hungrig** .  = I'm <u>hungry</u>.

thirsty: durstig

Nein danke, ich habe keinen **Hunger** .  = No thanks, I'm not <u>hungry</u>.

# OK, forget the pepper — just pass your exams...

This is pretty <u>easy</u>. They're bound to ask what you <u>like and don't like</u> — so you need to know what to say. And make sure you can ask questions <u>politely</u>... so you don't go offending anyone.

# Mealtimes

This is stuff you <u>should know</u> — especially if you want a <u>top grade</u>. Again, a lot of it could be used in <u>different</u> sorts of situations — <u>not just</u> in conversations at the dinner table.

## Hat das geschmeckt? — Did that taste good?

A fairly <u>common</u> question. Learn these answers and it won't cause you any <u>trouble</u>.

Das Essen hat **gut** geschmeckt. | = The food tasted <u>good</u>.

| | |
|---|---|
| *very good:* | sehr gut |
| *not especially good:* | nicht besonders gut |
| *bad:* | nicht |
| *very bad:* | gar nicht |

Das Frühstück war **lecker**, danke. | = Breakfast was <u>delicious</u>, thanks.

Hat das geschmeckt?

## Möchten Sie...? — Would you like...?

It's that word '<u>möchten</u>' again. These sentences are <u>dead important</u> — you can use them to make <u>different</u> sorts of offers, not just ones about <u>food</u>.

Möchten Sie **das Salz** haben? | = Would you like <u>the salt</u>?

This is <u>similar</u> to what's on the previous page — see <u>page 13</u> for more possible <u>vocab</u>.

| | |
|---|---|
| *the pepper:* | den Pfeffer |
| *the red wine:* | den Rotwein |
| *the butter:* | die Butter |

Kann ich Ihnen **eine Serviette** reichen? | = Can I pass you <u>a napkin</u>?

## Ein wenig... — A little...

These quantity words are dead <u>useful</u>. There'll be loads of times in your speaking and writing tasks that you can use them and bag yourself <u>more marks</u>.

Ich möchte **viel** Zucker, bitte. | = I would like <u>lots</u> of sugar, please.

*a bit:* ein bisschen/ein wenig

See <u>page 1</u> for more on quantities.

Ich möchte **ein großes Stück** Torte. | = I would like <u>a big piece</u> of cake.

Ich habe **genug** gegessen, danke. | = I've eaten <u>enough</u>, thanks.

Ich bin satt. | = I'm full.

# Ooh, I'd like a nice cuppa tea please...

These quantity words are really <u>handy</u> — learn them and you're cooking on gas. There are loads of ways you can use this stuff, so get cracking and make sure you know it <u>inside out</u>.

# Daily Routine

More useful stuff for if you're staying with someone.

## Wann isst du...? — When do you eat...?

Meals are important — so get learning these phrases.

**Wann | isst du | zu Abend ?** = When do you eat dinner?

See page 2 for more times.

do you eat (plural, informal): esst ihr
do you eat (formal): essen Sie

breakfast: das Frühstück
lunch: zu Mittag
tea (the meal): das Abendbrot

**Wir essen | um sieben Uhr | zu Abend .** = We eat dinner at seven o'clock in the evening.

## Musst du zu Hause helfen?
### — Do you have to help at home?

Even if you never help at home — learn these words.

**Ich wasche zu Hause ab.** = I wash up at home.

I tidy my room: Ich räume mein Zimmer auf.
I make my bed: Ich mache mein Bett.
I vacuum: Ich sauge Staub.
I clean: Ich putze.
I dust: Ich wische Staub.

**Ich muss | abwaschen .** = I have to wash up.

clean: putzen
dust: Staub wischen
tidy up: aufräumen
make my bed: mein Bett machen
empty the dishwasher: die Spülmaschine leeren

'Abwaschen' and 'aufräumen' are separable verbs.
If you don't know much about these, have a look at page 108.

## Brauchst du etwas? — Do you need anything?

These are easy phrases — so there's no excuse for not knowing them.
Remember to use the formal 'Sie' if you're asking someone older.

**Darf ich mich | duschen ?** = May I have a shower?

a bath: baden

**Kann ich bitte | etwas Zahnpasta | haben?** = Can I have some toothpaste please?

a towel: ein Handtuch
some soap: etwas Seife

Have you (informal): Hast du

**Haben Sie | Zahnpasta ?** = Have you any toothpaste?

## Essen — the ESSENtials of life...

You should have no problem learning the meals — but those separable verbs take a bit of getting used to. Learn one, and all the others follow the same pattern. It's almost as fun as washing up...

# About Yourself

You'll probably have to give all sorts of <u>personal details</u> about yourself in your speaking and writing tasks. You should <u>know</u> all this already, just make <u>sure</u> you <u>really</u> know it backwards.

## Erzähl mir etwas von dir... — Tell me about yourself...

You might need to answer these questions in your <u>speaking assessment</u>:

What are you called?: **Wie heißt du?**

Ich heiße George . = I'm called <u>George</u>.

How old are you?: **Wie alt bist du?**

Ich bin fünfzehn Jahre alt. = I'm <u>15</u> years old.

When is your birthday?: **Wann hast du Geburtstag?**

Ich habe am 12. Dezember Geburtstag. = My birthday is on the <u>12th of December</u>.

Where do you live?: **Wo wohnst du?**

Ich wohne in Lancaster . = I live in <u>Lancaster</u>.

What do you like?: **Was magst du?**

Ich mag Fußball . = I like <u>football</u>.

Use this to say you like or dislike any person or thing, e.g. I like you: ich mag dich.

See <u>pages 61-62</u> for where you live, <u>page 1</u> for more numbers and <u>page 3</u> for more dates.

## Wie siehst du aus? — What do you look like?

You might have to <u>describe</u> how gorgeous you are as well — shouldn't be too hard should it?

Ich bin groß . = I am <u>tall</u>.

| medium height: | mittelgroß |
| small: | klein |
| fat: | dick |
| thin: | dünn |
| slim: | schlank |

Ich habe braune Augen. = I have <u>brown</u> eyes.

blue: blaue
green: grüne

Ich trage eine Brille. = I wear <u>glasses</u>.

Ich habe lange Haare. = I have <u>long</u> hair.

| short: | kurze | straight: | glatte | dark: | dunkle | red: | rote |
| shoulder-length: | schulterlange | wavy: | wellige | light: | helle | brown: | braune |
| quite long: | ziemlich lange | curly: | lockige | blond: | blonde | black: | schwarze |

Ich habe einen Bart . = I have a <u>beard</u>.

moustache: Schnurrbart

OK — so <u>you</u> might not have a beard, but you might have to describe someone <u>who does</u>.

## Wie schreibt man das? — How do you spell that?

You may have to <u>spell</u> your name and home town letter by letter in your <u>speaking assessment</u> or <u>listen</u> to someone spell something in the listening exam.

Kannst du das buchstabieren? = Can you spell that?

Noooo!!!!
...er... I mean...
Nein!!!

That means you have to be able to <u>pronounce</u> the German alphabet.
Helpfully, the alphabet's all written out on the <u>inside front cover</u> for you.

## Appearances matter — to the exam board...

<u>Learn</u> how to <u>describe</u> how scrumptious you look — so you can do it without a second thought. You have to be able to <u>pronounce</u> the German <u>alphabet</u> as well — so get <u>practising</u>.

# Family and Pets

You might have to talk about <u>family</u> and <u>pets</u> in your speaking assessments or writing tasks.

## Ich habe eine Schwester — I have one sister

If you're talking about <u>more than one person</u>, use 'heißen', not 'heißt'.

Meine Mutter heißt Janet . = <u>My mother</u> <u>is called</u> <u>Janet</u>.

| | |
|---|---|
| *my father:* | mein Vater |
| *my brother:* | mein Bruder (meine Brüder) |
| *my sister:* | meine Schwester (-n) |
| *my stepmother:* | meine Stiefmutter |
| *my stepfather:* | mein Stiefvater |
| *my aunt:* | meine Tante (-n) |
| *my uncle:* | mein Onkel (-) |
| *my female cousin:* | meine Cousine (-n) |
| *my male cousin:* | mein Cousin (-s) |
| *my grandmother:* | meine Großmutter (meine Großmütter) |
| *my grandfather:* | mein Großvater (meine Großväter) |
| *my male friend:* | mein Freund (-e) |
| *my female friend:* | meine Freundin (-nen) |
| *my parents:* | meine Eltern |
| *my siblings:* | meine Geschwister |

Remember, it's 'meine' for plurals.

Ich habe einen Bruder . = I have <u>one brother</u>.

Ich bin ein Einzelkind. = I am <u>an only child</u>.

To <u>describe</u> your relatives, use these sentences:

Er ist zwölf Jahre alt. = He's <u>12</u> years old.

Er hat blaue Augen. = He has <u>blue</u> eyes.

Sie hat glatte Haare. = She has <u>straight</u> hair.

Sie ist groß . = She is <u>tall</u>.

You can stick the other words from <u>page 17</u> in the white boxes.

## Hast du Haustiere? — Have you any pets?

Ich habe einen Hund . = I have <u>a dog</u>.

| | |
|---|---|
| *a dog:* | einen Hund (-e) |
| *a cat:* | eine Katze (-n) |
| *a budgie:* | einen Wellensittich (-e) |
| *a guinea pig:* | ein Meerschweinchen (-) |
| *a rabbit:* | ein Kaninchen (-) |
| *a snake:* | eine Schlange (-n) |
| *a horse:* | ein Pferd (-e) |
| *a goldfish:* | einen Goldfisch (-e) |

Mein Hund heißt Rudi .

= My dog is called <u>Rudi</u>.

See <u>page 38</u> for colours and <u>page 17</u> for sizes and things like fat and thin.

Er ist gelb . = He is <u>yellow</u>.

Swap in <u>any</u> descriptive word here.

Who are you calling yellow?

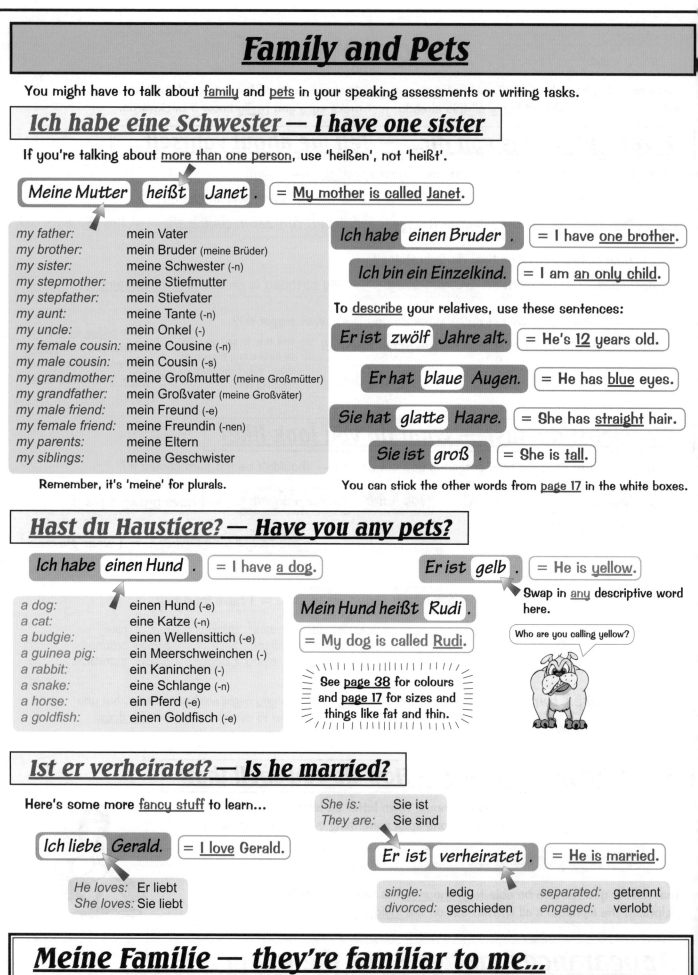

## Ist er verheiratet? — Is he married?

Here's some more <u>fancy stuff</u> to learn...

Ich liebe Gerald. = <u>I love</u> Gerald.

*He loves:* Er liebt
*She loves:* Sie liebt

*She is:* Sie ist
*They are:* Sie sind

Er ist verheiratet . = <u>He is</u> <u>married</u>.

| | | | |
|---|---|---|---|
| *single:* | ledig | *separated:* | getrennt |
| *divorced:* | geschieden | *engaged:* | verlobt |

## Meine Familie — they're familiar to me...

Most of this page is <u>basic stuff</u> you have to <u>know</u> — like how to say what <u>relations</u> you have (or don't have). If you don't <u>already</u> know it like the back of your hand — get <u>learning</u>.

# Personality

Personality, <u>character</u>, whatever you want to call it, I'm sure you've got bags of it.
It'd probably be <u>useful</u> if you could talk about it in <u>German</u> though...

## Meine Persönlichkeit — My personality

You might have to <u>describe your personality</u> in one of your speaking assessments — here's how...

Ich bin **fantastisch**.

= I am <u>fantastic</u>.

| | | | |
|---|---|---|---|
| *nice:* | sympathisch | *helpful:* | hilfsbereit |
| *intelligent:* | intelligent | *patient:* | geduldig |
| *funny:* | lustig | *busy:* | beschäftigt |
| *friendly:* | freundlich | *hard-working:* | fleißig |
| *sweet:* | goldig | *dynamic:* | dynamisch |
| *happy:* | glücklich | *responsible:* | verantwortlich |

*quite/fairly:* ziemlich
*very:* sehr

Ich bin **ein bisschen** **schüchtern**.

= I am <u>a bit</u> <u>shy</u>.

| | | | |
|---|---|---|---|
| *annoying:* | lästig | *boring:* | langweilig |
| *stupid:* | blöd / dumm | *serious:* | ernst |
| *disgusting:* | ekelhaft | *impolite:* | unhöflich |
| *moody:* | launisch | *impatient:* | ungeduldig |
| *noisy:* | laut | *untidy:* | unordentlich |
| *lazy:* | faul | *unfriendly:* | unfreundlich |

## Die Persönlichkeiten anderer Leute
## — Other people's personalities

So you know how to talk about <u>yourself</u>, here's how to talk about <u>other people</u>...

Mein kleiner Bruder ist sehr **lästig**. | = My little brother is very <u>annoying</u>.

Meine Schwester ist wirklich **sympathisch**, aber sie kann ein bisschen **ernst** sein.

= My sister is really <u>nice</u>, but she can be a bit <u>serious</u>.

You can put any of the personality traits above in these white boxes.

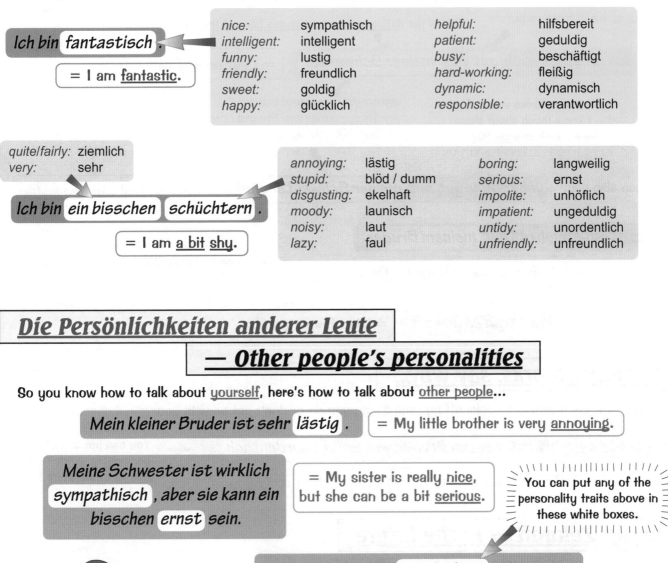

'Dad, can you lend me a tenner?'

'DAD! It's stuck up my nose!'

'Dad, I crashed the car...'

No matter what his kids threw at him, Colin was always happy. His secret was cotton wool...

Mein Vater ist oft **beschäftigt**, aber er ist auch sehr **lustig** und immer **glücklich**.

= My father is often <u>busy</u>, but he is also very <u>funny</u> and always <u>happy</u>.

## I'm intelligent, dynamic, responsible — and a born liar...

There's quite a bit of <u>vocab</u> on this page, but <u>learn it</u> and you're sure to impress those pesky examiners. Make sure you know how to <u>write</u> this stuff as well as <u>say</u> it — that's important.

20

# Relationships and Future Plans

OK, we're about to get all <u>deep and meaningful</u> here.
Tissues at the ready?  Let's plough on...

Rob didn't have much in common with his brother and sister.

## Wir verstehen uns gut — We get on well

Now's your chance to pour out all your <u>relationships woes</u> in German.

*not so well:*  nicht so gut

This is the <u>dative case</u> — see <u>pages 85 and 92</u> for more info.

**Ich verstehe mich gut mit meiner Schwester .** = I get on <u>well</u> with <u>my sister</u>.

This is a reflexive verb.  If you don't know much about these, take a look at <u>page 107</u>.

*my brother:* meinem Bruder
*my friend:* meinem Freund / meiner Freundin
*my parents:* meinen Eltern

You can also say:  **Ich komme gut mit meiner Schwester aus.** = I get on well with <u>my sister</u>.

**Ich streite mich oft mit meinem Bruder .**

= I often argue with <u>my brother</u>.

'Auskommen' is a separable verb. Take a look at <u>page 108</u> to find out more.

**Wir streiten uns oft.**  = We often argue.

## Get more marks, say why...

Really knock the examiner's socks off by saying <u>why</u> you do or don't get on with your <u>loved ones</u>...

**Ich streite mich oft mit meinem Bruder, weil er so unordentlich ist.**

= I often argue with my brother because he's so <u>untidy</u>.

You can put any of the personality words from <u>page 19</u> in the white box.

## In der Zukunft — In the future

You need to be able to say what your <u>relationship plans</u> for the <u>future</u> are in German.
If you don't have any yet, learn how to <u>say so</u>.

There's more about future plans on <u>page 75</u>.

**Ich möchte heiraten .**  = I would like to <u>get married</u>.

*to get engaged:*  mich verloben
*to have a family:*  eine Familie haben
*to be in a relationship:*  in einem Verhältnis sein

**Im Moment, weiß ich nicht.**

= At the moment, I don't know.

## We're just one big happy family...

OK, so this page might involve you <u>thinking</u> a bit, but once you've learnt a few <u>key phrases</u> you should be just fine.  You know what I'm going to say: <u>look</u>, <u>cover</u>, <u>scribble</u>... Lovely jubbly.

*Section 2 — Lifestyle*

# Social Issues and Equality

Argh, social issues... Talking about them can seem <u>daunting</u> enough in your own language, let alone another one, but keep a <u>cool head</u> and don't start anything you can't <u>finish</u>.

## Die Arbeitslosigkeit und die Obdachlosigkeit
## — Unemployment and Homelessness

There's not really very much that needs saying here. These things suck whichever way you look at it.

**Es gibt** viele **Arbeitslose** in meiner **Stadt** . = There are <u>lots of unemployed</u> <u>people</u> in my <u>town</u>.

*few:* wenige
*some:* einige

*homeless*
*people:* Obdachlose

*area:* Gegend
*city:* Großstadt

*homelessness:* Obdachlosigkeit

*no:* kein

**Die** Arbeitslosigkeit **in Großbritannien ist** ein großes **Problem heutzutage.**

= <u>Unemployment</u> in Britain is <u>a big</u> problem nowadays.

*young:* junge
*some:* einige

Viele **Leute haben ein Problem Arbeit zu finden.**

= <u>Many</u> people have a problem finding work.

## Die Gleichberechtigung — Equal Opportunities

This is your chance for a good <u>rant</u>, in German of course.

**Ich halte Gleichberechtigung für** sehr wichtig .

= I think equal opportunities are <u>very important</u>.

*unimportant:* unwichtig

**Manche Leute sind** gemein **zu mir, weil ich** aus Indien komme .

= Some people are <u>mean</u> to me because I <u>come from India</u>.

*nasty:* böse
*unfriendly:* unfreundlich

*am a girl:* ein Mädchen bin
*wear glasses:* eine Brille trage
*am foreign:* ausländisch bin

For more countries see <u>page 43</u>.

*poverty:* Armut
*vandalism:* Vandalismus

*discrimination:* Diskriminierung
*AIDS:* AIDS

*violence:* Gewalt

**Ich denke, dass** Rassismus **ein großes Problem in unserer Gesellschaft ist.**

= I think that <u>racism</u> is a big problem in our society.

**Das ist** rassistisch .

= That's <u>racist</u>.

*unfair:* unfair
*sexist:* sexistisch

**Es geht mir auf die Nerven.**

= It gets on my nerves.

## Phew — serious stuff this...

There are some really <u>important</u> topics on this page and examiners just love testing you on 'em. They could come up anywhere from <u>speaking</u> to <u>reading</u> too, so make sure you <u>learn</u> this vocab.

# Feeling Ill

You've got to be able to <u>tell</u> the doctor <u>what's wrong</u> with you. To do that, you've got to know the names of all the <u>parts of your body</u> in German. It's not hard, so get <u>learning</u>.

## Der Körper — The body

der Kopf: **the head**

der Hals: **the neck / throat**

der Bauch (**or** der Magen): **the stomach**

der Rücken: **the back**

der Arm (-e): **the arm**

die Hand (die Hände): **the hand**

das Bein (-e): **the leg**

das Knie (-): **the knee**

der Finger (-): **the finger**

der Fuß (die Füße): **the foot**

die Zehe (-n): **the toe**

## Der Kopf — The head

Remember, plurals are always 'die'.

die Haare (plural): **hair**

das Auge (-n): **the eye**

das Ohr (-en): **the ear**

der Zahn (die Zähne): **the tooth**

die Nase: **the nose**

der Mund: **the mouth**

## All together now — heads, shoulders, knees and toes...

When you think you know <u>all</u> those body parts, <u>cover</u> the page and scribble down a rough body picture with <u>all</u> the German words — <u>with</u> the <u>der</u>, <u>die</u> or <u>das</u>. Keep learning till you can get them <u>all</u> — <u>without</u> looking back. Der <u>Arm</u>, die <u>Hand</u> and der <u>Finger</u> should be pretty <u>easy</u>...

# Feeling Ill

Pain, illness and suffering... ah, it's all good fun. OK, roll your sleeves up and get stuck in.

## Wie fühlen Sie sich? — How do you feel?

An important question, this. You want to be able to answer it.

**Mir ist schlecht .** = I am ill.

hot: heiß
cold: kalt

The alternative words you can use in each sentence here are different.

**Ich bin krank .** = I am ill.

hungry: hungrig
thirsty: durstig
tired: müde

**Ich muss zum Arzt gehen.** = I need to go to the doctor's.

to the hospital: ins Krankenhaus
to the pharmacy: zur Apotheke
to the chemists: zur Drogerie
to the dentist: zum Zahnarzt

Cuthbert thought he had
Foot and Mouth disease.

## Was tut weh? — What hurts?

Here's how you say what bit hurts. The parts of the body are all on the previous page.

Use 'mein' for 'der' and 'das' words — and 'meine' for 'die' words.

**Mein Bein tut weh .** = My leg hurts.

hurt (plural): tun weh

My head: Mein Kopf
My hand: Meine Hand

## Was ist los? — What's wrong?

If you want to say your stomach aches, you stick '-schmerzen' ('pains') on the end of the word for stomach and make one long word. Bauch+schmerzen = Bauchschmerzen.

**Ich habe Bauchschmerzen .** = I have stomach ache.

a headache: Kopfschmerzen
earache: Ohrenschmerzen
flu: die Grippe
a cold: eine Erkältung

a stiff neck: einen steifen Hals
a sore throat: Halsschmerzen
backache: Rückenschmerzen
a temperature: Fieber

The German words for neck and throat are the same — 'der Hals'. You need to learn the difference between 'Halsschmerzen' and 'ein steifer Hals'.

**Ich habe mich am Bein geschnitten.** = I've cut my leg.

finger: am Finger
hand: an der Hand

You might need to say what's wrong with other people too...

**Er hat Atembeschwerden .** = He is having difficulty breathing.

is unconscious: ist bewusstlos

# Going to the doctor's — it's a pain in the neck...

It's not the most pleasant page in the world, but you've got to learn it.
You know the score — cover the page, scribble it down, and check you've got it right.

# Health and Health Issues

First up, how to live a <u>healthy lifestyle</u>. Ah the joys of GCSE German.
There's a fair bit to say on this topic, mind...

## Diät — Diet

No, I'm not talking about any ridiculous <u>lettuce-only</u>, weight-loss diet.
This is about your normal everyday diet and how <u>healthy</u> it is, or isn't.

Isst du **gesund**? = Do you eat <u>healthily</u>?

*unhealthily:* ungesund

For more food see
<u>page 13</u>.

### NEIN!

Nein, ich esse Pommes fast jeden Tag und ich trinke nur Cola.

= No, I eat chips almost every day and I only drink cola.

Nein, ich bin wahrscheinlich ein bisschen übergewichtig.

= No, I'm probably a bit overweight.

### JA!

*organic food:* Biokost

Ja, ich esse viel **Salat und frisches Obst**.

= Yes, I eat a lot of <u>salad and fresh fruit</u>.

Ja, ich mache eine relativ fettarme Diät.

= Yes, I'm on a relatively low fat diet.

Ja, ich versuche zu viel Fett und Zucker zu vermeiden.

= Yes, I try to avoid too much fat and sugar.

## Bewegung — Exercise

It doesn't matter if you don't do any, just be able to say so.

Was machst du, um fit zu bleiben?

= What do you do to stay fit?

For more sports
see <u>page 27</u>.

Ich treibe viel Sport. = I play a lot of sport.

Ich spiele Rugby gewöhnlich zweimal in der Woche.

= I usually play rugby twice a week.

Ich mache oft Aerobic, weil es sehr gut für das Herz ist.

= I often do aerobics because it's very good for the heart.

Sport isn't always good for you...

Ich bin sehr aktiv und ich spiele regelmäßig Fußball und Tennis.

= I am very active and I regularly play football and tennis.

## Of course I eat healthily — a chip is a vegetable, right?

There's loads you might want to say about these <u>exciting</u> things, but learning the stuff on this page is a <u>good start</u>. <u>Think</u> about what else you might want to say, write it down, and <u>practise</u> it.

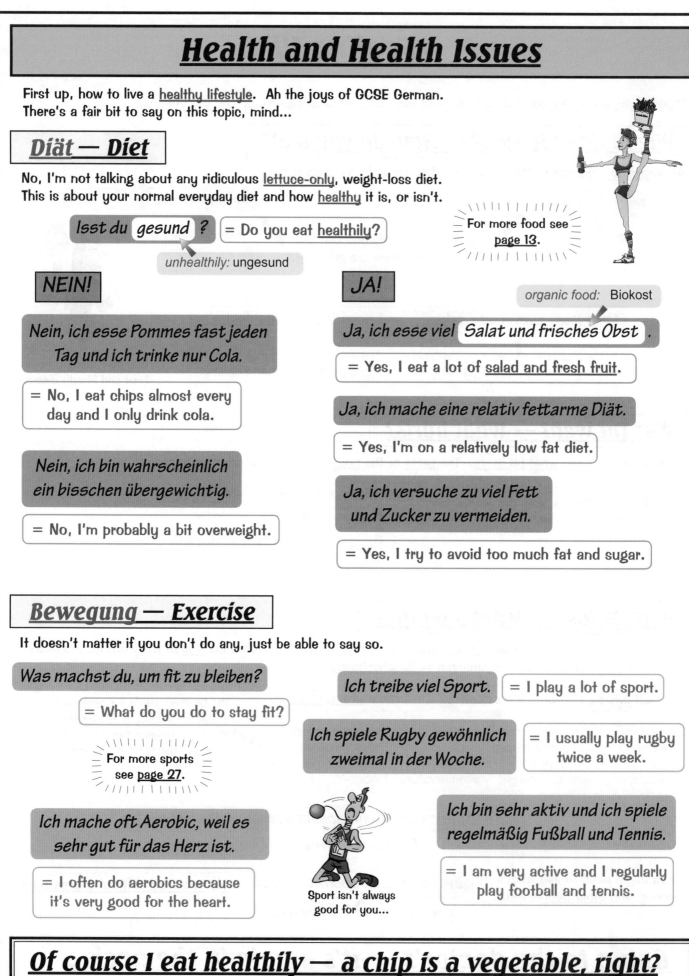

# Health and Health Issues

This bit's all about smoking, drugs, alcohol and rock 'n' roll. All right. I'm lying about the rock 'n' roll part. It's still pretty interesting though and you should at least have an opinion on this stuff without having to try too hard.

## Rauchen und Trinken — Smoking and drinking

Was ist deine Meinung über Rauchen ? = What do you think about smoking?

alcohol: Alkohol
drugs: Drogen

Ich rauche nicht. = I don't smoke.

drink: trinke

Ich rauche gern. = I like to smoke.

Rauchen ist cool. Mir ist es egal, ob es ungesund ist, Image ist alles. = Smoking is cool. I don't care if it is unhealthy, image is everything.

Rauchen ist widerlich. Ich hasse es wenn andere rauchen, es stinkt so. Es verursacht auch Krebs. = Smoking is disgusting. I hate it when others smoke, it really stinks. It also causes cancer.

Ich rauche, aber ich würde nie Drogen nehmen, weil es zu gefährlich ist. = I smoke, but I would never take drugs because it's too dangerous.

## Drogen — Drugs

You could get asked about your views on drugs, so here's some vocab you might need to know:

drugs/narcotics are: Rauschgifte ... sind
alcoholism is: Alkoholismus ... ist

Ich glaube, dass Drogen immer noch ein großes Problem in unserer Gesellschaft sind. = I think that drugs are still a big problem in our society.

Man kann abhängig werden. = You can become dependent.

an alcoholic: Alkoholiker

Man könnte eine Überdosis nehmen. = You could take an overdose.

Es gibt Drogenberatungsstellen. Hier kann man sich über Drogen und Entziehungskuren informieren. = There are drug advice centres. Here, you can get information about drugs and withdrawal treatments.

## Just say 'nein'...

I admit, this page is pretty heavy going, but at least it's interesting. Again, there's plenty more to say about this lot — so get your thinking cap on. And learn as much of the tricky vocab as you can.

# Revision Summary

The idea isn't that you just do these questions and <u>stop</u>.  To <u>really</u> make sure you've learnt this stuff, you need to <u>go back</u> through the section and look up the ones you couldn't do.  Then try them all again.  Your aim is to eventually be able to <u>glide</u> through them all with the greatest of ease.

1)  You're making a fruit salad for a party.  Think of the German words for as many fruits as you can to put in it — at least 5.  Make a list of 5 drinks you could offer people at the party.

2)  Write down how you'd say that you like vegetables but don't like sausage.
Also that you're very hungry.

3)  You're staying with a German family.  Thank your hosts for the meal, say you enjoyed it and it was delicious.  Offer to pass your hostess the milk (remember to use the right form of 'you').

4)  You're telling your host family about your home life.  Say that you make your bed and sometimes vacuum and clean at home.  You have breakfast at 8 o'clock and lunch at 1 o'clock.

5)  Introduce yourself to someone in German.  Tell them your name, age and when your birthday is.

6)  In German, describe three of your friends and say how old they are.
Spell out loud their names and the names of the towns where they live.

7)  Tell your German pen friend what relations you have — including how many aunts, cousins etc.

8)  Your animal-loving friend has six rabbits, a budgie, a guinea pig and two cats.
How will she say what these are in her German speaking assessment?

9)  Describe in German the personalities of two of your family members.
Say how well you get on with them.

10) A German news reporter asks your opinion on unemployment in the UK.
What would you say to them?

11) Say in German that you feel ill.  You have a temperature and your arms, back and legs hurt.

12) Do you play a lot of sport?  Why?  Why not?
Write down how you'd explain this to your German friend.

13) What's your opinion on smoking?  Give your answer in German.

# Sports and Hobbies

Loads of <u>dead useful vocab</u>.  Look back to this page if you need to know the name of a <u>hobby</u>.

## Treibst du Sport? — Do you do any sport?

Quite a lot of the stuff you'll be expected to say about yourself will be to do with <u>sport</u>.
Even if you're no demon on the pitch, you <u>need</u> to be good at talking about it.

Usually when you talk about sports you just say their name, e.g. 'Fußball', not 'der Fußball'.

**VERBS FOR OUTDOOR SPORTS**

| | | | |
|---|---|---|---|
| *to fish:* | angeln | *to ski:* | Ski fahren |
| *to go out:* | ausgehen | *to go for a walk:* | spazieren gehen |
| *to run:* | laufen | *to play:* | spielen |
| *to cycle:* | Rad fahren | *to walk, hike:* | wandern |
| *to swim:* | schwimmen | *to jog:* | joggen |

Remember, plurals are always 'die'.

**NAMES OF SPORTS**

| | |
|---|---|
| *badminton:* | das Badminton |
| *football:* | der Fußball |
| *tennis:* | das Tennis |
| *table tennis:* | das Tischtennis |
| *squash:* | das Squash |
| *hockey:* | das Hockey |

**PLACES YOU CAN DO SPORTS**

| | |
|---|---|
| *fitness centre:* | das Fitnesszentrum (-zentren) |
| *open-air pool:* | das Freibad (die Freibäder) |
| *swimming pool:* | das Schwimmbad (die Schwimmbäder) |
| *indoor swimming pool:* | das Hallenbad (die Hallenbäder) |
| *sports field:* | der Sportplatz (die Sportplätze) |
| *sports centre:* | das Sportzentrum (die Sportzentren) |
| *bowling alley:* | die Kegelbahn (-en) |
| *park:* | der Park (-s) |

## Hast du ein Hobby? — Do you have a hobby?

There are <u>other things</u> to do apart from sports — that's where these <u>tasty selections</u> come into play.

**GENERAL BUT VITAL**

| | |
|---|---|
| *hobby:* | das Hobby (-s) |
| *interest:* | das Interesse (-n) |
| *fan (supporter):* | der Fan (-s) |
| *club:* | der Club / Klub (-s) |
| *member:* | das Mitglied (-er) |
| *game:* | das Spiel (-e) |

To see how to use verbs with different people, see <u>pages 100 to 105</u>.

**OTHER IMPORTANT NOUNS**

| | |
|---|---|
| *chess:* | das Schach |
| *film:* | der Film (-e) |
| *performance:* | die Vorstellung (-en) |
| *play (in a theatre):* | das Theaterstück (-e) |

**VERBS FOR INDOOR ACTIVITIES**

| | |
|---|---|
| *to meet:* | (sich) treffen |
| *to dance:* | tanzen |
| *to sing:* | singen |
| *to collect:* | sammeln |
| *to bowl:* | kegeln |
| *to read:* | lesen |

**MUSICAL INSTRUMENTS**

| | |
|---|---|
| *violin:* | die Geige |
| *flute:* | die Querflöte |
| *drums (plural):* | das Schlagzeug |
| *clarinet:* | die Klarinette |
| *guitar:* | die Gitarre |
| *trumpet:* | die Trompete |
| *piano:* | das Klavier |
| *cello:* | das Cello |

**MUSICAL WORDS**

| | |
|---|---|
| *band, group:* | die Band (-s) |
| *CD:* | die CD (-s) |
| *instrument:* | das Instrument (-e) |
| *cassette:* | die Kassette (-n) |
| *concert:* | das Konzert (-e) |
| *stereo:* | die Stereoanlage (-n) |

## I've got hobbies — what's 'eating cheese' auf Deutsch?

This is dead <u>important</u>.  You can <u>look back</u> at this page while you're learning the rest of the section
— but you'll <u>still have to learn it</u> in the end.  <u>Cover</u> up the <u>German</u> bits and <u>scribble</u> down the ones
you know.  <u>Look back</u>, find out the ones you don't know and <u>try again</u>... and again... and again...

# Sports and Hobbies

You might be asked about what you do in your <u>free time</u> in either your speaking assessment or writing task. Chances are you'll get asked for your <u>opinions</u> on other <u>hobbies</u> too, so you've got to learn this page.

## Was machst du in deiner Freizeit?
## — What do you do in your free time?

You'll get asked this question <u>a lot</u> — so <u>learn it</u>.

Ich spiele | am Wochenende | Fußball | .   = I play <u>football</u> <u>at the weekend</u>.

*every day:*   jeden Tag
*every week:*   jede Woche
*twice a month:* zweimal im Monat

*badminton:* Badminton
*tennis:*   Tennis

For more about times, see <u>pages 2–3</u>.

Ich spiele | Klavier | .   = I play the <u>piano</u>.

Put in any of the instruments on <u>page 27</u> here.

Ich bin Mitglied eines | Tennisklubs | .

*chess club:*   Schachklubs
*squash club:* Squashklubs

= I'm a member of a <u>tennis club</u>.

**IMPORTANT**
In German, you just say, '<u>I play piano</u>' — you don't need to use '<u>the</u>'.

**Handy Hint:**
If you need to talk about any sport club, just add '<u>-klub</u>' to the end of the sport.

The '<u>-s</u>' on '<u>-klubs</u>' isn't to make a plural — it's the <u>genitive case</u> (see <u>page 85</u>). This is a little bit tricky because the plural of 'der Klub' is also 'Klubs' — be careful.

## Wie findest du Fußball? — What do you think of football?

Here's how to say what you <u>think</u> of different hobbies — <u>learn</u> these phrases even if you don't really <u>care</u>.

Ich finde | Fußball | okay | .   = I think <u>football</u>'s <u>okay</u>.

*the cinema:* das Kino
*hiking:*   Wandern

*good:*   gut
*bad:*   schlecht
*excellent:* ausgezeichnet
*terrible:*  furchtbar

Put 'gern' here if you like doing something, or 'ungern' if you don't.

Ich spiele | gern | Fußball | .

= I <u>like</u> playing <u>football</u>.

*I think that too:* Das denke ich auch.
*I don't think that:* Das denke ich nicht.
*That's true:*   Das ist wahr.
*That's not true:* Das ist nicht wahr.

For <u>agreeing</u> and <u>disagreeing</u> you can use these phrases.

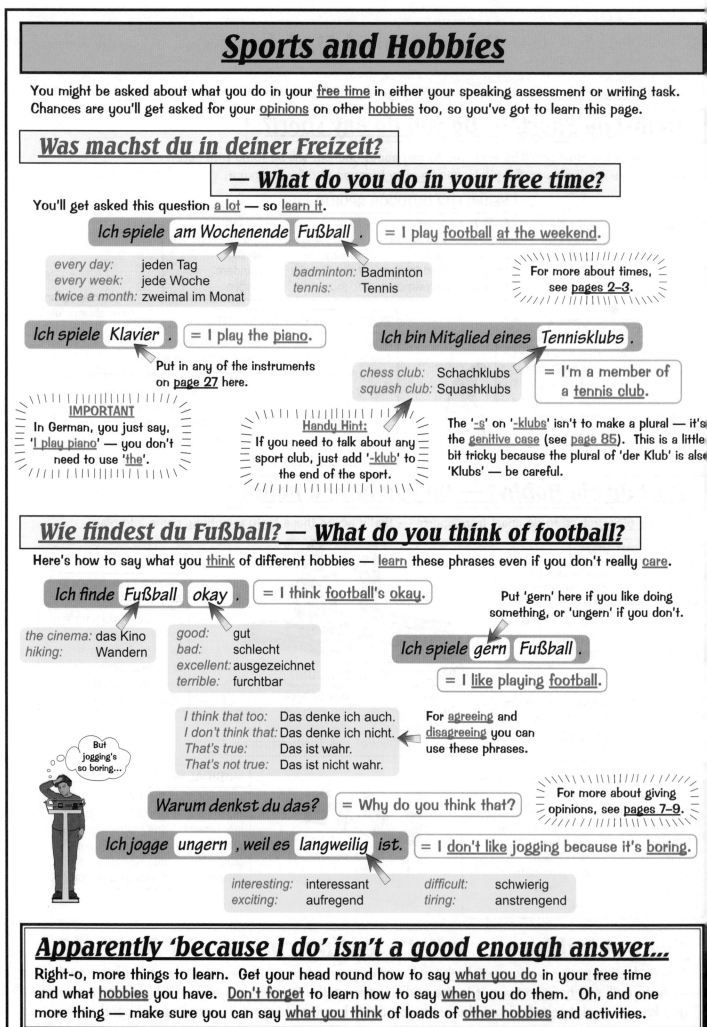

But jogging's so boring...

Warum denkst du das?   = Why do you think that?

For more about giving opinions, see <u>pages 7–9</u>.

Ich jogge | ungern | , weil es | langweilig | ist.   = I <u>don't like</u> jogging because it's <u>boring</u>.

*interesting:* interessant
*exciting:*   aufregend

*difficult:* schwierig
*tiring:*   anstrengend

## Apparently 'because I do' isn't a good enough answer...

Right-o, more things to learn. Get your head round how to say <u>what you do</u> in your free time and what <u>hobbies</u> you have. <u>Don't forget</u> to learn how to say <u>when</u> you do them. Oh, and one more thing — make sure you can say <u>what you think</u> of loads of <u>other hobbies</u> and activities.

# Television

This page is about <u>TV</u> — dead easy. It also covers <u>explaining</u> the kind of things you've done recently. This is dead important. <u>Learn it well</u>.

## Meine Lieblingssendung ist...
### — My favourite programme is...

You've probably got quite a bit to say about <u>TV</u> — here's how to do it <u>auf Deutsch</u>:

Welche **Fernsehsendungen** **siehst** du gern? = Which <u>TV programmes</u> do you like to <u>watch</u>?

*radio stations:* Radiosender
*books:* Bücher

*listen to:* hörst
*read:* liest

Ich **sehe** gern **Westenders** . = I like to <u>watch</u> <u>Westenders</u>.

*listen to:* höre
*read:* lese

Put what you like to watch, listen to or read here.

For more about giving opinions, see <u>pages 7–9</u>.

When I said, "Ich mag fernsehen", this wasn't quite what I meant...

**TELEVISION VOCAB**

| | | | |
|---|---|---|---|
| *programme:* | die Sendung (-en) | *documentary:* | der Dokumentarfilm (-e) |
| *series:* | die Serie (-n) | *quiz show:* | die Quizsendung (-en) |
| *weather report:* | der Wetterbericht (-e) | *comedy:* | die Komödie (-n) |
| *news:* | die Nachrichten (plural) | *cartoon:* | der Zeichentrickfilm (-e) |
| *soap opera:* | die Seifenoper (-n) | *feature film:* | der Spielfilm (-e) |

Remember, plurals are always 'die'.

Die Sendung fängt um **acht Uhr** an und endet um **halb zehn** . = The programme starts at <u>8 o'clock</u> and finishes at <u>half past nine</u>.

For more on telling the time, see <u>page 2</u>.

## Was hast du neulich gemacht?
### — What have you done recently?

This <u>past tense</u> stuff is <u>really</u> important — to get <u>top marks</u>, you have to be able to <u>use it</u>. See <u>pages 104-105</u> for more info.

Ich habe **neulich** **Godzilla** **gesehen** . = I <u>saw</u> <u>Godzilla</u> <u>recently</u>.

*heard:* gehört
*read:* gelesen

*last week:* letzte Woche
*two weeks ago:* vor zwei Wochen
*a month ago:* vor einem Monat

*the new song by Antarctic Apes:* das neue Lied von Antarctic Apes
*a great book:* ein tolles Buch

For more about times and dates, see <u>pages 2–3</u>.

## Godzilla — ein Dokumentarfilm about a giant lizard...

OK, so it turns out that talking about TV in German isn't <u>quite</u> as much fun as actually watching TV in real life. But (you guessed it) you've got to learn it anyway. Saying what you've done and <u>when you did it</u> is another <u>handy</u> thing that'll get you loads of gorgeous <u>marks</u>.

# Talking About the Plot

It could be last night's Westenders episode or the twists and turns of the last book you read, but you might well get asked to talk about the plot.

## Welche Filme hast du neulich gesehen?
## — Which films have you watched recently?

Another great opportunity to practise using the past tense. If you need some help, see pages 104-105.

Letzte Woche habe ich 'Pirates of the Mediterranean' gesehen.

= I saw 'Pirates of the Mediterranean' last week.

Was für ein Film ist das? = What sort of film is that?

Das ist ein Abenteuerfilm . = It is an adventure film.

Kannst du den Film beschreiben? Was ist passiert?

= Can you describe the film? What happened?

| a horror film: | ein Horrorfilm |
| a comedy: | eine Komödie |
| a romance: | ein Liebesfilm (literally: a love film) |
| a crime drama: | ein Krimi |
| a love story: | eine Liebesgeschichte |

When it comes to talking about this sort of thing, don't panic. Just pick a film (or a book, or a play...) that's got a relatively simple plot and remember to use the past tense.

Here are some helpful bits and pieces, for when it comes to describing what happened:

| at the beginning: | zu Beginn | a man called...: | ein Mann namens... |
| at the start: | am Anfang | a woman called...: | eine Frau namens... |
| at the end: | am Ende | | |

## Wie fandest du den Film?
## — What did you think of the film?

You're bound to get asked for your opinion at some point — so get learning these little gems...

Was hielst du vom Film? = What did you think of the film?

Er war interessant . = It was interesting.

For more on giving opinions, see pages 7–9.

| amusing: | amüsant | quite good: | ziemlich gut |
| fascinating: | faszinierend | very good: | sehr gut |
| exciting/tense: | spannend | bad: | schlecht |
| sad: | traurig | terrible: | furchtbar |

Er hat mir gefallen. = I liked it.

Er hat mir nicht gefallen. = I didn't like it.

Ich fand den Film langweilig . = I found the film boring.

| the book: | das Buch | the play: | das Theaterstück |
| the novel: | den Roman | the performance: | die Vorstellung |

This sentence uses the imperfect tense — 'fand' comes from the strong verb 'finden'. See pages 104-105 for more info.

# Der Film war gut — that's my gut reaction...

There's some pretty useful vocab on this page, so make sure you know it. Also, even if you couldn't really care less, make sure you have an opinion to give. That's what grabs you marks.

# Music

Whether it's Kylie or Bach, everybody likes a bit of <u>music</u>. You need to be able to talk about your <u>musical preferences</u>, as well as saying <u>where</u> and <u>when</u> you listen to it.

## Was für Musik magst du?
## — What sort of music do you like?

This bit's about <u>giving your opinion</u> again. Try and find something a bit <u>interesting</u> to say and <u>jazz</u> up those sentences.

*Ich höre gern* Popmusik. = I like listening to <u>pop music</u>.

| rock music: | Rockmusik |
| rap music: | Rapmusik |
| modern music: | moderne Musik |

Magst du Rapmusik?

Nicht so viel. Ich höre lieber Handel.

*Volksmusik gefällt mir nicht.*

= I don't like <u>folk music</u>.

*Ich spiele klassische Musik am Klavier, aber ich höre lieber modernere Musik.*

= I play classical music on the piano, but I prefer listening to more modern music.

Like in English, you can add '<u>-er</u>' onto the end of an adjective to mean '<u>more</u>' e.g. small → small<u>er</u>, klein → klein<u>er</u> — '<u>moderner</u>' just means '<u>more modern</u>' (the extra '-e' on the end is because 'Musik' is feminine). See <u>pages 91 & 94</u>.

*Meine Lieblingssängerin* ist Beyoncé. = <u>My favourite (female) singer</u> is <u>Beyoncé</u>.

| my favourite (male) singer: | Mein Lieblingssänger |
| my favourite group: | Meine Lieblingsgruppe |

For more on giving opinions, see <u>pages 7–9</u>.

## Wo magst du Musik hören?
## — Where do you like listening to music?

This is all about <u>how</u> and <u>where</u> you listen to music. Easy peasy.

| in the shower: | in der Dusche |
| in the car: | im Auto |

*Ich höre gern Musik* im Radio *, wenn ich* in meinem Zimmer *bin.*

| on my iPod®: | auf meinem iPod® |
| on my MP3 player: | auf meinem Mp3-Player/Mp3-Spieler |
| on CD: | auf CD |

= I like listening to music <u>on the radio</u> when I'm <u>in my room</u>.

Examiners will <u>love it</u> if you talk about the <u>latest technologies</u>.

## German — it's music to my ears...

Now this is fairly <u>straightfoward</u> stuff, but you still have to <u>learn it</u>. It could really come in handy. Also, if you happen to have heard any German pop music then <u>say so</u>. Not only does it make life <u>more interesting</u>, the examiners will be over the moon that you've taken an interest in German culture.

# Famous People

Now this choice of topic seems a tad weird to me, but apparently you are supposed to be <u>fascinated</u> by celebs. So much so that you wanna <u>talk</u> about them in German with your pen friends and <u>exchange partners</u>.

## Welche berühmten Persönlichkeiten findest du gut?

### Which celebrities do you like?

Talking about celebrities and famous people you admire mostly involves all the same old <u>straightforward</u> stuff that you need to talk about yourself and your family.
Start with their <u>name</u>, then <u>what</u> they do, and follow that up with <u>why</u> you like them.

**WHO** *Ich finde Beyoncé fantastisch.* = I think Beyoncé is fantastic.

**WHAT** *Sie ist eine berühmte amerikanische Popsängerin.* = She is a famous American pop singer.

**WHY** *Beyoncé sieht so hübsch aus und trägt immer schicke modische Klamotten.* = Beyoncé looks so pretty and always wears smart trendy clothes.

*Noch dazu singt sie wie ein Engel.* = She sings like an angel as well.

*Sie ist meine absolute Heldin.* = She is my absolute heroine.

## Der Einfluss berühmter Persönlichkeiten

### The Influence of Celebrities

Celebrities are often <u>role models</u> for young people. You may be expected to have an <u>opinion</u> on this and the role the media plays in the whole cult of celebrity.

*Sollten berühmte Persönlichkeiten als positive Beispiele für junge Leute dienen?* = Should celebrities serve as positive examples for young people?

### JA!

*Sicher. Sie sind erfolgreiche Menschen.* = Of course. They are successful people.

*Sie sind Vorbilder für viele Jugendliche.* = They are role models for a lot of young people.

*Man kann sie bewundern.* = You can admire them.

### NEIN!

*Keineswegs. Sie sind gar keine normale Menschen.* = No way. They aren't normal people.

*Manche Mädchen glauben sie müssen so dünn wie die 'Supermodels' sein. Dann kommen oft Probleme mit Magersucht oder Bulimie vor.* = Some girls think they have to be as thin as the 'Supermodels'. Then problems with anorexia or bulimia often occur.

---

**PRETTY DARNED USEFUL VOCAB:  RELATIV NÜTZLICHE VOKABELN**

| | | | | | | |
|---|---|---|---|---|---|---|
| *famous:* | bekannt / berühmt | *role model:* | das Vorbild (-er) | *hero / heroine:* | Held / Heldin |
| *pop singer:* | Popsänger / Popsängerin | *example:* | das Beispiel (-e) | *the media (plural):* | die Medien |
| | | *actor / actress:* | Schauspieler / Schauspielerin | *influence:* | der Einfluss |
| *on the stage:* | auf der Bühne | | | *admire:* | bewundern |
| *anorexia:* | die Magersucht | *celebrity (person):* | die berühmte Persönlichkeit | *responsible:* | verantwortlich |
| *bulimia:* | die Bulimie | *responsibility:* | die Verantwortung | *occur:* | vorkommen |

# New Technology

Computers are taking over the world, or so they say.
They'll almost definitely be cropping up somewhere in GCSE German.

## Computer und das Internet
### — Computers and the internet

It's a good idea to be able to talk about what you use computers for...

Ich habe eine Website für meinen Schachclub gemacht.

= I have made a website for my chess club.

Wir chatten über MSN®.

= We chat over MSN®.

football team: meine Fußballmannschaft
band: meine Band

Ich will meine Fotos downloaden.

= I want to download my photos.

download: herunterladen
upload: hochladen

**COMPUTER HARDWARE**

computer: der Computer
printer: der Drucker
screen/monitor: der Bildschirm
keyboard: die Tastatur

Our computer really is like a member of the team...

Foolish humans! Soon I shall render you all obsolete! Mwa-ha-ha-haa!

**INTERNET-SPEAK**

website: die Website
webpage: die Webseite / die Internetseite
server: der Server
search engine: die Suchmaschine

Your writing task might involve you writing a blog.

Ich schreibe ein Online-Tagebuch seit zwei Jahren.

= I've been writing a blog for two years.

You can also just say 'ein Blog'.

Ich surfe im Internet.

= I surf the internet.

## Technologie: Vorteile und Nachteile
### — Technology: Advantages and Disadvantages

There are lots of things you can say about the pros and cons of computers.
Here are a few to get you started:

Computer sind wirklich nützlich. Ohne Computer könnte ich nicht meine Schularbeit machen.

= Computers are really useful. Without a computer I couldn't do my schoolwork.

Computer können viel Zeit sparen.

= Computers can save a lot of time.

Man kann zu viel Zeit vor dem Computer verbringen. Es ist nicht gut für die Gesundheit.

= You can spend too much time in front of the computer. It's not good for your health.

## It were all done wit' horses back in my day...

You're probably familiar with the arguments for and against modern technology, so just think about what you'd say to someone asking you in English. Make sure you can talk about how you use computers too.

# E-mail and Texting

Ah, the joys of <u>digital communication</u>. Exam boards like to move with the times, so here's a bit about text messages and electronic-post. Great stuff.

## Ich möchte eine E-Mail senden
### — I would like to send an e-mail

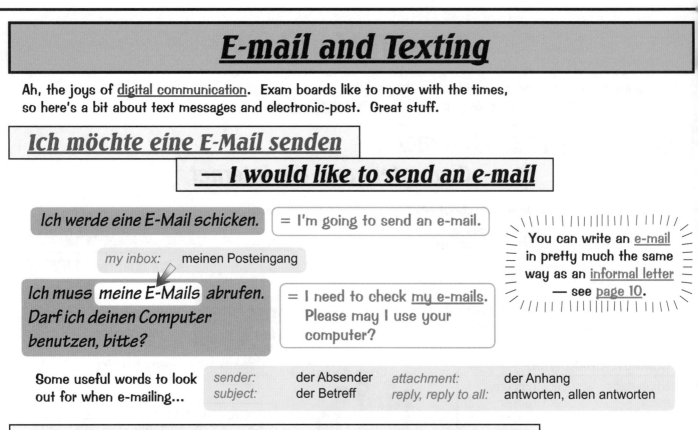

**Ich werde eine E-Mail schicken.** = I'm going to send an e-mail.

*my inbox:* meinen Posteingang

**Ich muss meine E-Mails abrufen. Darf ich deinen Computer benutzen, bitte?** = I need to check <u>my e-mails</u>. Please may I use your computer?

> You can write an <u>e-mail</u> in pretty much the same way as an <u>informal letter</u> — see <u>page 10</u>.

Some useful words to look out for when e-mailing...

| | | | |
|---|---|---|---|
| *sender:* | der Absender | *attachment:* | der Anhang |
| *subject:* | der Betreff | *reply, reply to all:* | antworten, allen antworten |

## Simsen — To text — eine SMS — A text message

<u>Text messages</u> could crop up anywhere. You might get asked to <u>write</u> a text message in one of your writing tasks, or <u>read</u> one in the reading exam.

If you do get asked to write a text, <u>don't panic</u>.

You probably send them all the time in English — just think about the sort of things you'd <u>normally say</u> to your friends and remember to use the <u>informal</u> '<u>du</u>'. Same goes for <u>e-mails</u>.

*text message:* die SMS, die (SMS-)Mitteilung
*mobile phone:* das Handy

> 16:04
>
> Hallo Berta. Wie geht's? Möchtest du heute Abend mit mir ins Kino gehen? Der neue Film von Danny Kraig beginnt um 20h00. Bis später. Alex.

= Hello Berta. How's it going? Do you want to go to the cinema with me tonight? The new Danny Kraig film starts at 8 o'clock. See you later. Alex.

## Ich blogg, du bloggst... — I blog, you blog...

A blog is basically just 'a day in the life of...'. Here's an <u>example</u> to get you started:

> Cumbria     11/05/2009     22h15
>
> Heute habe ich einen tollen Tag gehabt. Ich bin mit meinen Freunden ins Kino gegangen und wir haben den neuen Film von Danny Kraig gesehen. Normalerweise mag ich keine Abenteuerfilme aber er war eigentlich sehr lustig. Ich würde diesen Film bestimmt empfehlen!

> Cumbria     11/05/2009     22h15
>
> Today I've had a great day. I went to the cinema with my friends and we saw the new Danny Kraig film. Normally I don't like adventure films, but it was actually very funny. I would definitely recommend this film!

This blog is written (mainly) in the <u>perfect tense</u>. See <u>page 104</u> for help.

## It's pretty 'Handy', this mobile phone thing...

This is the sort of stuff that might appear in one of your <u>writing tasks</u>, so it's <u>important</u> you're familiar with it. Be warned though: your e-mail, text or blog could be about a whole host of <u>different topics</u>. And <u>don't</u> try and <u>use txt spk</u>* in your writing assessment or the exam. * That's 'text speak' by the way.

# Shopping

This is bread-and-butter stuff and you really have to <u>know it</u>. Basically, if you learn this stuff, you'll be able to use it when it comes up. You'd be <u>nuts</u> not to.

## Wo ist...? — Where is...?

A <u>dead useful</u> question — and luckily the word order is the <u>same</u> in English and German.

**Wo ist** der Supermarkt **, bitte?** = Where is <u>the supermarket</u>, please?

butcher's: die Metzgerei (-en)
bakery: die Bäckerei (-en)
grocer's: der Lebensmittelladen (die Lebensmittelläden)
greengrocer's: der Gemüsehändler (-)

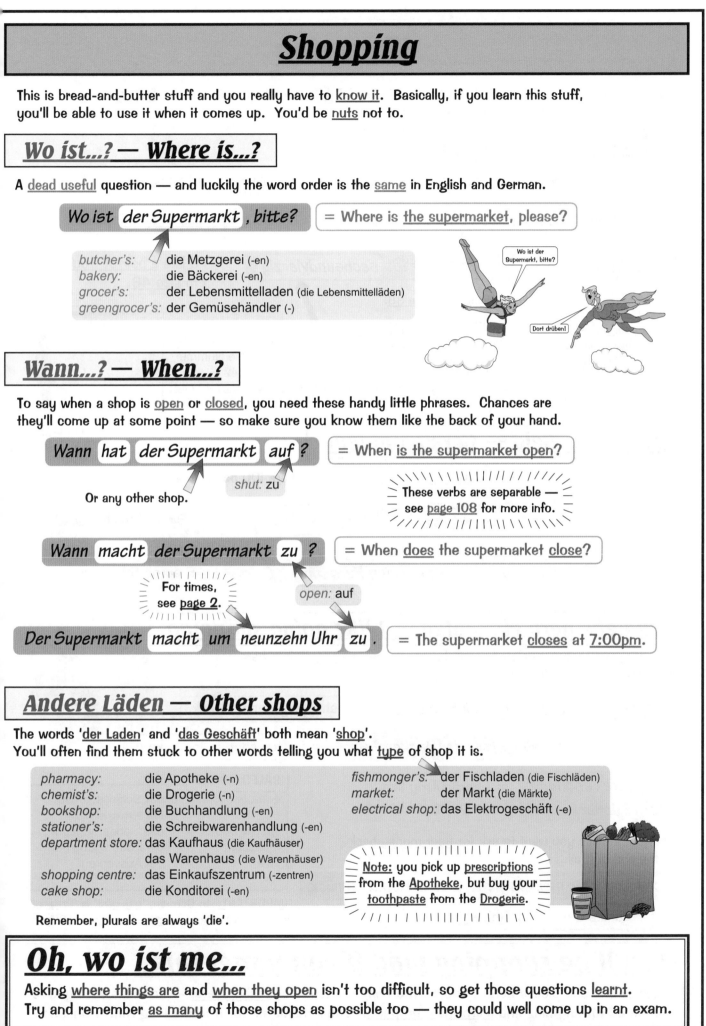

Wo ist der Supermarkt, bitte?

Dort drüben!

## Wann...? — When...?

To say when a shop is <u>open</u> or <u>closed</u>, you need these handy little phrases. Chances are they'll come up at some point — so make sure you know them like the back of your hand.

**Wann** hat der Supermarkt auf **?** = When <u>is the supermarket open</u>?

Or any other shop. shut: zu

These verbs are separable — see <u>page 108</u> for more info.

**Wann** macht der Supermarkt zu **?** = When <u>does</u> the supermarket <u>close</u>?

For times, see <u>page 2</u>. open: auf

**Der Supermarkt** macht um neunzehn Uhr zu **.** = The supermarket <u>closes</u> at <u>7:00pm</u>.

## Andere Läden — Other shops

The words '<u>der Laden</u>' and '<u>das Geschäft</u>' both mean '<u>shop</u>'.
You'll often find them stuck to other words telling you what <u>type</u> of shop it is.

pharmacy: die Apotheke (-n)
chemist's: die Drogerie (-n)
bookshop: die Buchhandlung (-en)
stationer's: die Schreibwarenhandlung (-en)
department store: das Kaufhaus (die Kaufhäuser)
das Warenhaus (die Warenhäuser)
shopping centre: das Einkaufszentrum (-zentren)
cake shop: die Konditorei (-en)

fishmonger's: der Fischladen (die Fischläden)
market: der Markt (die Märkte)
electrical shop: das Elektrogeschäft (-e)

<u>Note:</u> you pick up <u>prescriptions</u> from the <u>Apotheke</u>, but buy your <u>toothpaste</u> from the <u>Drogerie</u>.

Remember, plurals are always 'die'.

# Oh, wo ist me...

Asking <u>where things are</u> and <u>when they open</u> isn't too difficult, so get those questions <u>learnt</u>.
Try and remember <u>as many</u> of those shops as possible too — they could well come up in an exam.

# Shopping

These are the kind of phrases that can be used in lots of different situations, so it's definitely going to be worth learning them. Well, get to it — and enjoy.

## Ich möchte... — I would like...

You'll be using this all the time. You should be pretty comfortable with 'Ich möchte' by now.

Ich möchte ein großes Stück Brot , bitte. = I'd like a big piece of bread, please.

Ich möchte eine Hose . Meine Größe ist sechsundvierzig . = I'd like a pair of trousers. I'm size 46.

For clothing, see page 38.

**Important Bit:**
Another good way to say 'I would like' is 'Ich hätte gern'.

**CONTINENTAL SIZES**

| size: | die Größe / die Nummer |
|---|---|
| dress size 10 / 12 / 14 / 16: | 36 / 38 / 40 / 42 |
| shoe size 5 / 6 / 7 / 8 / 9 / 10: | 38 / 39 / 41 / 42 / 43 / 44 |

Do you think my bum looks big in this?   I do.

## Deutsches Geld — German money

German money's easy. There are 100 cents in a euro, like there are 100 pence in a pound.

This is what you'd see on a German price tag: → € 5,50

For numbers, see page 1.

This is how you'd say the price: → 'Fünf Euro fünfzig Cent' = 5 euros 50 cents

## Ich gehe gern einkaufen — I like going shopping

Lots of useful shopping-related vocab for you to get your teeth into here.
First up, how to talk about your shopping habits...

Ich gehe einmal pro Woche einkaufen. = I go shopping once a week.

Ich kaufe oft in der Bäckerei ein. = I often shop in the bakery.

Ich kaufe besonders gern Bücher ein. = I particularly like shopping for books.

And just in case you want to ask for your money back at the end of it all...

Ich hätte gern mein Geld für dieses Hemd zurück.

= I'd like a refund on this shirt.

**SALES VOCAB**

| end-of-season sale: | der Schlussverkauf |
|---|---|
| | (die Schlussverkäufe) |
| special offer: | das Sonderangebot (-e) |
| reduction: | die Ermäßigung (-en) |
| sale: | der Ausverkauf |
| | (die Ausverkäufe) |

**IMPORTANT:** In German, 'per cent' is 'Prozent'.
So, '10% reduction' = 'zehn Prozent Ermäßigung'.

# You'll be shopping mad if you forget this...

Lots of bits and pieces here, I know. The thing is they're all really useful — so make sure you're prepared for anything and learn them properly. You'll thank me for it in the long run. Honest.

# Shopping

Another important topic that you might well need to know. It's not a difficult one —
and there are some standard questions and answers that save you having to think.

## Kann ich Ihnen helfen? — Can I help you?

Use 'Ich möchte...' or 'Ich hätte gern...' for saying what you'd like:

**Ich hätte gern fünfhundert Gramm Zucker, bitte.** = I'd like 500 g of sugar, please.

1 kg: ein Kilo
2 kg: zwei Kilo

1) You don't need to make words like 'Gramm' and 'Kilo' plural. Just say, 'Ein Kilo...', 'Zwei Kilo...' and so on.

2) In German, you can also just say '500 g sugar' — you don't need to use 'of'.

**USEFUL VOCAB**
| | |
|---|---|
| several: | mehrere |
| a dozen: | ein Dutzend |
| a tin/box of: | eine Dose |
| a bottle of: | eine Flasche |
| a jar of: | ein Glas |
| a slice of: | eine Scheibe |
| a piece of: | ein Stück |
| a bag of: | eine Tüte |
| a bar of: | eine Tafel |

The shop assistant may say:

**Sonst noch etwas?** ...or... **Sonst noch einen Wunsch?**

= Will there be anything else?

You could reply:

**Nein danke.** = No thank you.

two apples: zwei Äpfel
three pears: drei Birnen

See page 1 for numbers.

...or...

**Ja, ich möchte auch eine Kartoffel, bitte.** = Yes, I'd like a potato as well, please.

## Haben Sie...? — Do you have...?

Maybe you're not sure this shop will have what you want — in which case, you'll have to ask.

**Entschuldigung, haben Sie Brot, bitte?** = Excuse me, do you have any bread, please?

milk: Milch    cheese: Käse

Can I help you?

**Ja, hier ist es.** = Yes, here it is. **Nein, haben wir nicht.** = No, we don't.

it: er / sie / es

## Nehmen Sie das? — Will you be taking that?

Decision time. It happens every time you go into a shop. Make sure you know these.

**Ich nehme es.** = I'll take it.

it: ihn / sie / es

Which word you use for 'it' depends on the gender and case of the noun — see page 97.

I'll leave it. I'm not sure this shade of blue suits me.

**Ich lasse es. Die Farbe gefällt mir nicht.** = I'll leave it. I don't like the colour.

It's the wrong size: Es ist die falsche Größe    It's too expensive: Es ist zu teuer

## Will you be taking that? — No, I was going to pay...

There's lots of important stuff here. You don't have to make those 'quantity words' like 'Gramm' and 'Kilo' plural — just use them as they are. Also, you don't need to use 'of' like in English. Remember — there are no tricks or catches in the tasks — you just need to know your stuff.

# Shopping

This is the sort of vocab you'll need if you ever have to give a <u>description</u> of somebody.
Useful if your best mate ever goes missing in Germany...

## Die Kleidung — Clothing

Most of this stuff is <u>pretty common</u> — so you <u>need</u> to know it.

| Dieser Mantel | gefällt mir (nicht). | = I (don't) like <u>this coat</u>. |

*Watch out:* 'die Hose' is <u>feminine singular</u>, <u>not plural</u> as in the English 'trousers'. Same with '<u>die Strumpfhose</u>'.

fashionable: modisch      old-fashioned: altmodisch

| Dieser Mantel | ist wirklich | bequem | . | = <u>This coat</u> is really <u>comfortable</u>. |

*Remember, plurals are always 'die'.*

| shirt: | das Hemd (-en) | coat: | der Mantel (die Mäntel) | scarf: | der Schal (-e) |
|---|---|---|---|---|---|
| blouse: | die Bluse (-n) | hat: | der Hut (die Hüte) | glove: | der Handschuh (-e) |
| trousers: | die Hose (-n) | cap: | die Mütze (-n) | miniskirt: | der Minirock (die Miniröcke) |
| skirt: | der Rock (die Röcke) | T-shirt: | das T-Shirt (-s) | tie: | die Krawatte (-n), der Schlips (-e) |
| sock: | die Socke (-n) | suit: | der Anzug (die Anzüge) | tights: | die Strumpfhose (-n) |
| shoe: | der Schuh (-e) | jacket: | die Jacke (-n) | shorts: | die Shorts (plural), die kurze Hose (-n) |
| dress: | das Kleid (-er) | jumper: | der Pullover (-) | a pair of socks: | ein Paar Socken |

Examiners love it if you talk about <u>fashion</u> too...

| Es ist sehr schwierig richtig individuell zu sein. | = It's very difficult to be truly individual. |

fashionable clothes: die modischen Klamotten

| Man muss immer | die Markenklamotten | tragen, und die sind wirklich teuer. |

= You always have to wear <u>brand-named clothes</u> and they are really expensive.

## Welche Farbe...? — What colour...?

Another <u>vital</u> little topic...

For adjective endings, see <u>page 91</u>.

| Ich möchte eine | blaue | Jacke. |

= I'd like a <u>blue</u> jacket.

**COLOURS: DIE FARBEN**

| black: | schwarz | brown: | braun |
|---|---|---|---|
| white: | weiß | orange: | orange |
| red: | rot | pink: | rosa |
| yellow: | gelb | purple: | lila |
| green: | grün | light blue: | hellblau |
| blue: | blau | dark brown: | dunkelbraun |

The colours '<u>rosa</u>', '<u>lila</u>' and '<u>orange</u>' don't take endings.

| Ich möchte einen | rosa | Rock. | = I'd like a <u>pink</u> skirt. |

## Es besteht aus... — It's made out of...

| Ich hätte gern eine neue Jacke aus | Leder | . |

= I'd like a new <u>leather</u> jacket.      wool: Wolle

**OTHER MATERIALS: ANDERE STOFFE**

| iron: | das Eisen | paper: | das Papier |
|---|---|---|---|
| wood: | das Holz | plastic: | das Plastik |
| metal: | das Metall | silver: | das Silber |
| silk: | Seide | cotton: | Baumwolle |

## He's got a Hut on his head — in German, that's normal...

Lots of these clothes are pretty easy to remember — <u>Schuh</u>, <u>Socke</u>, <u>Hut</u>, <u>Bluse</u> and so on.
Others need a bit more effort. It's <u>important stuff</u> though, so it's worth it. Honestly.

# Inviting People Out

As well as finding out <u>how much</u> things cost, <u>when</u> they're open and <u>where</u> they are, you've <u>got to learn</u> how to <u>ask someone</u> to come <u>with you</u>.

## Gehen wir aus — Let's go out

These are all really <u>useful</u> phrases, so get them <u>learnt</u>.

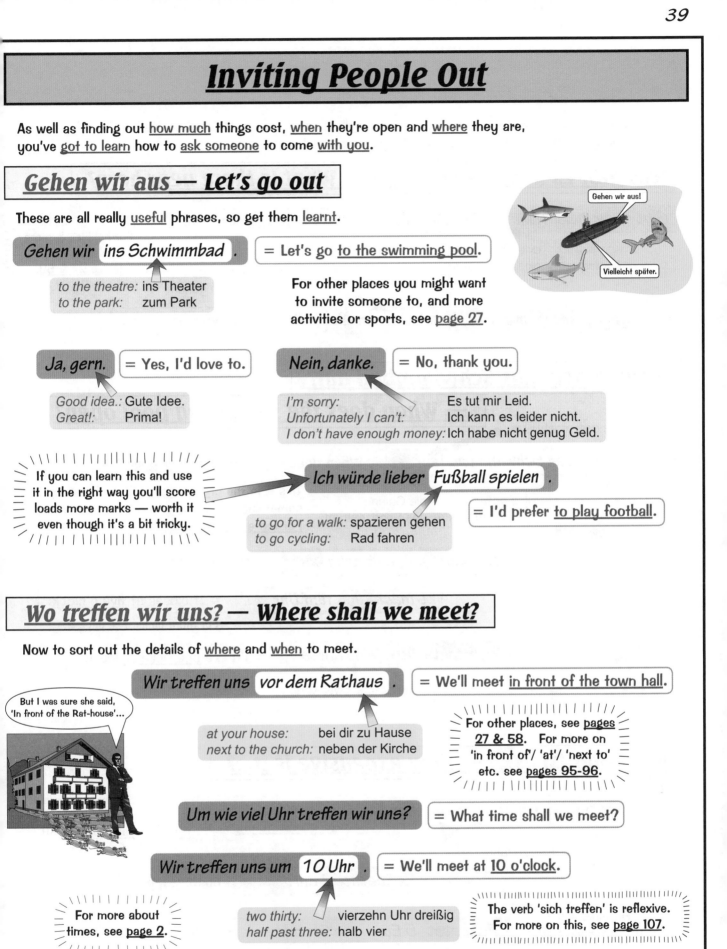

*Gehen wir* **ins Schwimmbad** . = Let's go <u>to the swimming pool</u>.

*to the theatre:* ins Theater
*to the park:* zum Park

For other places you might want to invite someone to, and more activities or sports, see <u>page 27</u>.

Gehen wir aus!

Vielleicht später.

*Ja, gern.* = Yes, I'd love to.

*Good idea.:* Gute Idee.
*Great!:* Prima!

*Nein, danke.* = No, thank you.

*I'm sorry:* Es tut mir Leid.
*Unfortunately I can't:* Ich kann es leider nicht.
*I don't have enough money:* Ich habe nicht genug Geld.

If you can learn this and use it in the right way you'll score loads more marks — worth it even though it's a bit tricky.

*Ich würde lieber* **Fußball spielen** .

*to go for a walk:* spazieren gehen
*to go cycling:* Rad fahren

= I'd prefer <u>to play football</u>.

## Wo treffen wir uns? — Where shall we meet?

Now to sort out the details of <u>where</u> and <u>when</u> to meet.

*Wir treffen uns* **vor dem Rathaus** . = We'll meet <u>in front of the town hall</u>.

But I was sure she said, 'In front of the Rat-house'...

*at your house:* bei dir zu Hause
*next to the church:* neben der Kirche

For other places, see <u>pages 27 & 58</u>. For more on 'in front of'/ 'at'/ 'next to' etc. see <u>pages 95-96</u>.

*Um wie viel Uhr treffen wir uns?* = What time shall we meet?

*Wir treffen uns um* **10 Uhr** . = We'll meet at <u>10 o'clock</u>.

For more about times, see <u>page 2</u>.

*two thirty:* vierzehn Uhr dreißig
*half past three:* halb vier

The verb 'sich treffen' is reflexive. For more on this, see <u>page 107</u>.

## Es tut mir Leid, I'm washing my hair...

Now you've got that <u>sorted</u> you should be able to ask Boris Becker out to the theatre or arrange to meet Claudia Schiffer in front of the park. If you <u>can't</u> then <u>go back</u> over it until you darn well can.

# Going Out

You're going to <u>need</u> this stuff — you may need to <u>talk</u> about it and you'll definitely have to be able to <u>understand it all</u>. Don't just sit there, <u>get into gear</u> and get down to it.

## <u>Was gibt es hier in der Nähe?</u> — <u>What is there near here?</u>

Gibt's hier in der Nähe | ein Theater | ? = Is there <u>a theatre</u> near here?

*a sports field:* einen Sportplatz
*a bowling alley:* eine Kegelbahn

*play tennis:* Tennis spielen
*go for walks:* spazieren gehen

*For hobbies & more places, see <u>pages 27 & 58</u>.*

Kann man hier in der Nähe | schwimmen | ? = Can people <u>swim</u> near here?

## <u>Wann macht das Schwimmbad auf?</u>
## — <u>When does the swimming pool open?</u>

*close:* macht ... zu

Wann | macht | das Schwimmbad | auf | ? = When does <u>the swimming pool</u> <u>open</u>?

*For more on verbs like this one, see <u>page 108</u>.*

*the gallery:* die Galerie
*the sports centre:* das Sportzentrum

This is in the <u>present tense</u>, but it's talking about something that's going to happen in the <u>future</u>. <u>For more info see page 103</u>.

Es macht um | halb zehn | auf . = It opens at <u>half past nine</u>.

Es macht um | fünf Uhr | zu. = It closes at <u>five o'clock</u>.

For more times, see <u>page 2</u>.

Ich möchte bitte | eine Karte | . = I'd like <u>one ticket</u>, please.

*two tickets:* zwei Karten

## <u>Wie teuer ist es...?</u> — <u>How expensive is it...?</u>

Wie viel kostet es, | schwimmen zu gehen | ? = How much does it cost <u>to go swimming</u>?

*For other sports and activities, see <u>pages 27 and 58</u>.*

*to go cycling:* Rad zu fahren
*to play tennis:* Tennis zu spielen

Es kostet | 2 Euro | . = It costs <u>2 euros</u>.

*For more about prices see <u>page 36</u>.*

Es kostet | 5 Euro | pro Stunde. = It costs <u>5 euros</u> per hour.

## <u>A noisy horse near here — a 'Nähe'...</u>

Before you move on, make sure you can ask <u>how much</u> it <u>costs</u> to do something, <u>when</u> something <u>opens</u> and if something's <u>nearby</u>. So <u>cover</u> the <u>page</u> and see if you've got them all <u>sussed</u> out.

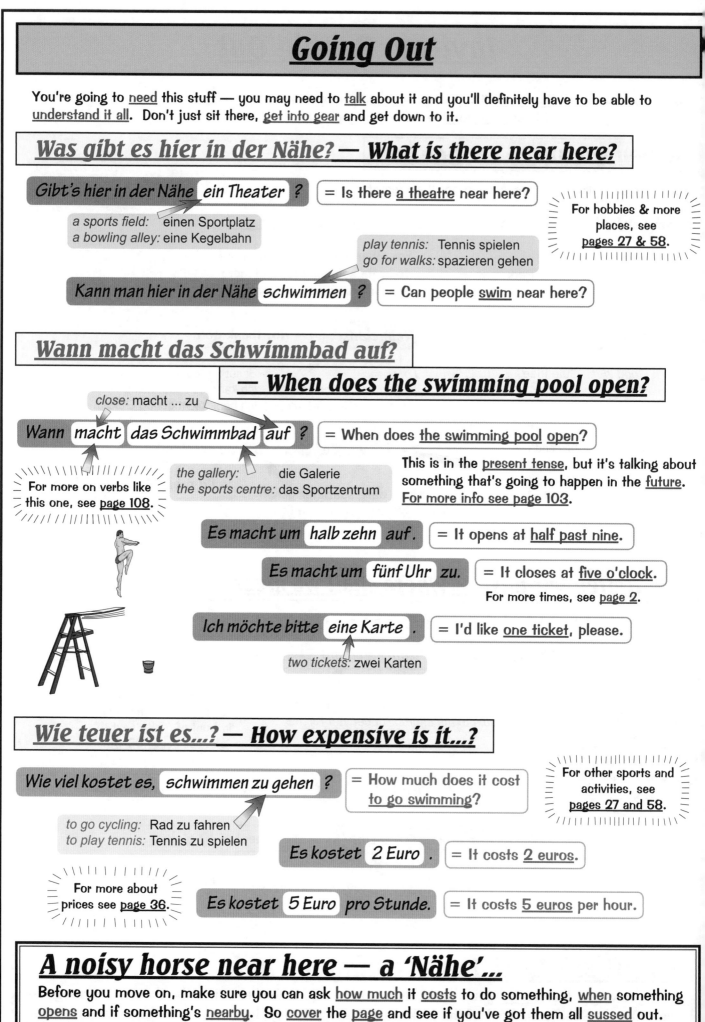

# Going Out

Almost everyone likes the cinema, and whatever kind of films tickle your fancy you're gonna need to know how to arrange going there with someone else. Away you go.

## Was läuft im Kino? — What's on at the cinema?

Some useful cinema-related phrases for you:

**Wie viel kostet eine Eintrittskarte ?**  = How much does one entry ticket cost?

*How much do two entry tickets cost?:*
Wie viel kosten zwei Eintrittskarten?

**Eine Karte kostet 10 Euro.**  = One ticket costs 10 euros.

Plural ending — see page 101.

'Eintrittskarte' means 'entry ticket' and 'Karte' means 'ticket', so they're basically the same thing. You'll get more marks if you can use the longer word, but you need to understand it.

**Ich möchte zwei Karten , bitte.**  = I'd like two tickets, please.

*one ticket:* eine Karte
*three tickets:* drei Karten

If you want to know how to describe a film you've seen, see page 30.

## Um wie viel Uhr...? — At what time...?

It's no good if you don't know what time the film starts.
You'll miss all the nice adverts at the beginning for one thing...

**Um wie viel Uhr beginnt die Vorstellung?**  = What time does the performance begin?

'fängt ... an' comes from 'anfangen', which is a separable strong verb. See page 108 for more info.

**Wann fängt die Vorstellung an?**  = When does the performance start?

*the film:* der Film    *the play:* das Theaterstück    *the concert:* das Konzert

**Wann endet die Vorstellung ?**  = When does the performance end?

**Sie fängt um acht Uhr an.**  = It starts at 8 o'clock.

**Sie endet um halb elf .**  = It finishes at half past ten.

You use 'sie' here because 'die Vorstellung' is feminine.
For 'der Film' use 'er' and for 'das Konzert' use 'es'.

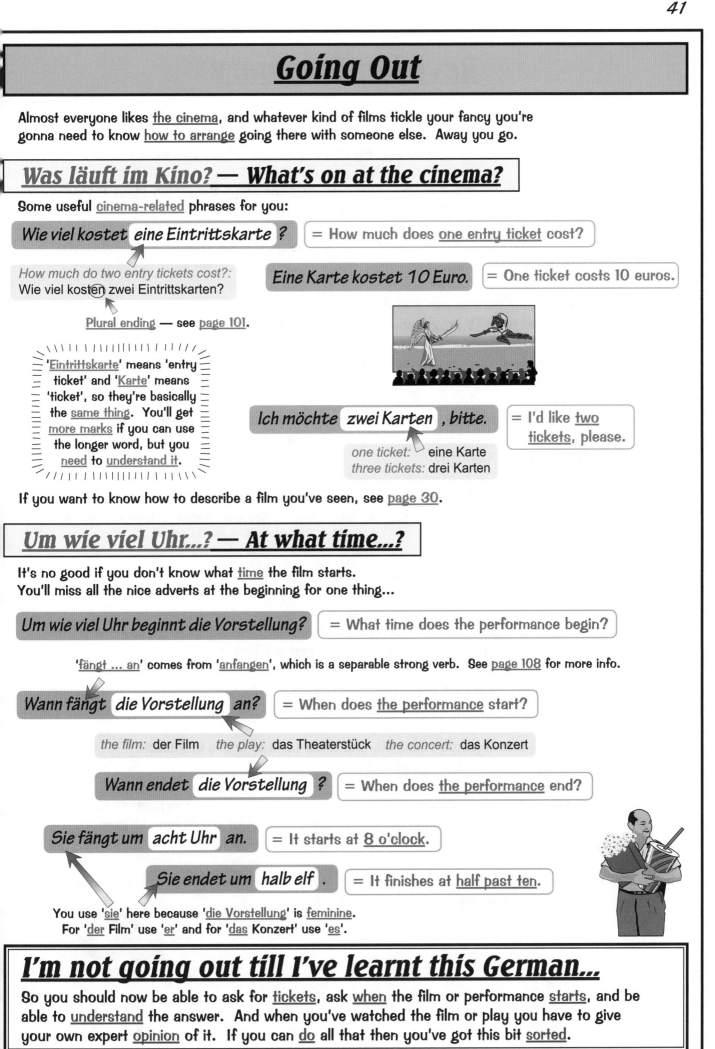

# I'm not going out till I've learnt this German...

So you should now be able to ask for tickets, ask when the film or performance starts, and be able to understand the answer. And when you've watched the film or play you have to give your own expert opinion of it. If you can do all that then you've got this bit sorted.

# Revision Summary

These questions really do check what you <u>know</u> and don't know — which means you can spend your time learning the bits you're shaky on. But it's not a good idea to do this one day, then forget about it. <u>Come back</u> to these a day later and try them again. And then a week later...

1) Franz asks Christine if she has a hobby. She says that she plays the guitar, plays football and reads books. Write down their conversation in German.

2) Hermann and Bob are having an argument. Hermann says that he likes tennis because it's exciting. Bob finds tennis boring and tiring. Write down their conversation in German.

3) You're talking to your German pen friend.
How do you tell her what TV programmes you like to watch?

4) Tell your German friend you went to see 'Night of the Zombie-Mummies 26' at the cinema last week. Tell her it was a horror film and that you thought it was very sad.

5) You and your pen friend are having an unlikely conversation about where and how you listen to music. Your friend says she listens to her iPod® when she's in the car.
How did she say that in German?

6) Nadja thinks she's fallen in love with Justin Timberlake. Write a paragraph in German to her saying what you think of him, and telling her which celebrities you admire. Don't forget to give reasons.

7) Give one advantage of using a computer and one disadvantage.
Don't cheat — give them in German.

8) Write out a text message in German asking your friend Joe if he wants to go swimming with you on Saturday. Don't forget to be a good friend and ask how he is.

9) What are the German names for the shops where you'd buy: paper, a cake, some sausages, some soap? (And don't just say 'Supermarkt' for all four.)

10) You need to buy a brown jumper, size 48, and three pairs of socks in Munich.
How do you say this to the shop assistant?

11) Dave wants to see 'Romeo und Julia' at the cinema, but Gabriela says they should see 'Otto — der Katastrophenfilm'. They arrange to meet in front of the cinema at 8pm. Write down their conversation in German. (Watch out for word order here.)

12) You're in Germany and you want to play squash. Ask when the sports centre is open and how much it costs to play squash. Ask for two tickets.

## Holiday Destinations

I know there's a lot to <u>learn</u> on this page, but it's really pretty <u>important</u>. It could come up <u>anywhere</u>.

### Learn these foreign places

You need to <u>understand</u> where <u>other people</u> are from when they tell you. And you're bound to have to talk about <u>holidays</u> and <u>trips abroad</u> at some point. So get <u>learning</u> this little lot:

| | Place | People (male/female) | Adjective |
|---|---|---|---|
| Germany: | Deutschland | Deutscher/Deutsche | deutsch |
| France: | Frankreich | Franzose/Französin | französisch |
| Italy: | Italien | Italiener(in) | italienisch |
| Spain: | Spanien | Spanier(in) | spanisch |
| Austria: | Österreich | Österreicher(in) | österreichisch |
| Holland: | Holland | Holländer(in) | holländisch |
| Greece: | Griechenland | Grieche/Griechin | griechisch |
| America: | Amerika | Amerikaner(in) | amerikanisch |
| Belgium: | Belgien | Belgier(in) | belgisch |
| Denmark: | Dänemark | Däne/Dänin | dänisch |
| Russia: | Russland | Russe/Russin | russisch |
| Africa: | Afrika | Afrikaner(in) | afrikanisch |
| Ireland: | Irland | Ire/Irin | irisch |
| India: | Indien | Inder(in) | indisch |
| Poland: | Polen | Pole/Polin | polnisch |
| China: | China | Chinese/Chinesin | chinesisch |
| Australia: | Australien | Australier(in) | australisch |

> An adjective is a describing word. See pages 91-92.

So your (male) German friend might say:

**Ich bin Deutscher.**
**Ich komme aus Deutschland.**

= I am <u>German</u>.
I come from <u>Germany</u>.

And you'd describe him as:

**Mein deutscher Freund.**

= My <u>German</u> friend.

For more on talking about where <u>you're</u> from, including countries in the <u>UK</u>, see <u>page 60</u>.
Women and girls need the <u>feminine versions</u> — usually that just means adding '<u>-in</u>' to the end.

### Some countries are a bit more tricky...

1) <u>Watch out:</u> you always have to put '<u>die</u>' before these countries:

| | Place | People (male/female) | Adjective |
|---|---|---|---|
| Turkey: | die Türkei | Türke/Türkin | türkisch |
| Switzerland: | die Schweiz | Schweizer(in) | schweizerisch |
| The Netherlands: | die Niederlande | Niederländer(in) | niederländisch |
| The USA: | die USA, die Vereinigten Staaten | Amerikaner(in) | amerikanisch |

> Don't forget — <u>Holland</u> and the <u>Netherlands</u> are the <u>same place</u>.

There's no people/adjective to go with 'the USA', so just use these.

2) <u>BUT</u> after '<u>aus</u>', the '<u>die</u>' changes to '<u>der</u>' for Turkey and Switzerland (because they're singular and feminine) and '<u>den</u>' for the others (cos they're plural). See <u>pages 90 and 95</u> for stuff about 'die' and 'aus'.

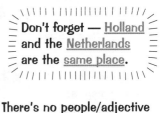

**Ich komme aus den USA.**

= I come from the USA.

### You need to know these holiday destinations

Um... not that I'm really suggesting you go on holiday in the Channel Tunnel, but I'm sure you catch my drift — <u>learn</u> this little lot, they just might come in <u>handy</u>:

| | | | | | |
|---|---|---|---|---|---|
| the English Channel: | der Ärmelkanal | the Black Forest: | der Schwarzwald | the Rhine: | der Rhein |
| the Channel Tunnel: | der Tunnel | Lake Constance: | der Bodensee | the Danube: | die Donau |
| the Alps (plural): | die Alpen | Bavaria: | Bayern | | |

### We're all going on a summer holiday...

You've got to <u>learn</u> all those <u>countries</u> and <u>nationalities</u>. With ones that are <u>similar</u> in German and English, make sure you get the <u>spelling</u> right. There's a pretty ridiculous amount of vocab here, but keep <u>testing yourself</u> until you know it back to front. It's really the <u>only way</u>.

# Catching the Train

Trains, planes and automobiles... Well, just trains for now. You'll need loads of vocab if you want the best marks. And you must know a few bog-standard sentences — things you'll always need.

## Ich möchte mit dem Zug fahren

Fährt ein Zug nach Berlin ?

### — I'd like to travel by train

= Is there a train to Berlin?

| Cologne: | Köln | Geneva: | Genf |
| Munich: | München | Vienna: | Wien |

Some German-speaking cities have different names in German and English.

Einmal einfach nach Berlin, erste Klasse .

= One single to Berlin, first class.

| Two: | Zweimal | return(s): hin und zurück | second class: zweite Klasse |
| Three: | Dreimal |

There's another word for 'return ticket' — 'die Rückfahrkarte':

Eine Rückfahrkarte nach Berlin, bitte.

= One return ticket to Berlin, please.

## Wann fahren Sie? — When are you travelling?

This stuff is more complicated, but it's still dead important.

Ich möchte am Samstag nach Köln fahren.

= I would like to travel to Cologne on Saturday.

today: heute     next Monday: nächsten Montag     on the tenth of June: am zehnten Juni

'Abfahren' and 'ankommen' are separable verbs. See page 108 for more info.

Wann fährt der Zug nach Köln ab?

= When does the train for Cologne leave?

Wann kommt der Zug in Köln an?

= When does the train arrive in Cologne?

Von welchem Gleis fährt der Zug ab?

= Which platform does the train leave from?

More vocab... Yes, it's as dull as a big dull thing, but it's also vital to know as much as you can.

Remember, plurals are always 'die'.

| to depart: | abfahren | ticket: | die Fahrkarte (-n) | | |
| to arrive: | ankommen | ticket window: | der Fahrkartenschalter | | |
| to change (trains): | umsteigen | ticket machine: | der Fahrkartenautomat | fast-stopping train: | der Eilzug |
| platform: | das Gleis (-e) | timetable: | der Fahrplan | regional train: | der Nahverkehrszug |
| departure: | die Abfahrt | to get on: | einsteigen | suburban train: | die S-Bahn |
| arrival: | die Ankunft | to get out: | aussteigen | intercity express train: | der ICE-Zug |
| the waiting room: | der Warteraum | through train: | der D-Zug | cross-country train: | der Inter-Regio-Zug |

## Whoops, I've dropped the train...

Be careful with verbs like 'abfahren' and 'einsteigen'. They're 'separable' — you say 'der Zug fährt ab', not 'der Zug abfährt'. Apart from that, this is all fairly straightforward — so learn it. Then getting around in Germany will be a whole lot easier — more importantly, so will your GCSE.

# All Kinds of Transport

Here's what you need to know about other forms of transport. This is another of those topics that you'll need to know really well — and you need to know loads of vocab for it, too.

## Wie kommst du dahin? — How do you get there?

You'll need to say how you get about. Use the verb 'fahren' with most vehicles, but 'gehen' if you're on foot. Also, you have to use 'mit...' with most vehicles — but if you're on foot, say 'zu Fuß'.

Ich gehe zu Fuß. = I'm going on foot.

Ich fahre mit dem Zug. = I'm travelling by train.

| by bus: | mit dem Bus |
| by tram: | mit der Straßenbahn |
| on the underground: | mit der U-Bahn |
| by bike: | mit dem Fahrrad |
| by car: | mit dem Auto |
| by motorbike: | mit dem Motorrad |
| by coach: | mit dem Reisebus |
| by boat: | mit dem Boot |

Normalerweise fahre ich mit dem Bus in die Stadt. = I normally go into town by bus.

You can't use 'Ich fahre...' for travelling by plane. Instead, you can use one of these:

Ich reise mit dem Flugzeug. = I'm travelling by plane. Ich fliege. = I'm flying.

## Abfahrt und Ankunft — Departure and arrival

These are the kinds of questions you'd have to ask at a station.

This doesn't look like Stuttgart - I must've taken the wrong bus...

Fährt ein Bus nach Mannheim? = Is there a bus that goes to Mannheim?

a tram: eine Straßenbahn  a boat: ein Boot
a coach: ein Reisebus

Wann fährt der nächste Bus nach Stuttgart ab? = When does the next bus to Stuttgart leave?

the (next) coach: der (nächste) Reisebus
the (next) boat: das (nächste) Boot

Wann kommt das Flugzeug in Frankfurt an? = When does the plane arrive in Frankfurt?

## Welcher Bus...? — Which bus...?

No doubt about it — you need to be able to ask which bus or train goes where. Just learn this.

Welcher Bus fährt zum Stadtzentrum, bitte? = Which bus goes to the town centre, please?

Which tram: Welche Straßenbahn
Which underground line: Welche U-Bahn-Linie

to the bus stop: zur Bushaltestelle
to the airport: zum Flughafen
to the harbour/port: zum Hafen

# Take the bus — no, leave it there...

Think about how you usually get around, and how you get around when you're on holiday. Then tell someone in German. They'll be dead impressed by your language skills, and really interested to hear about all the different modes of transport you use for different occasions. Promise.

# Planning Your Holiday

So you've finally made it to your destination. Now you need to know what there is to do.
Unfortunately there are quite a lot of things to learn about this. Better get started then...

## Das Verkehrsamt — The Tourist Information Office

Here's where you find out what a town's got to offer. Get these phrases between your ears:

Können Sie mich über **den Zoo** informieren, bitte? = Can you give me information about the zoo, please?

the sights of Stuttgart: die Sehenswürdigkeiten von Stuttgart
the museum: das Museum

the exhibition: die Ausstellung
the gallery: die Galerie

**IMPORTANT:**
When 'über' means 'about', it's followed by the accusative. See page 84.

Wann **macht** **das Museum** **auf**? = When does the museum open?

close: zu

See page 59 for info on asking for directions.

## Ausflüge — Excursions

Learning this lot'll get you big bonus marks.

Haben Sie Broschüren über **Ausflüge von München aus**? = Do you have any leaflets about excursions from Munich?

the museums in Cologne: die Museen in Köln

Was für einen Ausflug würden Sie gern machen? = What kind of excursion would you like to go on?

Ich möchte **Neuschwanstein besichtigen**. = I'd like to look round Neuschwanstein.

go to a museum: in ein Museum gehen
see the castle: das Schloss sehen

Ooooooooohhhhhh!
A Magical Mystery Tour!

Was kostet es? = What does it cost?

Es kostet fünf Euro pro Person. = It costs 5 euros for one person.

Dieser Bus fährt nach Neuschwanstein.
**Der Bus** fährt um **halb drei** **vom Rathaus** ab. = This bus goes to Neuschwanstein. The bus leaves from the town hall at half past two.

The train: Der Zug

2 pm: vierzehn Uhr
3.15 pm: fünfzehn Uhr fünfzehn

from the church: von der Kirche
from the marketplace: vom Marktplatz

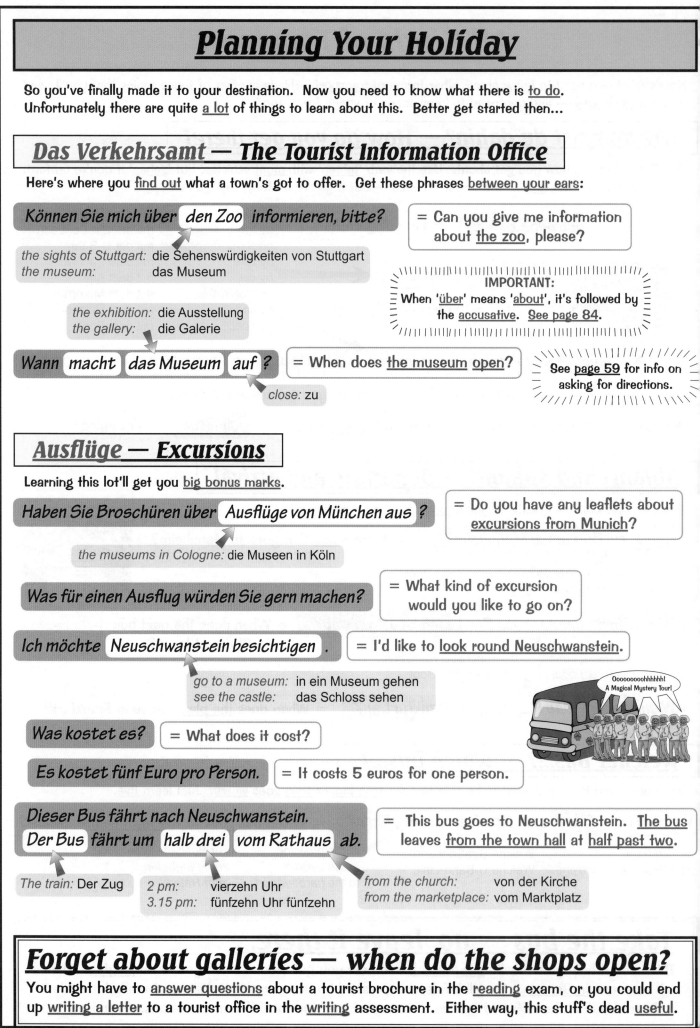

# Forget about galleries — when do the shops open?

You might have to answer questions about a tourist brochure in the reading exam, or you could end up writing a letter to a tourist office in the writing assessment. Either way, this stuff's dead useful.

# Holiday Accommodation

Okay, this page has all the words you need to know about <u>hotels</u>, <u>hostels</u> and <u>camping</u>.
You may not find it exactly riveting, but it <u>is</u> dead useful.  Better get <u>learning</u> then...

## Der Urlaub — Holiday

They like to <u>test</u> you on booking the right kind of <u>room</u> in the right kind of hotel — <u>learn it</u>...

**GENERAL VOCABULARY**

| | |
|---|---|
| holiday: | der Urlaub (-e) |
| abroad: | im Ausland |
| person: | die Person (-en) |
| night: | die Nacht (die Nächte) |
| overnight stay: | die Übernachtung (-en) |

**VERBS USED IN HOTELS**

| | |
|---|---|
| to reserve: | reservieren |
| to stay the night: | übernachten |
| to stay: | bleiben |
| to cost: | kosten |
| to leave: | abreisen/abfahren |

**THINGS YOU MIGHT ASK FOR**

| | |
|---|---|
| room: | das Zimmer (-) |
| double room: | das Doppelzimmer (-) |
| single room: | das Einzelzimmer (-) |
| place/space: | der Platz (die Plätze) |
| room service: | der Zimmerservice (-s) |

**TYPES OF ACCOMMODATION**

| | |
|---|---|
| full board: | die Vollpension |
| half board: | die Halbpension |
| bed and breakfast: | Übernachtung mit Frühstück |

For more on meals see <u>pages 51-52</u>.

**Remember: plurals are always 'die'.**

hotel: das Hotel (-s)

guest house: das Gasthaus (die Gasthäuser)

campsite: der Campingplatz (die Campingplätze)

youth hostel: die Jugendherberge (-n)

## Die Rechnung — The bill

After all that, you need to be able to ask about your <u>room</u>, where <u>things are</u>... and <u>paying the bill</u>.

**PARTS OF A HOTEL**

| | |
|---|---|
| reception: | der Empfang (die Empfänge) |
| restaurant: | das Restaurant (-s) |
| dining room: | der Speisesaal (die Speisesäle) |
| lift: | der Aufzug (die Aufzüge) |
| stairs: | die Treppe (-n) |
| car park: | der Parkplatz (die Parkplätze) |
| games room: | der Aufenthaltsraum (die Aufenthaltsräume) |

Donnie had finally located the drinking water.

**OTHER HOTEL VOCAB**

| | |
|---|---|
| key: | der Schlüssel (-) |
| balcony: | der Balkon (-e) |
| bath: | das Bad (die Bäder) |
| shower: | die Dusche (-n) |
| washbasin: | das Waschbecken (-) |

**PAYING FOR YOUR STAY**

| | |
|---|---|
| bill: | die Rechnung (-en) |
| price: | der Preis (-e) |

**EXTRA WORDS FOR CAMPING**

| | |
|---|---|
| tent: | das Zelt (-e) |
| sleeping bag: | der Schlafsack (die Schlafsäcke) |
| to camp: | zelten |
| to pitch the tent: | das Zelt aufstellen |
| pitch: | der Platz (die Plätze) |
| drinking water: | das Trinkwasser |

## You'll need a holiday after this...

A page bristling with vocab — <u>learn</u> all the stuff on this page and you're <u>well away</u> if anything on hotels comes up... and it often does.  Check you know the words by <u>covering</u> the page and <u>scribbling</u> them down.

# Booking a Room / Pitch

Looking for a relaxing post-exam break this summer? Here's how to <u>book yourself a room</u> in Deutschland.

## Haben Sie Zimmer frei? — Do you have any rooms free?

You'll have to say <u>what sort</u> of room you want and <u>how long</u> you'll be staying.

Ich möchte ein **Einzelzimmer** . = I'd like a <u>single room</u>.

*double room:* Doppelzimmer

You could be a bit more specific and use these:
*room with a bath:* Zimmer mit Bad
*room with a balcony:* Zimmer mit Balkon

Ich möchte **zwei Nächte** hier bleiben. = I'd like to stay here for <u>two nights</u>.

On the plus side this is only costing us 5.95 a night.

See <u>page 1</u> for more numbers.

If you're staying for one night, use 'eine Nacht' (not ein Nacht).

Was kostet es pro Nacht für **eine Person** ? = How much is it per night for <u>one person</u>?

If there's more than one person, use '<u>zwei Personen</u>', '<u>drei Personen</u>' etc.

Ich nehme es. = I'll take it.    Ich nehme es nicht. = I won't take it.

## Kann man hier zelten? — Can I camp here?

Whether you like the <u>outdoor life</u> or not — you'll <u>need</u> these phrases.

Ich möchte einen **Platz** für **drei Nächte** , bitte. = I'd like a <u>pitch</u> for <u>three nights</u>, please.

Put how long you want to stay here.

pitch (place for a tent): der Platz (die Plätze)

tent: das Zelt (-e)

You might need these phrases too:
*Is there drinking water here?:* Gibt es hier Trinkwasser?
*Can I light a fire here?:* Kann man hier Feuer machen?
*Where can I get...?:* Wo bekomme ich...?

caravan: der Wohnwagen (-)

sleeping bag: der Schlafsack (die Schlafsäcke)

Remember, plurals are always 'die'.

You may have to book ahead. See <u>page 11</u> for information on how to write a formal letter.

## Do you have any rooms free — no, you have to pay...

Going to a <u>hotel</u> or <u>campsite</u> could well come up somewhere like your <u>listening</u> exam. So even if you're <u>never</u> going to go on holiday to Germany, get this page <u>learnt</u>.

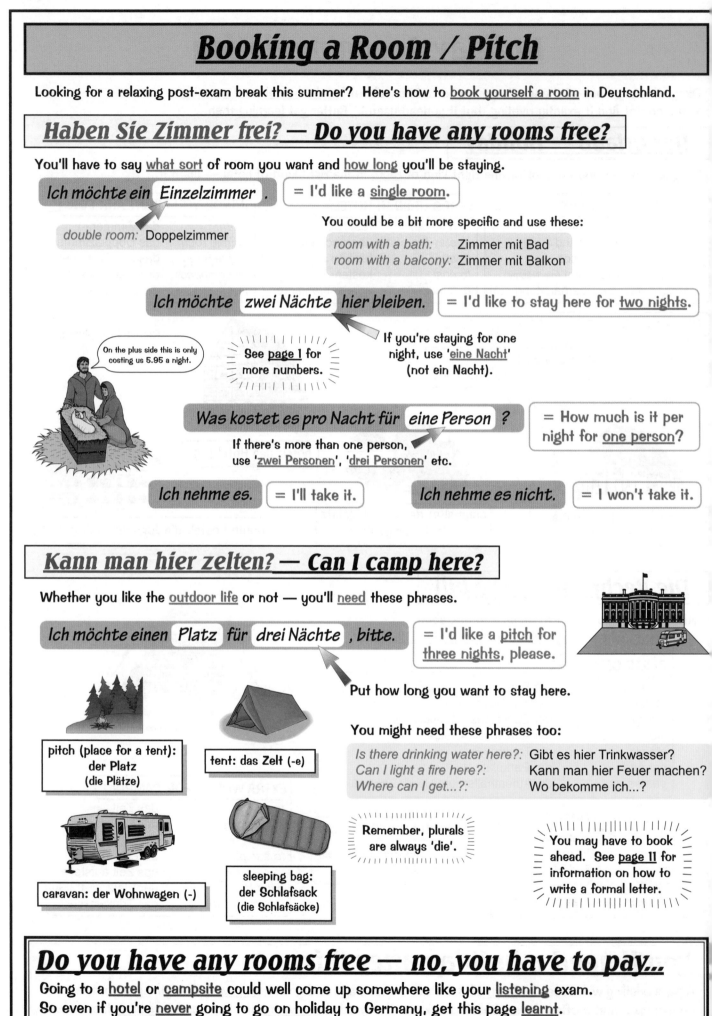

# Where / When is... ?

Being able to <u>ask questions</u> is pretty darn useful — as is <u>understanding</u> the answers.
This lot'll also help when you go on holiday...

## Wo ist... ? — Where is... ?

Knowing how to ask <u>where</u> things are is essential — get these <u>learnt</u>:

**Wo ist** der Speisesaal **, bitte?** = Where is <u>the dining room</u>, please?

| | |
|---|---|
| *the car park:* | der Parkplatz (die Parkplätze) |
| *the games room:* | das Spielzimmer (-) |
| *the play area:* | der Spielplatz (die Spielplätze) |
| *the toilet:* | die Toilette (-n) |
| *the loo:* | das Klo (-s) |

See <u>page 47</u> for more things you might need to ask about.

Remember, plurals are always 'die'.

The floor number takes a <u>dative</u> ending here. See <u>page 91</u>.

**Er ist im** dritten Stock **.** = It's on the <u>third floor</u>.

Only 13 more floors to go...

| | |
|---|---|
| *fourth floor:* | vierten Stock |
| *second floor:* | zweiten Stock |
| *first floor:* | ersten Stock |
| *ground floor:* | Erdgeschoss |

For higher floor numbers, see <u>page 1</u>.

These are other words you might need when you describe where something is.

| | |
|---|---|
| *outside:* | draußen |
| *on the left / right:* | links / rechts |
| *upstairs:* | oben |
| *downstairs:* | unten |
| *at the end of the corridor:* | am Ende des Ganges |

## Wann ist... ? — When is... ?

And then when you've found out <u>where</u> everything is, you'll need to know <u>when</u> things happen...

**Wann wird** das Frühstück **serviert, bitte?** = When is <u>breakfast</u> served, please?

| | |
|---|---|
| *lunch:* | das Mittagessen (-) |
| *evening meal:* | das Abendessen (-) |

For more times, see <u>page 2</u>.

Wann wird das Abendessen serviert?

Gulp!

**Es wird um** acht Uhr **serviert.** = It's served at <u>eight o'clock</u>.

# What d'you mean 'das Klo' is on the 49th floor?

That stuff on <u>1st floor</u>, <u>2nd floor</u> etc. comes up for <u>other</u> things, like <u>shops</u>... — so it's well worth <u>learning</u>. You need to <u>know</u> all of this vocab to get good <u>marks</u>. The best way to make sure you know it is to <u>cover up</u> the page and try to <u>scribble</u> the words down. If you can't, you haven't learnt it.

# Problems with Accommodation

Whatever your problem, sometimes it's good to get it all off your chest. Nobody wants their holiday ruined by dodgy plumbing and itchy sheets, so here's how to make yourself heard auf Deutsch...

## Es gibt ein Problem mit... — There's a problem with...

Here are a few common complaints to be getting on with:

*The room:* Das Zimmer → **Das Wasser ist kalt .** = **The water** is **cold**.

*too hot:* zu heiß

**Es gibt keine Handtücher in meinem Zimmer.** = There are no <u>towels</u> in my room.

*soap:* Seife

Once you get started it's hard to stop...

**Der Fernseher ist kaputt.** = **The television** is broken.

*The radiator:* Der Heizkörper    *The air conditioning:* Die Klimaanlage
*The heating:* Die Heizung    *The telephone:* Das Telefon

**Die Dusche funktioniert nicht.** = **The shower** doesn't work.

**Es ist zu laut. Ich kann nicht schlafen.** = It's too loud. I can't sleep.

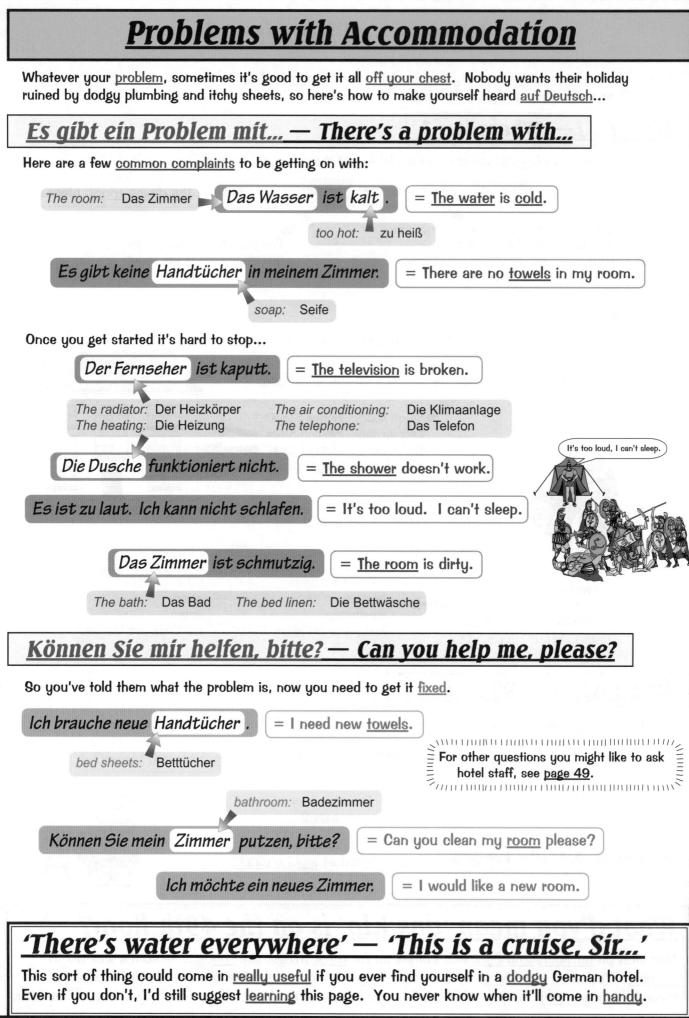

It's too loud, I can't sleep.

**Das Zimmer ist schmutzig.** = **The room** is dirty.

*The bath:* Das Bad    *The bed linen:* Die Bettwäsche

## Können Sie mir helfen, bitte? — Can you help me, please?

So you've told them what the problem is, now you need to get it fixed.

**Ich brauche neue Handtücher .** = I need new <u>towels</u>.

*bed sheets:* Betttücher

> For other questions you might like to ask hotel staff, see page 49.

*bathroom:* Badezimmer

**Können Sie mein Zimmer putzen, bitte?** = Can you clean my <u>room</u> please?

**Ich möchte ein neues Zimmer.** = I would like a new room.

## 'There's water everywhere' — 'This is a cruise, Sir...'

This sort of thing could come in <u>really useful</u> if you ever find yourself in a <u>dodgy</u> German hotel. Even if you don't, I'd still suggest <u>learning</u> this page. You never know when it'll come in <u>handy</u>.

# At a Restaurant

You might've seen <u>some</u> of these sentences before in <u>different situations</u> and with <u>different</u> vocabulary. That's because they're <u>important</u>, so get them <u>learnt</u>.

## Im Restaurant — At the restaurant

*Entschuldigen Sie* = Excuse me!

This is what you'd use to call the waiter or waitress over...

waiter: der Kellner (-)
waitress: die Kellnerin (-nen)

...and these are the names of the jobs.

*Darf ich bitte* **die Karte** *haben?* = May I have <u>the menu</u>, please?

*the menu of the day:* die Tageskarte

See <u>page 49</u> on 'hotels' for asking where things are.

*Wo ist* **die Toilette** *, bitte?* = Where's <u>the toilet</u>, please?

*the phone:* das Telefon

## Ich hätte gern... — I'd like...

This stuff could be used in <u>other situations</u> too, like shops — so <u>learn it well</u>.

*Haben Sie* **Bockwurst** *?* = Do you have <u>boiled sausage</u>?

*fried sausage:* Bratwurst
*German noodles:* Spätzle

*the steak:* das Steak
*the chicken:* das Hähnchen

*Ich hätte gern* **das Schnitzel** *mit* **Pommes** *.* = I'd like <u>the schnitzel</u> with <u>chips</u>.

*rice:* Reis
*pickled cabbage:* Sauerkraut

See <u>page 13</u> for more food vocab.

## Wie schmeckt es? — What does it taste like?

You might want to know what something's like before you scoff it all — so <u>be sure</u> to learn this:

*Wie schmeckt* **Sauerkraut** *?* = What does <u>Sauerkraut</u> taste like?

*German Christmas cake:* Stollen

## Sind Sie fertig? — Are you finished?

There's <u>no</u> getting away from having to know <u>this</u>. You can't leave without paying.

*Die Rechnung, bitte.* = The bill, please.

*Darf ich bitte zahlen?* = May I pay, please?

The bill, sir.

# The day of Rechnung — it's time to pay...

These <u>important phrases</u> are just the sort of thing your exam board loves, so <u>learn them now</u>. You could even test some of them out on your mum at tea time... on second thoughts maybe not.

# At a Restaurant

All this restaurant stuff's not hard — but your exam could well be if you don't make an effort to memorise it.

## Haben Sie einen Tisch frei? — Do you have a table free?

This part's easy, so it's definitely worth learning.

**Einen Tisch für vier Personen, bitte.** = A table for four, please.

See page 1 for more about numbers.

*two:* zwei
*three:* drei

*two:* zu zweit
*three:* zu dritt

**Wir sind zu viert.** = There are four of us.

**Wir möchten drinnen sitzen.** = We'd like to sit inside.

*outside:* draußen   *on the terrace:* auf der Terrasse

## Ich bin nicht zufrieden — I'm not satisfied

Once you've learnt this first phrase, you can complain about anything. Useful.

**Ich möchte mich beklagen.** = I'd like to make a complaint.

**Das Rindfleisch ist nicht gar.** = The beef is underdone.

*The steak:* Das Steak
*The pork:* Das Schweinefleisch
*The soup:* Die Suppe
*The sausage:* Die Wurst

*overcooked:* verbraten
*too hot:* zu heiß
*too cold:* zu kalt
*too salty:* zu salzig

See page 13 for more food vocab.

## Die Speisekarte — The Menu

A few other bits and pieces for you to learn...

**Ist die Bedienung inbegriffen?** = Is service included?

If you see these words or their abbreviations on a menu, it means service is 'included'.

inbegriffen
inklusive
(or inkl.)

inklusive Bedienung

Bedienung inbegriffen

It's always handy to know which bit of the menu you're looking at.

**COURSES: DIE GÄNGE**
*starter:* die Vorspeise (-e)
*main course:* das Hauptgericht (-e) / der Hauptgang (die Hauptgänge)
*dessert:* der Nachtisch (-e)

## Es gibt eine Fliege in meiner Suppe...

Being at a restaurant could easily come up somewhere, so you need to know all about it. If you've learnt all the stuff on this page, then it'll be easy. So no skiving out of anything.

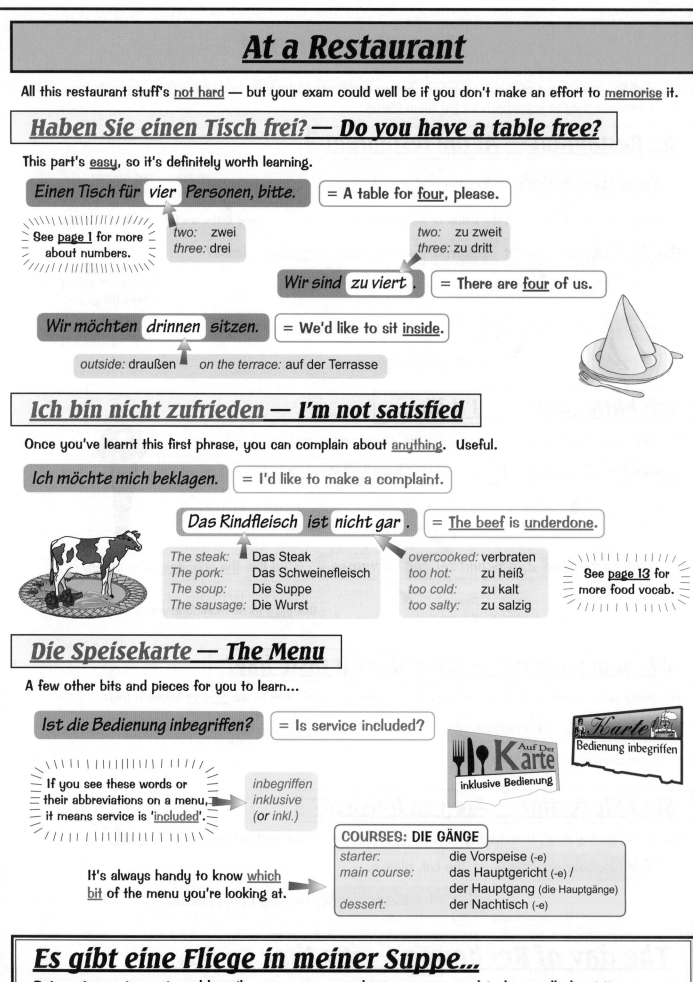

# Talking About Your Holiday

When you've been on <u>holiday</u> you want to bore everyone by <u>telling</u> them all about it.
After this page you'll be able to bore people in <u>German</u> too... and get good <u>marks</u>.

## Wohin bist du gefahren? — *Where did you go?*

Talking about your holiday is a great place to use the <u>perfect tense</u>.
Get it right and the examiners will be dead <u>impressed</u>. For help, see <u>page 104</u>.

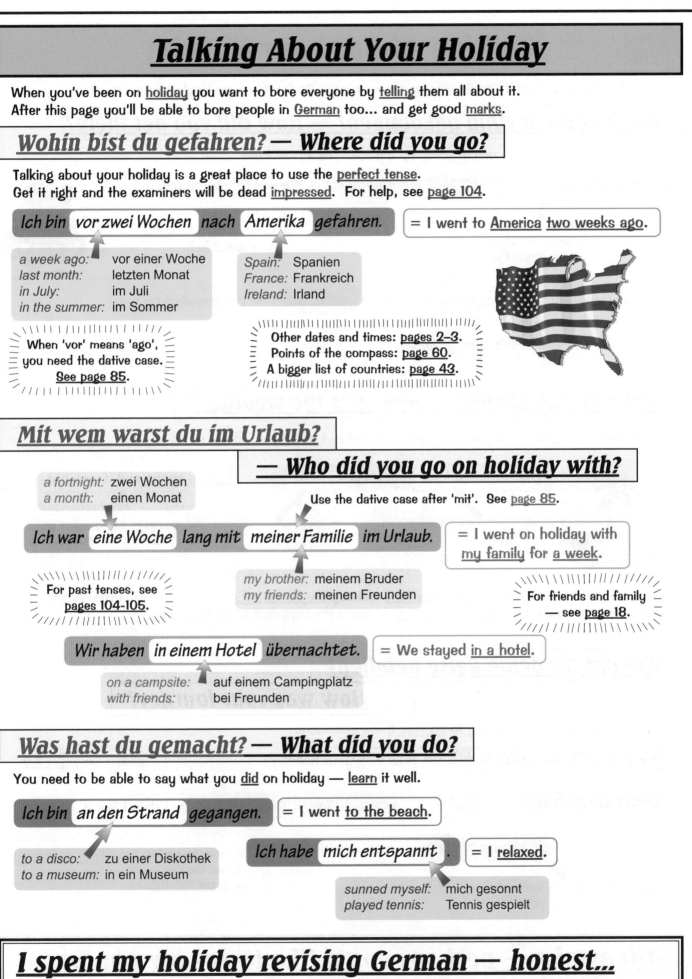

Ich bin | vor zwei Wochen | nach | Amerika | gefahren.
= I went to <u>America</u> <u>two weeks ago</u>.

*a week ago:* vor einer Woche
*last month:* letzten Monat
*in July:* im Juli
*in the summer:* im Sommer

*Spain:* Spanien
*France:* Frankreich
*Ireland:* Irland

When 'vor' means 'ago',
you need the dative case.
See page 85.

Other dates and times: pages 2–3.
Points of the compass: page 60.
A bigger list of countries: page 43.

## Mit wem warst du im Urlaub?

### — *Who did you go on holiday with?*

*a fortnight:* zwei Wochen
*a month:* einen Monat

Use the dative case after 'mit'. See <u>page 85</u>.

Ich war | eine Woche | lang mit | meiner Familie | im Urlaub.
= I went on holiday with <u>my family</u> for <u>a week</u>.

For past tenses, see
pages 104-105.

*my brother:* meinem Bruder
*my friends:* meinen Freunden

For friends and family
— see page 18.

Wir haben | in einem Hotel | übernachtet.
= We stayed <u>in a hotel</u>.

*on a campsite:* auf einem Campingplatz
*with friends:* bei Freunden

## Was hast du gemacht? — *What did you do?*

You need to be able to say what you <u>did</u> on holiday — <u>learn</u> it well.

Ich bin | an den Strand | gegangen.
= I went <u>to the beach</u>.

*to a disco:* zu einer Diskothek
*to a museum:* in ein Museum

Ich habe | mich entspannt |.
= I <u>relaxed</u>.

*sunned myself:* mich gesonnt
*played tennis:* Tennis gespielt

# I spent my holiday revising German — honest...

You need to be able to <u>talk</u> about holidays in your <u>speaking</u> and <u>writing</u> tasks, and <u>understand</u> other people going on about <u>their holidays</u>. Cover up the page and see how much you can <u>remember</u>.

# Talking About Your Holiday

This is the kind of stuff that'll really impress the examiner. So for lots more lovely marks, plough on...

## Wie bist du dorthin gekommen? — How did you get there?

'Dorthin' means 'there' when you're going 'to' a place. It's a useful one.

**Wir sind mit** dem Wagen **dorthin gekommen.** = We went there by car.

train: dem Zug
boat: dem Boot
bike: dem Fahrrad

For more types of transport, see pages 44–45.

You could also say: **Wir sind mit** dem Auto **gefahren.** = We travelled by car.

Or even: **Wir sind geflogen.** = We flew.

## Wie war das Wetter? — How was the weather?

No description of your holiday would be complete without giving a run-down of the weather.

**Die Sonne schien** und es war heiß. = The sun shone and it was hot.

It rained: Es hat geregnet
It snowed: Es hat geschneit

cold: kalt
rainy: regnerisch

See page 56 for more ways of talking about the weather.

You could use the perfect tense (see page 104) and say 'die Sonne hat geschienen' for 'the sun shone', but it's more normal to say 'die Sonne schien' — that's the imperfect tense (see page 105).

## Wie hat dir deine Reise gefallen?
### — How was your journey?

Giving your opinion is a great way to impress those examiners.

For more on giving opinions see pages 7-9.

**Wie fandst du deinen Urlaub?** = How was your holiday?

**Er hat mir gefallen.** = I liked it. **Er hat mir nicht gefallen.** = I didn't like it.

**Er war in Ordnung.** = It was OK.

For more on talking about the past, see pages 104-105.

'Urlaub' is masculine — that's why it's 'er war', not 'es' or 'sie'.

## Still awake — perhaps you'd like to see my photos...

You need to know all this vocab for writing and talking about holidays. You can always make up a holiday you didn't have, if you know the German words for it. Smile — it could be worse. Just.

# Talking About Your Holiday

You're not done yet — oh no. There's <u>plenty more</u> you can say about holidays. Just you <u>wait and see</u>...

## Wohin wirst du fahren? — Where will you go?

You've got to be able to talk about the <u>future</u> — things that you <u>will be doing</u>...

These are all in the future tense...

| Where will you go?
Wohin wirst du fahren? |

| Who will you go on holiday with?
Mit wem wirst du in den Urlaub fahren? |

| What will you do?
Was wirst du machen? |

| How will you get there?
Wie wirst du dorthin kommen? |

...and these are in the present future tense...

| I'm going to America in two weeks.
Ich fahre in zwei Wochen nach Amerika. |

| I'm going on holiday for a month with my family.
Ich fahre einen Monat lang mit meiner Familie in den Urlaub. |

| I'm going to the beach.
Ich gehe an den Strand. |

| I'm going by car.
Ich fahre mit dem Wagen. |

For more info about the future tense, see <u>page 103</u>.

## Ein deutscher Austausch — A German Exchange

Finally, you might want to talk about an <u>exchange</u> visit you did with school.

Letztes Jahr bin ich nach Deutschland gefahren, um meinen Brieffreund zu besuchen.
= Last year I went to Germany in order to visit <u>my pen friend</u>.

*my pen friend (female):* meine Brieffreundin

For more about '<u>um... zu...</u>' ('in order to') see <u>page 112</u>.

Ich habe Deutschland mit der Schule besucht. Ich habe bei einer deutschen Familie gewohnt.
= I visited Germany with school. I stayed with a <u>German family</u>.

*host family:* Gastfamilie

Während meines Austausches habe ich die Schule meines Freundes besucht.
= During my exchange I visited <u>my friend's</u> school.

*my (female) friend:* meiner Freundin

Wir haben uns sehr gut verstanden.
= We got on really well.

Finding a way to sneak the <u>future tense</u> in will always impress...

It's usual to use the accusative here, so it's 'diese<u>n</u>' not 'diese<u>r</u>'.

Diesen Sommer wird mein Brieffreund nach England kommen.
= This summer my pen friend will come to England.

## I've got a pen friend — his name's Parker...

So, that just about wraps up talking about your holiday. There's <u>loads</u> of stuff you can say, which makes this a <u>really important</u> topic. Make sure you know it <u>well</u>. I mean <u>ultra</u>-well.

# The Weather

You may well have to talk about the <u>weather</u> yourself, or understand a <u>forecast</u> in your <u>listening</u> exam. But don't worry — just learn these few <u>easy sentences</u> and this bit of <u>vocab</u>.

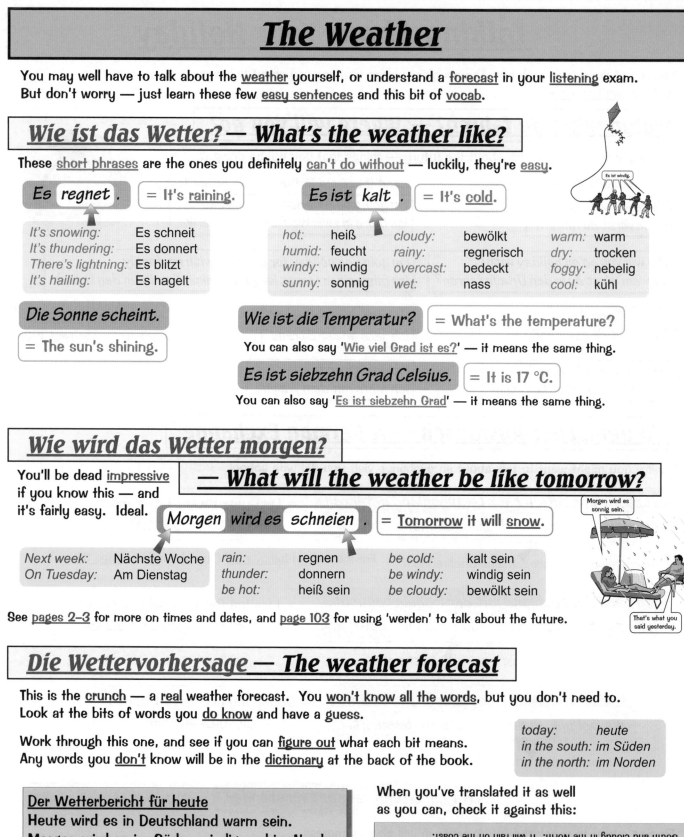

## Wie ist das Wetter? — What's the weather like?

These <u>short phrases</u> are the ones you definitely <u>can't do without</u> — luckily, they're <u>easy</u>.

**Es regnet .** = It's <u>raining</u>.

**Es ist kalt .** = It's <u>cold</u>.

| | |
|---|---|
| *It's snowing:* | Es schneit |
| *It's thundering:* | Es donnert |
| *There's lightning:* | Es blitzt |
| *It's hailing:* | Es hagelt |

| *hot:* | heiß | *cloudy:* | bewölkt | *warm:* | warm |
|---|---|---|---|---|---|
| *humid:* | feucht | *rainy:* | regnerisch | *dry:* | trocken |
| *windy:* | windig | *overcast:* | bedeckt | *foggy:* | nebelig |
| *sunny:* | sonnig | *wet:* | nass | *cool:* | kühl |

**Die Sonne scheint.**

= The sun's shining.

**Wie ist die Temperatur?** = What's the temperature?

You can also say '<u>Wie viel Grad ist es?</u>' — it means the same thing.

**Es ist siebzehn Grad Celsius.** = It is 17 °C.

You can also say '<u>Es ist siebzehn Grad</u>' — it means the same thing.

## Wie wird das Wetter morgen?

You'll be dead <u>impressive</u> if you know this — and it's fairly easy. Ideal.

## — What will the weather be like tomorrow?

**Morgen wird es schneien .** = <u>Tomorrow</u> it will <u>snow</u>.

| *Next week:* | Nächste Woche | *rain:* | regnen | *be cold:* | kalt sein |
|---|---|---|---|---|---|
| *On Tuesday:* | Am Dienstag | *thunder:* | donnern | *be windy:* | windig sein |
| | | *be hot:* | heiß sein | *be cloudy:* | bewölkt sein |

See <u>pages 2–3</u> for more on times and dates, and <u>page 103</u> for using 'werden' to talk about the future.

## Die Wettervorhersage — The weather forecast

This is the <u>crunch</u> — a <u>real</u> weather forecast. You <u>won't know all the words</u>, but you don't need to. Look at the bits of words you <u>do know</u> and have a guess.

Work through this one, and see if you can <u>figure out</u> what each bit means. Any words you <u>don't</u> know will be in the <u>dictionary</u> at the back of the book.

| | |
|---|---|
| *today:* | *heute* |
| *in the south:* | *im Süden* |
| *in the north:* | *im Norden* |

**Der Wetterbericht für heute**
Heute wird es in Deutschland warm sein.
Morgen wird es im Süden windig und im Norden bewölkt sein. An der Küste wird es regnen.

When you've translated it as well as you can, check it against this:

Today's Weather Report
Today it will be warm in Germany. Tomorrow it will be windy in the South and cloudy in the North. It will rain on the coast.

# Learn this page — Wetter you like it or not...

All I want to know is "Do I need a coat?" and "Will I get a tan?" Still, this stuff comes up in the exams so you've got to do it — luckily it's <u>not</u> that <u>hard</u>. All you need to do is <u>learn</u> the main <u>sentences</u> on this page and the <u>vocab</u>, and you'll be working for the Met Office in no time...

# Revision Summary

These questions are here to make sure you really <u>know your stuff</u>. Work through them all, and <u>make a note</u> of the ones you couldn't do. Look back through the section to <u>find out</u> how to answer them. Try those problem questions again. Then look up any you still can't do. <u>Keep at it</u> until you can do them all — cos that'll mean you've really learnt it.

1) Write down ten countries in German.
How would you say that you came from each one of these countries?

2) Ask for three return tickets to Dresden, second class. Ask what platform the train leaves from and where the waiting room is. Ask if you have to change trains.

3) Say in German that you go to school by car, but your friend walks.
(Make sure you use the right verb for these.)

4) You've missed the bus to Frankfurt.
Ask when the next bus leaves and when it arrives in Frankfurt.

5) You arrive in Tübingen and go to the tourist information office.
Ask for information about the sights.

6) There's an excursion to a nearby museum. Ask for a leaflet about the excursion.
Ask what time the bus departs from the town hall.

7) You get to a hotel in Germany. Ask them if they have any free rooms.

8) Say you want one double room and two single rooms. Say you want to stay five nights.
Say you'll take the rooms.

9) Ask where the games room is.

10) Ask the staff in your German hotel when breakfast is served.

11) You get to your room and find that's it's dirty and the shower doesn't work.
Tell the hotel staff this and say that you would like the room cleaned.

12) You're going out for a meal. Ask if you can have a table for two and ask where the toilet is.

13) Order steak and chips for you, and roast chicken with potatoes for your friend.
Attract the waitress's attention and tell her that the potatoes are cold.

14) Attract the waiter's attention and say that you'd like the bill.

15) You've just been on holiday to Italy. You went for two weeks with your sister. You went there by plane. You relaxed and sunned yourself. The weather was hot and sunny.
You enjoyed the holiday and are going to go to Spain next year.
Phew — say that lot in German.

16) Your German pen friend wants to know what the weather is like where you are.
Say that it is cloudy and raining, but that tomorrow the sun will shine.

# Names of Buildings

You'll be able to talk about your town much better if you know what buildings there are in it — and the examiners will think you're pretty cool too. Which means bucketloads of marks.

## Die Gebäude — Buildings

These are the basic, bog-standard 'learn-them-or-else' buildings. (Building = das Gebäude.) Don't go any further until you know all of them.

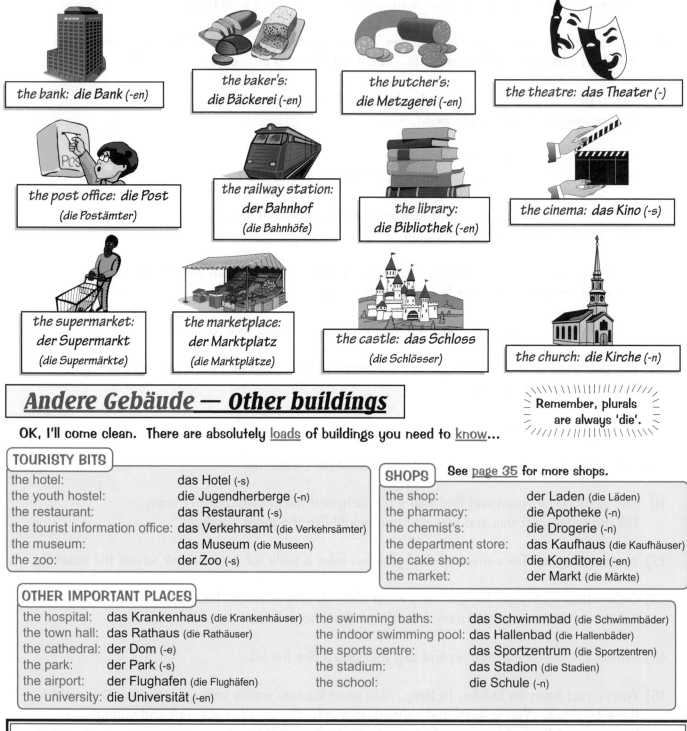

| | |
| --- | --- |
| the bank: die Bank (-en) | the baker's: die Bäckerei (-en) | the butcher's: die Metzgerei (-en) | the theatre: das Theater (-) |
| the post office: die Post (die Postämter) | the railway station: der Bahnhof (die Bahnhöfe) | the library: die Bibliothek (-en) | the cinema: das Kino (-s) |
| the supermarket: der Supermarkt (die Supermärkte) | the marketplace: der Marktplatz (die Marktplätze) | the castle: das Schloss (die Schlösser) | the church: die Kirche (-n) |

## Andere Gebäude — Other buildings

*Remember, plurals are always 'die'.*

OK, I'll come clean. There are absolutely loads of buildings you need to know...

### TOURISTY BITS

| | |
| --- | --- |
| the hotel: | das Hotel (-s) |
| the youth hostel: | die Jugendherberge (-n) |
| the restaurant: | das Restaurant (-s) |
| the tourist information office: | das Verkehrsamt (die Verkehrsämter) |
| the museum: | das Museum (die Museen) |
| the zoo: | der Zoo (-s) |

### SHOPS

See page 35 for more shops.

| | |
| --- | --- |
| the shop: | der Laden (die Läden) |
| the pharmacy: | die Apotheke (-n) |
| the chemist's: | die Drogerie (-n) |
| the department store: | das Kaufhaus (die Kaufhäuser) |
| the cake shop: | die Konditorei (-en) |
| the market: | der Markt (die Märkte) |

### OTHER IMPORTANT PLACES

| | | | |
| --- | --- | --- | --- |
| the hospital: | das Krankenhaus (die Krankenhäuser) | the swimming baths: | das Schwimmbad (die Schwimmbäder) |
| the town hall: | das Rathaus (die Rathäuser) | the indoor swimming pool: | das Hallenbad (die Hallenbäder) |
| the cathedral: | der Dom (-e) | the sports centre: | das Sportzentrum (die Sportzentren) |
| the park: | der Park (-s) | the stadium: | das Stadion (die Stadien) |
| the airport: | der Flughafen (die Flughäfen) | the school: | die Schule (-n) |
| the university: | die Universität (-en) | | |

## There's a butcher's, a baker's, *a lovely little candlestick place...*

There are lots of words to learn here. The best way to do it is to turn over the page and see if you can write them all down, have a look and then have another go... It's boring, but it works. Just reading the page isn't enough — you wouldn't remember them tomorrow, never mind in an exam.

# Asking Directions

You're probably going to get at least <u>one</u> question about asking <u>directions</u>. So this page is going to be really <u>important</u>. Start learning this stuff and get these phrases between your ears.

## Wo ist... ? — Where is... ?

It's dead easy to ask <u>where</u> a place is — say '<u>Wo ist...</u>' and stick the <u>place</u> on the end.
No dodgy word order — say it how you would in English.

> Wo ist **die Post** , bitte?

= Where is <u>the post office</u>, please?

*See <u>page 58</u> for more buildings.*

> Gibt es hier in der Nähe **eine Bibliothek** ?

= Is there <u>a library</u> near here?

*Realising her mistake, Phoebe began frantically searching for a trouser shop.*

## Wie weit ist es? — How far is it?

The place you're looking for might be <u>too far</u> to walk — you might need a <u>bus</u> or <u>tram</u> instead. Here's how you check the <u>distance</u>, before you let yourself in for a 3-hour trek to the airport.

> Wie weit ist es **zum Kino** ?

= How far is it <u>to the cinema</u>?

**IMPORTANT BIT:**
It's '<u>zur</u>' for '<u>die</u>' words and '<u>zum</u>' for '<u>der</u>' and '<u>das</u>' words.

> **Es** ist **zwei Kilometer** von hier.

= <u>It's two kilometres</u> from here.

*It:* Er/Sie/Es

*a hundred metres:* hundert Meter
*not far:* nicht weit

## Wie komme ich zu...? — How do I get to...?

If you're not standing right <u>in front</u> of it, you'll need <u>directions</u>.
Here's how you <u>ask</u> for them...

You can add '<u>am besten</u>' into the sentence (before the building) to ask the <u>best</u> way to get there.

> Entschuldigen Sie bitte, wie komme ich **zur Bank** ?

= Excuse me please, how do I get <u>to the bank</u>?

**IMPORTANT BIT:**
Swap this for any place, using '<u>zum</u>' or '<u>zur</u>' like in the last section.

*to the station:* zum Bahnhof
*to the library:* zur Bibliothek
*to the castle:* zum Schloss

> Wie komme ich **am besten** zum Bahnhof?

= What's the <u>best</u> way to the station?

You'll need <u>all</u> this vocabulary to <u>understand</u> any directions you're given:

| | | | |
|---|---|---|---|
| *go straight on:* | gehen Sie geradeaus | *right at the traffic lights:* | rechts an der Ampel |
| *go right:* | gehen Sie rechts | *straight on, past the church:* | geradeaus, an der Kirche vorbei |
| *go left:* | gehen Sie links | *take the first road on the left:* | nehmen Sie die erste Straße links |
| *on the corner:* | an der Ecke | *on the right/left:* | auf der rechten/linken Seite |
| *round the corner:* | um die Ecke | | |
| *over there:* | dort drüben/da drüben | | |

Look at <u>page 1</u> for more stuff on 1st, 2nd, etc.

# Everyone needs some direction in life...

This is another page of stuff you're almost <u>bound</u> to get in one of your papers, so it's time to <u>cover up</u> the page and see how much of the vocab you can <u>remember</u> — and <u>keep going</u> until you know it all. Use the phrases on <u>all</u> the buildings you can remember from <u>page 58</u>. No pain, no gain.

# Where You're From

At some point, you're probably going to get asked about <u>where</u> you're from. And you're going to <u>have</u> to be able to <u>answer</u>. So it's a good job you're reading this page then eh?

## Woher kommst du? — *Where do you come from?*

Get this phrase learnt <u>off by heart</u> — if the country you're from isn't here, look at <u>page 43</u>, or go look it up in a dictionary.

Ich komme aus England . Ich bin Engländer(in) .

= I come from <u>England</u>. I am <u>English</u>.

Wales: Wales
Northern Ireland: Nordirland
Scotland: Schottland
Great Britain: Großbritannien

Welsh: Waliser(in)
Northern Irish: Nordirländer(in)
Scottish: Schotte/Schottin
British: Brite/Britin

**IMPORTANT BIT:**
You must add '-in' on the end for <u>women and girls</u>.

With '<u>Schotte</u>' and '<u>Brite</u>' you also have to <u>remove</u> the '<u>-e</u>' from the end before you add on the '<u>-in</u>' to make the feminine versions.

Wo wohnst du?  = Where do you live?

Ich wohne in England .  = I live in <u>England</u>.

## Wo wohnst du? — *Where do you live?*

You're <u>bound</u> to get asked this at some point — so get your answer ready.

Ich wohne in Barrow .  = I live in <u>Barrow</u>.

Ich komme vom Mars.
Ich bin Marsmensch.

Barrow liegt in Nordwestengland .  = Barrow's <u>in the north-west of England</u>.

in the north: im Norden    in the south: im Süden    in south-east England: in Südostengland
in the east: im Osten    in the west: im Westen    in north Scotland: in Nordschottland

*a city:* eine Großstadt   *a village:* ein Dorf

Barrow ist eine Stadt mit ungefähr 60 000 Einwohnern und viel Industrie.

= Barrow is <u>a town</u> with about 60 000 inhabitants and a lot of industry.

See <u>page 85</u> for an explanation of the '-n' on the end of 'Einwohner'.

## Ein wohner, zwei wohner — this'll take for ever...

This page is fairly <u>straightforward</u>, which — after all that asking for directions stuff — is quite <u>nice</u>. It's so straightfoward in fact that you'd be a <u>fool</u> not to <u>learn it</u>. So I suggest you get to it...

# Talking About Where You Live

Whether you like where you live or not, you can still find <u>plenty</u> to say about it. Make sure you <u>learn</u> these phrases, then you can happily <u>regurgitate</u> them in your speaking and writing tasks without even thinking.

## Die Gegend von Plymouth... — The Plymouth area...

Come up with this <u>little lot</u> and you'll knock those examiners <u>for six</u>...

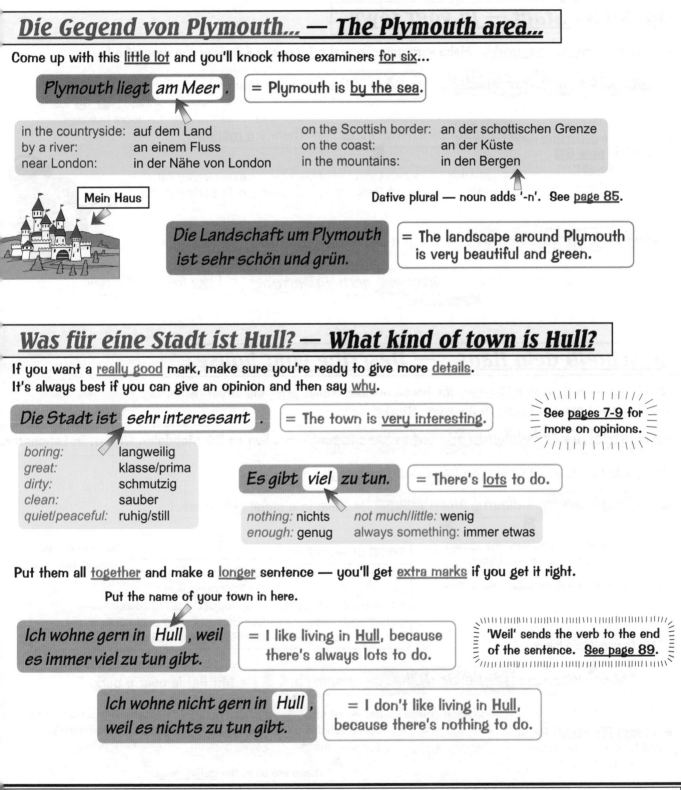

Plymouth liegt am Meer .   = Plymouth is <u>by the sea</u>.

| | | | |
|---|---|---|---|
| in the countryside: | auf dem Land | on the Scottish border: | an der schottischen Grenze |
| by a river: | an einem Fluss | on the coast: | an der Küste |
| near London: | in der Nähe von London | in the mountains: | in den Bergen |

Mein Haus

Dative plural — noun adds '-n'. See <u>page 85</u>.

Die Landschaft um Plymouth ist sehr schön und grün.   = The landscape around Plymouth is very beautiful and green.

## Was für eine Stadt ist Hull? — What kind of town is Hull?

If you want a <u>really good</u> mark, make sure you're ready to give more <u>details</u>.
It's always best if you can give an opinion and then say <u>why</u>.

Die Stadt ist sehr interessant .   = The town is <u>very interesting</u>.

See pages <u>7-9</u> for more on opinions.

| | |
|---|---|
| *boring:* | langweilig |
| *great:* | klasse/prima |
| *dirty:* | schmutzig |
| *clean:* | sauber |
| *quiet/peaceful:* | ruhig/still |

Es gibt viel zu tun.   = There's <u>lots</u> to do.

*nothing:* nichts   *not much/little:* wenig
*enough:* genug   *always something:* immer etwas

Put them all <u>together</u> and make a <u>longer</u> sentence — you'll get <u>extra marks</u> if you get it right.

Put the name of your town in here.

Ich wohne gern in Hull , weil es immer viel zu tun gibt.   = I like living in <u>Hull</u>, because there's always lots to do.

'Weil' sends the verb to the end of the sentence. <u>See page 89</u>.

Ich wohne nicht gern in Hull , weil es nichts zu tun gibt.   = I don't like living in <u>Hull</u>, because there's nothing to do.

## Hull — it's a little bit like Paris actually...

If you think you come from a really dreary place which has <u>nothing</u> going for it, you can <u>make things up</u> (within reason) — but chances are there'll be <u>something</u> to say about a place near you. Start with <u>whereabouts</u> it is and see how much you can say about it <u>without</u> looking at the page.

# Talking About Where You Live

More really important stuff — you'll need to be able to talk about the place where you live, where your home is and what it looks like.

## In deiner Stadt — In your town

This sort of thing is easy marks. Make sure you can reel off those buildings at the drop of a hat.

**Was gibt es in deiner Stadt?** = What is there in your town?

You need the accusative case (see page 84) after 'Es gibt'.

**Es gibt einen Markt.** = There's a market.

See page 58 for more buildings.

a cathedral: einen Dom    a university: eine Universität
a park: einen Park    a sports centre: ein Sportzentrum

**Wohnst du gern in Barrow?** = Do you like living in Barrow?

don't like: nicht gern    **Ich wohne gern in Barrow.** = I like living in Barrow.

## Beschreib dein Haus… — Describe your house…

Watch out — in German addresses, the house number comes after the street name, and the street name is joined to the word 'Straße'.

**Ich wohne in der Magdalenstraße 24 in Lancaster.** = I live at 24 Magdalen Street, in Lancaster.

Being able to talk about where you live is really important…

**Ich wohne in einem kleinen, alten Haus.** = I live in a small old house.

big: großen    modern: modernen
new: neuen    cold: kalten

See page 91 for more on adjective endings.

**TYPES OF HOUSE**

Remember, plurals are always 'die'.

house: das Haus (die Häuser)
flat: die Wohnung (-en)
semi-detached house: das Doppelhaus (die Doppelhäuser)
detached house: das Einfamilienhaus (die Einfamilienhäuser)
terraced house: das Reihenhaus (die Reihenhäuser)

My house: Mein Haus

**Meine Wohnung liegt in der Nähe von einem Park.** = My flat is near a park.

See pages 85 and 96 for 'in' and 'von' with the dative.

the town centre: der Stadtmitte    a shopping centre: einem Einkaufszentrum
the motorway: der Autobahn    a bus stop: einer Bushaltestelle
the shops: den Geschäften    a train station: einem Bahnhof

These are all in the dative case.

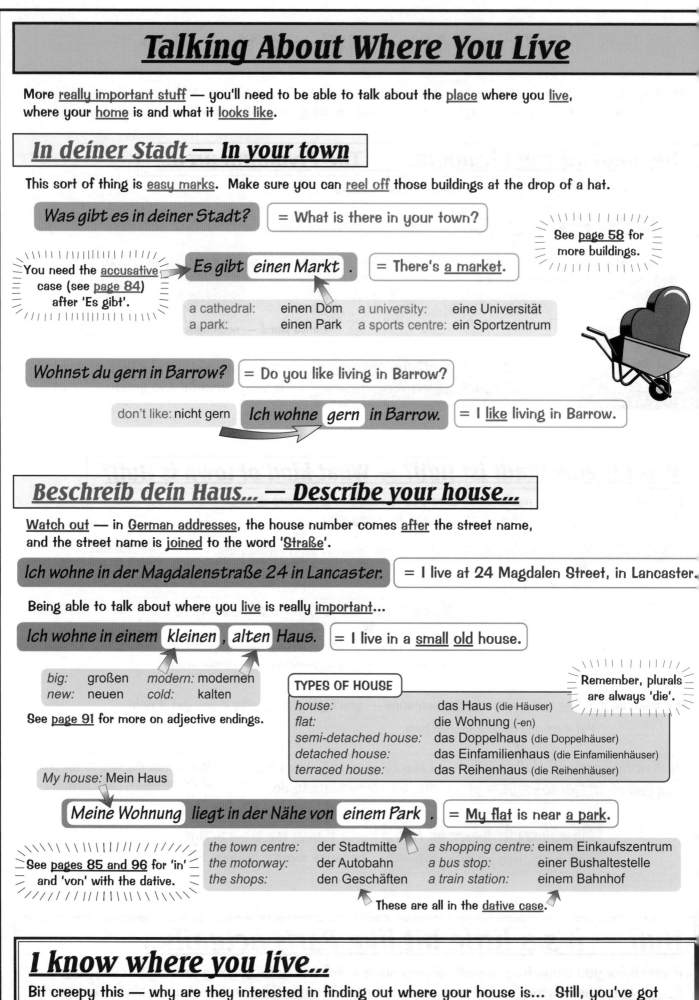

# I know where you live…

Bit creepy this — why are they interested in finding out where your house is… Still, you've got to learn it anyway, so cover the page, scribble it all down, and check how many you got right.

# Inside Your Home

You've got to be able to <u>describe</u> what's in your house. Luckily, you don't need to say <u>everything</u> that's in it — just some things. This may not look <u>exciting</u>, but ignore it at your <u>peril</u>.

## Wie ist dein Haus? — What's your house like?

Whether or not you need to ask where <u>rooms</u> are in your <u>exchange partner's</u> home, you <u>do</u> need to know this stuff for the exams. To make the first question a bit more <u>polite</u>, just add '<u>bitte</u>' on the end — <u>easy</u>.

**Wie sieht** die Küche **aus?** = What does <u>the kitchen</u> look like?

*the living room:* das Wohnzimmer (-)
*the bathroom:* das Badezimmer (-) / das Bad (die Bäder)
*the dining room:* das Esszimmer (-)
*the bedroom:* das Schlafzimmer (-)

**Ist die Küche** groß **?** = Is the kitchen <u>big</u>?

*small:* klein
*huge:* riesig
*tiny:* winzig

**Wo ist** die Küche **?** = Where is <u>the kitchen</u>?

<u>Get learning</u> the words below for what's in your room — and <u>remember</u> that if your room <u>doesn't</u> have any of these things in it, you can always <u>lie</u> — as long as you get the <u>vocab right</u>.

**Was für Möbel hast du im** Schlafzimmer **?** = What kind of furniture do you have in the <u>bedroom</u>?

**Im Schlafzimmer habe ich** ein Bett **,** zwei Stühle **und** einen kleinen Tisch **.** = <u>In the bedroom</u> I have <u>a bed</u>, <u>two chairs</u> and <u>a small table</u>.

You can use any of these words in the white boxes above, but you need to get the <u>right endings</u> for '<u>ein</u>' — the <u>accusative case</u> is used after 'habe'. See <u>pages 84 & 90</u> for more info.

| THINGS IN THE HOME | | |
|---|---|---|
| *armchair:* der Sessel (-) | *cupboard:* der Schrank (die Schränke) | *wallpaper:* die Tapete |
| *sofa:* das Sofa (-s) | *wall:* die Wand (die Wände) | *bed:* das Bett (-en) |
| *lamp:* die Lampe (-n) | *carpet:* der Teppich (-e) | *double bed:* das Doppelbett (-en) |
| *table:* der Tisch (-e) | *ceiling:* die Decke (-n) | *curtains (plural):* die Vorhänge |
| *chair:* der Stuhl (die Stühle) | *wardrobe:* der Kleiderschrank (die Kleiderschränke) | |

Remember, plurals are always 'die'.

## Hast du einen Garten? — Have you got a garden?

More stuff which will help you to do <u>really well</u>...

**Mein Haus** hat einen Garten. = <u>My house</u> has a garden.

*My flat:* Meine Wohnung

**Wir haben** Blumen **in unserem Garten.** = We have <u>flowers</u> in our garden.

*a tree:* einen Baum (die Bäume)
*a lawn:* einen Rasen

# Who would live in a house like this?

This is stuff they could easily chuck at you. If the <u>list</u> of things in your room looks a bit <u>grisly</u>, <u>start off</u> with just a <u>few</u> — but make sure you can <u>understand</u> all the words if you <u>read</u> or <u>hear</u> them.

# Celebrations

Time to get the <u>party poppers</u> out — this page is gonna be a hoot...
Now where did I put my balloon animals...

## Wann feierst du? — When do you celebrate?

There are <u>loads</u> of things you can celebrate — any excuse for a <u>party</u> and all that. Here are just a few:

**Wir feiern** | Weihnachten | **am** | fünfundzwanzigsten Dezember | **.**

= We celebrate <u>Christmas</u> on the <u>25th of December.</u>

| | |
|---|---|
| Christmas Eve: | Heiligabend |
| New Year's Eve: | Silvester |
| New Year: | Neujahr |
| my birthday: | meinen Geburtstag |

| | |
|---|---|
| Hanukkah: | Chanukka |
| Ramadan: | Ramadan |
| Easter: | Ostern |

Put the <u>date</u> you celebrate here. For more on dates see <u>page 3</u>.

## Mit wem feierst du? — Who do you celebrate with?

*Ich feiere meinen Geburtstag mit* | meiner Familie | **.**

= I celebrate my birthday with <u>my family.</u>

| | |
|---|---|
| my friends: | meinen Freunden |
| my parents: | meinen Eltern |

| | |
|---|---|
| in the restaurant: | im Restaurant |
| at a hotel: | in einem Hotel |

*Normalerweise habe ich eine Party* | zu Hause | **.**

= Normally I have a party <u>at home.</u>

## Wie feierst du? — How do you celebrate?

These examiners want to know <u>everything</u>, the nosy beggars...

*Zu Weihnachten* ...

= At Christmas...

| | |
|---|---|
| ...we have a Christmas tree: | ...haben wir einen Weihnachtsbaum |
| ...we send Christmas cards: | ...senden wir Weihnachtskarten |
| ...we give presents: | ...geben wir Geschenke |
| ...we sing carols: | ...singen wir Weihnachtslieder |

*An Neujahr* ...

= At New Year...

| | |
|---|---|
| ...we have fireworks: | ...haben wir Feuerwerk |
| ...we dance: | ...tanzen wir |
| ...we have fun: | ...machen wir uns Spaß |

## Deutsche Feste... — German Festivals...

You'll really <u>impress</u> those examiners if you know anything about <u>German</u> festivals and <u>how</u> they celebrate them

*Letztes Jahr war ich in Köln für Rosenmontag. Es gab große Umzüge mit Singen und Tanzen. Es hat viel Spaß gemacht.*

= Last year I was in Cologne for Rosenmontag. There were giant parades with singing and dancing. It was a lot of fun.

'<u>Rosenmontag</u>' is the high point of the German Catholic festival season, '<u>Karneval</u>' (also called '<u>Fasching</u>'). The main Karneval celebrations take place in the weeks leading up to <u>Lent</u> (Jan-Feb), but in some places start as early as <u>November</u>. There are parades, street parties, dances and much more.

## Rosenmontag — is that like Orange Wednesdays?

Well, that was fun... Admittedly not as fun as <u>actually</u> celebrating something, but still...
There's <u>loads</u> you can say about festivals and the like — just make sure you've <u>cracked</u> this lot first.

# The Environment

Things get <u>serious</u> when the environment comes up, and you're supposed to have an opinion. It's a chance for you to write or say what you <u>think</u> about something real and <u>important</u> — not just what colour <u>velour jumpsuit</u> you'd like to buy in the sale.

## Ist die Umwelt wichtig für dich..?
### Is the environment important to you..?

Ja, ich halte die Umwelt für total wichtig. = Yes, I think the environment is very important.

Always give a <u>reason why</u> — it makes the examiners go all tingly inside...

Ich habe große Angst um die Umwelt wegen des Treibhauseffekts. = I'm really worried about the environment <u>because of the greenhouse effect</u>.

because of the hole in the ozone layer: wegen des Ozonloches
because we don't recycle enough: weil wir nicht genug recyceln

Wir müssen die Umwelt schützen oder unsere Kinder werden leiden. = We must protect the environment or our children will suffer.

## Hast du Angst um die Umwelt..?
### Do you worry about the environment..?

Nein, ich interessiere mich ganz und gar nicht dafür. = No, I'm not at all interested in it.

Well, don't just leave it at that for Pete's sake...

Es geht mich nichts an. Ich bin sehr beschäftigt und ich habe keine Zeit zu recyceln. = It doesn't concern me. I am very busy and I don't have time to recycle.

Blumen und die Natur sind todlangweilig. Ich mag lieber Computerspiele. = Flowers and nature are dead boring. I prefer computer games.

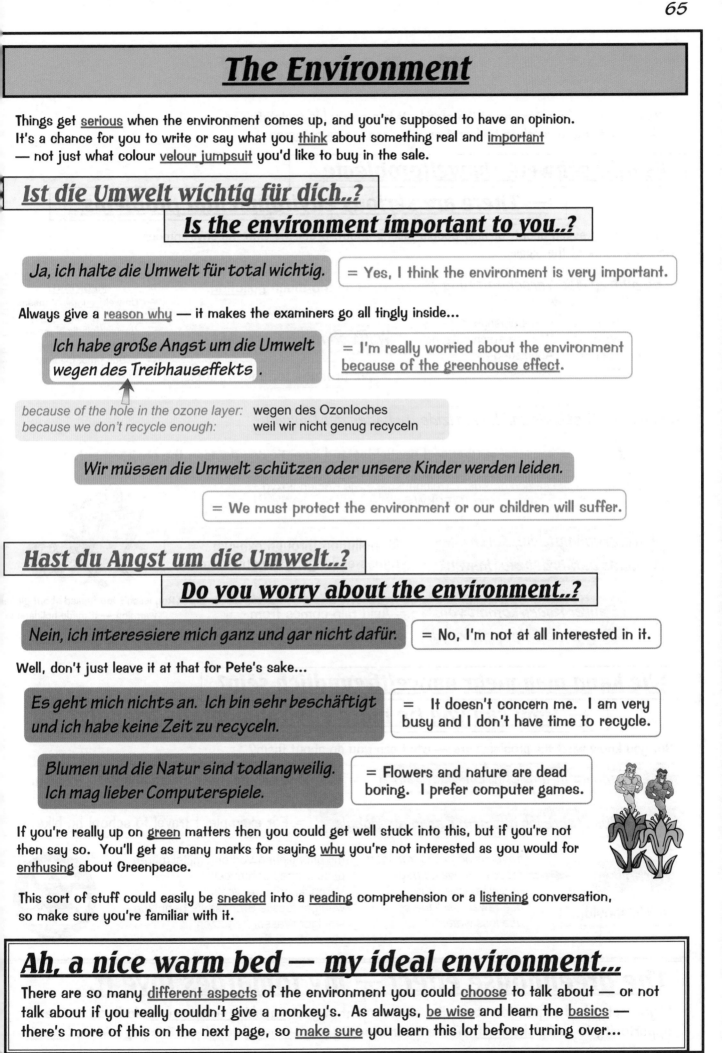

If you're really up on <u>green</u> matters then you could get well stuck into this, but if you're not then say so. You'll get as many marks for saying <u>why</u> you're not interested as you would for <u>enthusing</u> about Greenpeace.

This sort of stuff could easily be <u>sneaked</u> into a <u>reading</u> comprehension or a <u>listening</u> conversation, so make sure you're familiar with it.

## Ah, a nice warm bed — my ideal environment...

There are so many <u>different aspects</u> of the environment you could <u>choose</u> to talk about — or not talk about if you really couldn't give a monkey's. As always, <u>be wise</u> and learn the <u>basics</u> — there's more of this on the next page, so <u>make sure</u> you learn this lot before turning over...

# The Environment

Yep, more on the environment I'm afraid. It is a pretty big topic after all.
There's lots more vocab to be learnt on this page, so be prepared...

## Es gibt schwere Umweltprobleme...
### — There are serious environmental problems...

You might get asked about, or hear people talking about, problems with the environment.
Here are some of the biggies...

**Es gibt zu viel Verschmutzung.**  = There is too much pollution.

noise pollution: Lärmbelästigung
water pollution: Wasserverschmutzung
deforestation: Abholzung
consumption: Verbrauch

**Wir produzieren zu viel Müll.**

= We produce too much rubbish.

IMPORTANT:
'Umweltfreundlich' means
'environmentally friendly' —
'umweltfeindlich' means
'environmentally unfriendly'.
Don't mix them up.

**Chemische Pestizide und Insektizide schaden der Umwelt.**

= Chemical pesticides and insecticides damage the environment.

greenhouse gases like carbon dioxide: Treibhausgase wie Kohlendioxyd
CFCs: FCKWs

**Luftverschmutzung durch Abgase gefährdet die Umwelt.**  = Air pollution through exhaust fumes endangers the environment.

**Saurer Regen kommt von Gasen wie Schwefeldioxyd.**  = Acid rain comes from gases like sulphur dioxide.

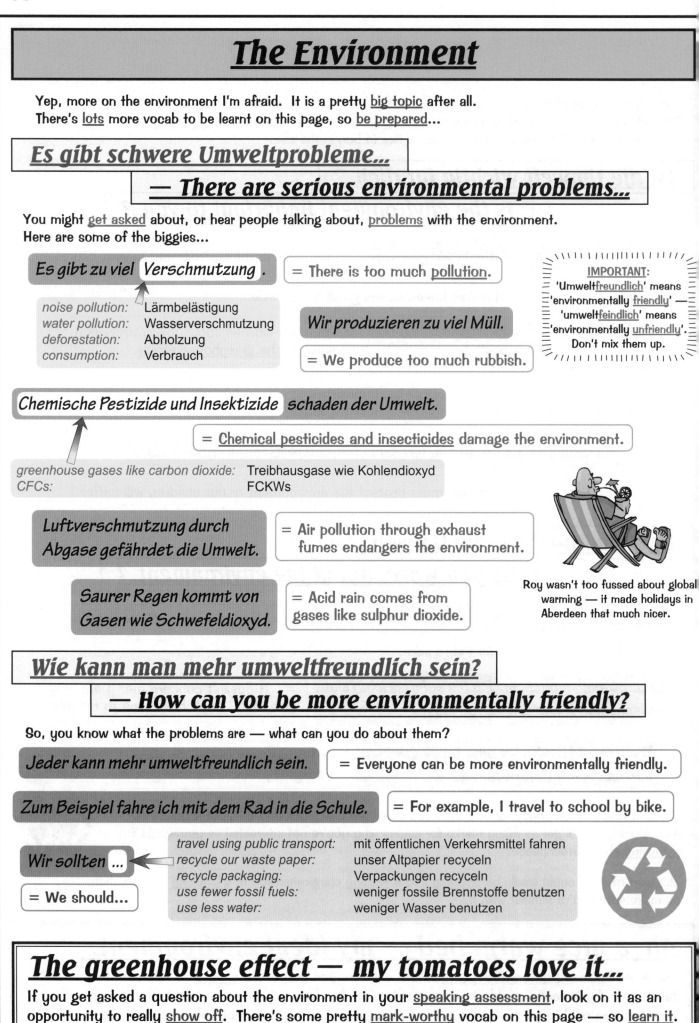

Roy wasn't too fussed about global warming — it made holidays in Aberdeen that much nicer.

## Wie kann man mehr umweltfreundlich sein?
### — How can you be more environmentally friendly?

So, you know what the problems are — what can you do about them?

**Jeder kann mehr umweltfreundlich sein.**  = Everyone can be more environmentally friendly.

**Zum Beispiel fahre ich mit dem Rad in die Schule.**  = For example, I travel to school by bike.

**Wir sollten ...**

travel using public transport: mit öffentlichen Verkehrsmittel fahren
recycle our waste paper: unser Altpapier recyceln
recycle packaging: Verpackungen recyceln
use fewer fossil fuels: weniger fossile Brennstoffe benutzen
use less water: weniger Wasser benutzen

= We should...

# The greenhouse effect — my tomatoes love it...

If you get asked a question about the environment in your speaking assessment, look on it as an opportunity to really show off. There's some pretty mark-worthy vocab on this page — so learn it.

# Revision Summary

The thing with doing GCSE German is that it's mainly about learning a few phrases, being able to change a few words in them, and stringing some of those phrases together. But if you don't <u>know the phrases</u>, you've got a problem. These questions will check you know what you need to know about this section. <u>Keep trying</u> them until you can do them <u>all</u>.

1) You've just arrived in Heidelberg and are writing to your pen friend about the sights. How do you say that there is a castle, a swimming pool, a university, a zoo, a museum and a theatre?

2) You need to go to the pharmacy in Germany. Ask where it is, and how far away it is.

3) A German tourist has come to see your home town and is looking for the youth hostel. Tell him to go straight on, turn left at the traffic lights and the youth hostel is on the right.

4) Tell your German pen friend where you live and whereabouts it is (which country and whether it's north-east etc.).

5) Say in German that you like living in your town, there's loads to do and it's quite clean. Say there's a sports centre and a cinema.

6) Say your address in German and describe the place where you live — is it a town or a village, is the landscape nice, and how many people live there?

7) Julia lives in a big house with a garden. It's near a shopping centre, a bus stop and a motorway. How would she say this in German?

8) Give the names of the rooms in your home in German and say how many bedrooms it has.

9) Tom has red wallpaper and a brown carpet in his bedroom. He has a bed, two lamps, a wardrobe and a cupboard. He doesn't have a sofa. How will he say all this in German?

10) You and Erika are talking about her birthday. She tells you that it's on the 24th of July, and that she and her family celebrate with a big party at her house. How would she say this in German?

11) Your German pen friend is writing an article about the environment for his school newspaper. He wants to know whether or not the environment is important to you. In German, tell him whether it is or isn't and make sure you give a reason why.

12) Your German pen friend is really struggling with this newspaper article. Now he wants to know two environmental problems and two things that we can do to be more environmentally friendly. Give him these in German. Honestly, you might as well be writing this thing for him...

I've told you Hermann, you're really going to have to write it yourself. Just put in a bit about recycling...

# School Subjects

School and jobs — maybe not what thrills you most in life. But never mind —
this stuff's really <u>important</u>, so learn it well and you'll have less to stress about.

## Welche Schulfächer hast du?

## — What school subjects do you do?

Go over each group of subjects until you can write them all out without looking.

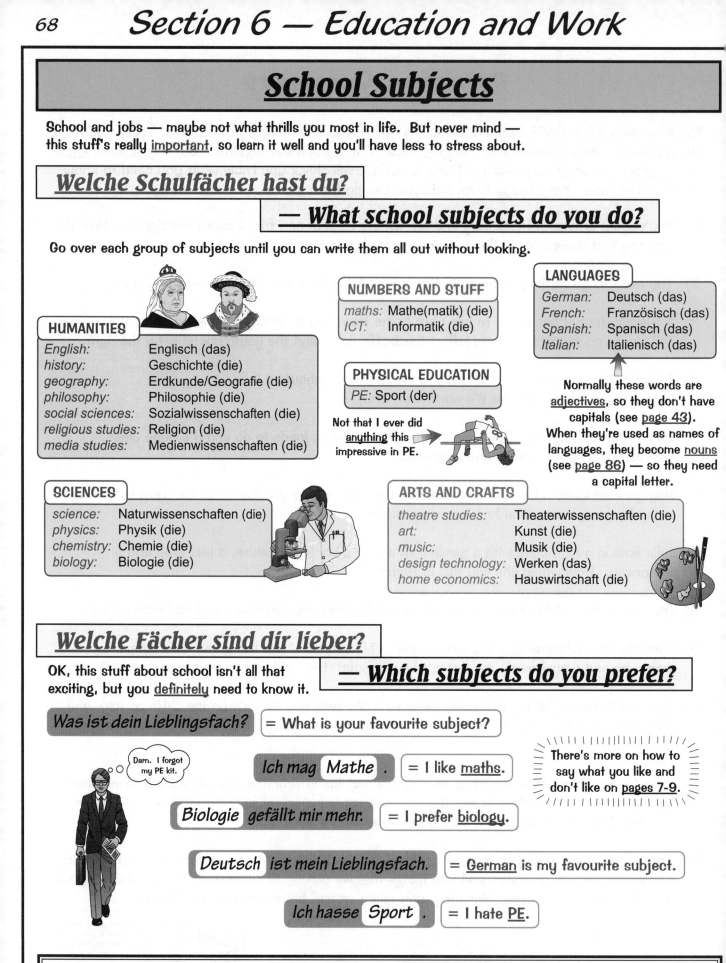

**HUMANITIES**

| | |
|---|---|
| *English:* | Englisch (das) |
| *history:* | Geschichte (die) |
| *geography:* | Erdkunde/Geografie (die) |
| *philosophy:* | Philosophie (die) |
| *social sciences:* | Sozialwissenschaften (die) |
| *religious studies:* | Religion (die) |
| *media studies:* | Medienwissenschaften (die) |

**NUMBERS AND STUFF**

| | |
|---|---|
| *maths:* | Mathe(matik) (die) |
| *ICT:* | Informatik (die) |

**PHYSICAL EDUCATION**

*PE:* Sport (der)

Not that I ever did <u>anything</u> this impressive in PE.

**LANGUAGES**

| | |
|---|---|
| *German:* | Deutsch (das) |
| *French:* | Französisch (das) |
| *Spanish:* | Spanisch (das) |
| *Italian:* | Italienisch (das) |

Normally these words are <u>adjectives</u>, so they don't have capitals (see <u>page 43</u>).
When they're used as names of languages, they become <u>nouns</u> (see <u>page 86</u>) — so they need a capital letter.

**SCIENCES**

| | |
|---|---|
| *science:* | Naturwissenschaften (die) |
| *physics:* | Physik (die) |
| *chemistry:* | Chemie (die) |
| *biology:* | Biologie (die) |

**ARTS AND CRAFTS**

| | |
|---|---|
| *theatre studies:* | Theaterwissenschaften (die) |
| *art:* | Kunst (die) |
| *music:* | Musik (die) |
| *design technology:* | Werken (das) |
| *home economics:* | Hauswirtschaft (die) |

## Welche Fächer sind dir lieber?

## — Which subjects do you prefer?

OK, this stuff about school isn't all that exciting, but you <u>definitely</u> need to know it.

**Was ist dein Lieblingsfach?** = What is your favourite subject?

Darn. I forgot my PE kit.

**Ich mag Mathe .** = I like <u>maths</u>.

There's more on how to say what you like and don't like on <u>pages 7-9</u>.

**Biologie gefällt mir mehr.** = I prefer <u>biology</u>.

**Deutsch ist mein Lieblingsfach.** = <u>German</u> is my favourite subject.

**Ich hasse Sport .** = I hate <u>PE</u>.

# Make sure you learn these lessons...

Make sure you can <u>say</u> all the subjects you do, and at least <u>understand</u> the ones you don't do. You <u>don't</u> need to use 'der', 'die' or 'das' when you're talking about a school subject — phew. You should have seen pretty much all of this stuff before — just make sure it's firmly lodged in your brain.

# The School Routine

This isn't the most thrilling set of sentences, but when it comes to the exams they're gold dust.
Keep each sentence <u>small</u> and <u>perfectly formed</u> — that way it's harder to mess it up.

## Wie kommst du in die Schule?

### — How do you get to school?

This could come up in the reading or listening exam, so make sure you learn <u>the lot</u>.

**Ich fahre mit dem Auto in die Schule.** = I go to school by <u>car</u>.

Use '<u>in die Schule</u>' for '<u>to school</u>'. '<u>Gehen</u>' means '<u>to go</u>' only for '<u>on foot</u>', so use '<u>fahren</u>' if you have any kind of <u>transport</u>.

*car:* dem Auto/dem Wagen    *bike:* dem Fahrrad
*bus:* dem Bus

**Ich gehe zu Fuß in die Schule.** = I go to school on foot.

## Der Stundenplan — The timetable

Write out all these sentences and slot in the <u>right times</u> and <u>numbers</u> for <u>your school</u> — then all you've got to do is <u>learn</u>, <u>learn</u> and <u>learn</u> some more, until you can reel them off like a robot.

**Die Schule fängt um neun Uhr an.** = School begins at <u>9.00</u>.

For more on times, see <u>page 2</u>.

**Die Schule ist um halb vier aus.** = School ends at <u>3.30</u>.

**Um elf haben wir Pause.** = We have <u>break</u> <u>at 11</u>.

*Lunch break:* Mittagspause

**BREAK'S OVER!!**

Watch out — 'Stunde' can mean 'lesson' or 'hour'. Sneaky.

**Wir haben acht Stunden pro Tag.** = We have <u>8</u> lessons per day.

**Jede Stunde dauert vierzig Minuten.** = Each lesson lasts <u>forty minutes</u>.

**Wir machen eine Stunde Hausaufgaben pro Tag.** = We do <u>one hour</u> of homework every day.

## Die Ferien — The holidays

So you can talk about just how much <u>lovely</u> holiday you get, learn this lot:

**Es gibt drei Trimester.** = There are <u>three</u> terms. ◄ If there are two terms, you say '<u>zwei Semester</u>'.

**Wir haben im Sommer sechs Wochen Ferien.** = We have <u>six weeks'</u> holiday <u>in the summer</u>.

*at Christmas:* zu Weihnachten    *eight weeks':* acht Wochen    *five days':* fünf Tage
*at Easter:* zu Ostern

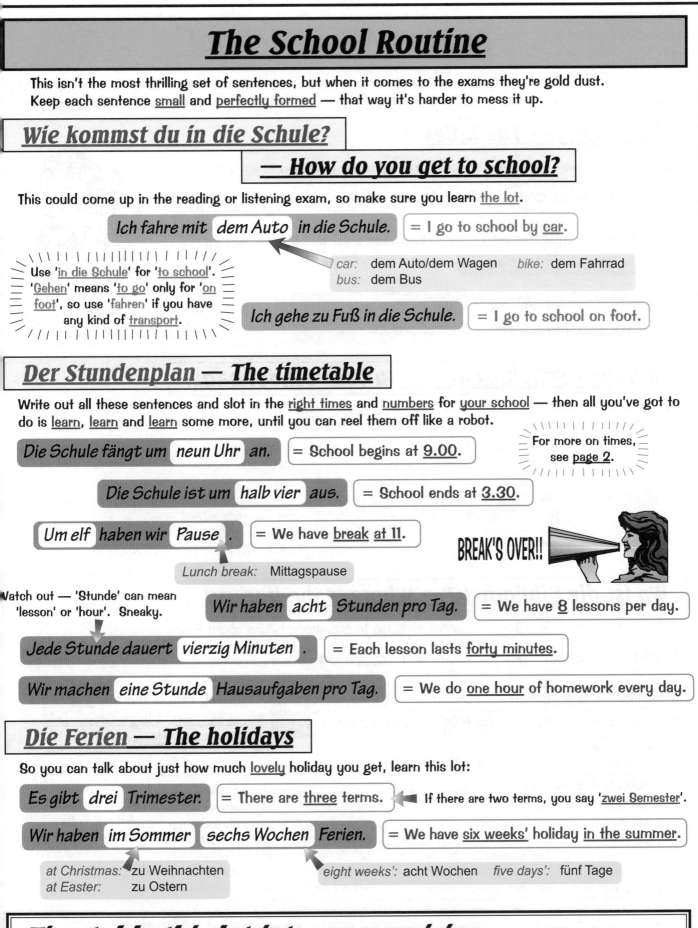

# Timetable this lot into your revision...

Next time your mum asks what you've been doing at school all day, why not reply in German... Don't worry, she already thinks you're weird. But this <u>is</u> all <u>useful</u> stuff and you'll feel like a right lemon if you don't <u>know it</u> when you need to. Remember the handy phrase '<u>pro Tag</u>' — it'll come in useful.

# Talking About School

This page is full of extra little bits that follow on from the basic school conversation. They can crop up in both the exams and things like the speaking and writing tasks — without them you'll miss out on some easy marks.

## Die Regeln — The Rules

This is all a bit more tricky, but if you want a top mark, you need to learn it.

Die Regeln sind streng.    = The rules are strict.

In der Schule müssen wir eine Uniform tragen.    = We must wear a uniform at school.

For more on clothes and colours, see page 38.

Mum says that I'll grow into it.

Billy's new school uniform was a little on the large side.

Unsere Uniform ist ein roter Pulli, eine graue Hose, ein weißes Hemd und ein grüner Schlips.    = Our uniform is a red jumper, grey trousers, a white shirt and a green tie.

## In deiner Schultasche... — In your school bag...

Learn this list of stuff you might find in your school bag — and I'm not talking about half-eaten sandwiches and an unwashed PE kit.

Remember, plurals are always 'die'.

| | | | |
|---|---|---|---|
| ballpoint pen: | der Kugelschreiber (-) / der Kuli (-s) | felt-tip pen: | der Filzstift (-e) |
| | | scissors: | die Schere (-n) |
| pencil: | der Bleistift (-e) | exercise book: | das Heft (-e) |
| sharpener: | der Anspitzer (-) | writing pad: | der Schreibblock (-s or die Schreibblöcke) |
| rubber: | der Radiergummi (-s) | calculator: | der Taschenrechner (-) |
| ruler: | das Lineal (-e) | school book: | das Schulbuch (die Schulbücher) |
| fountain pen: | der Füller (-) | chalk: | die Kreide (-n) |

## Wo ist die Bibliothek? — Where is the library?

You might need to describe your school, or listen to somebody talking about theirs.

Wo ist die Turnhalle ?    = Where is the gym?    ◄ For more on asking where something is see page 49.

In meiner Schule gibt es eine Bibliothek , eine Kantine , einen großen Sportplatz und viele Klassenzimmer .    = In my school there is a library, a canteen, a large sports field and many classrooms.

These are accusative endings. See pages 90-91 for more info.

You can put any of the 'Places in School' in the white boxes.

### PLACES IN SCHOOL

| | | | |
|---|---|---|---|
| assembly hall: | die Aula | corridor: | der Korridor (-e) |
| library: | die Bibliothek | staff room: | das Lehrerzimmer |
| canteen: | die Kantine | gymnasium: | die Turnhalle (-n) |
| classroom: | das Klassenzimmer (-) | sports hall: | die Sporthalle (-n) |
| laboratory: | das Labor (-s/-e) | sports field: | der Sportplatz (die Sportplätze) |
| language lab: | das Sprachlabor (-s/-e) | school yard: | der Schulhof |

## School rules — not as far as I'm concerned...

There's a lot of vocab for this section — make sure you learn it. The more you can reel off about your school, the better — close the book and see how much you can remember. Any Germans you meet will love to hear about your uniform, since they don't have them — pretty unfair.

# Classroom Language

This stuff is really <u>important</u> if you're not always word-perfect at understanding German.
It's really useful to be able to ask someone to <u>repeat</u> something, or <u>spell out</u> a word you're not sure about.

## Ich verstehe nicht — I don't understand

These phases can be <u>vital</u> in your <u>speaking assessment</u>. Even if the worst happens, it's far better to say
'I don't understand' <u>in German</u> than to shrug, give a cheesy smile and mumble something in English.

**Verstehst du?** = Do you understand? | **Ich verstehe (nicht).** = I (don't) understand.

**Wie spricht man das aus?** = How do you pronounce that?

**Wie sagt man das auf Deutsch?** = How do you say that in German?

**Wie buchstabiert man das?** = How do you spell that?

**Was bedeutet das, bitte?** = What does that mean, please?

**Kannst du** dieses Wort erklären? = <u>Can you</u> (informal) explain this word?

**Können Sie** das bitte wiederholen? = <u>Can you</u> (formal) repeat that, please?

**Ist das richtig?** = Is that right? | **Das ist falsch.** = That's wrong.

## Setzt euch! — Sit down!

Learn these three short phrases to avoid the wrath of a scary teacher.

> These phrases are all in the <u>imperative</u>. For more info see <u>page 106</u>.

**Steht auf!** = Stand up! | **Setzt euch!** = Sit down! | **Seid ruhig!** = Be quiet!

## Wie lange...? — How long...?

This isn't here because I like it. It's here because it could crop up somewhere. So <u>learn it</u>.

**Wie lange lernst du schon Deutsch?** = How long have you been learning German?

Be careful to use the present tense — you don't say 'I have been' as in English.

**Ich lerne seit** drei Jahren **Deutsch.** = I've been learning German for <u>three years</u>.

The word '<u>seit</u>' is really useful. It means '<u>since</u>' — this sentence literally translates as 'I am learning German <u>since</u> three years'. You use 'seit' and the <u>present tense</u> to say how long you've been doing anything — and you have to follow it with the <u>dative case</u> (see <u>pages 85 & 96</u>).

## Mind your language...

Learn <u>all</u> these <u>dead useful</u> phrases for your speaking — even if you haven't a <u>clue</u> what your teacher just said, you'll get credit for asking them to <u>repeat</u> something — and you'll save yourself from an embarrassing silence at the same time. <u>Don't panic</u> — things like that happen to everyone.

# More School Stuff

You're expected to know a little bit about how German schools work — you know, broaden your horizons and all that. It's really quite interesting actually. No, honestly.

## Meine Noten sind sehr gut — My grades are very good...

The German marking system works a bit differently to ours.
Instead of A, B, C etc., they have the numbers 1-6.
It's pretty simple — just make sure you're familiar with it...

Quite frankly, if we'd had a 7 you'd have got it.

**GERMAN GRADES**

| | |
|---|---|
| 1 = very good: | 1 = sehr gut |
| 2 = good: | 2 = gut |
| 3 = satisfactory: | 3 = befriedigend |
| 4 = adequate: | 4 = ausreichend |
| 5 = (fail) inadequate | 5 = mangelhaft |
| 6 = (fail) unsatisfactory | 6 = ungenügend |

## Deutsche Schulen — German Schools...

At first glance, the German school system seems mind-bogglingly complicated. Don't panic — again, just make sure you're familiar with the different terms.

**FOR LITTLE ONES**

der Kindergarten — *voluntary nursery school for 3-6 year olds*
die Grundschule — *primary school*

**SECONDARY SCHOOLS**

das Gymnasium — *takes the most academic pupils and prepares them for* das Abitur *('A-levels') and university*
die Hauptschule — *focuses on vocational and practical training*
die Realschule — *somewhere between a Gymnasium and a Hauptschule, covers a broader range of subjects*
die Gesamtschule — *combines all three of the schools above in one (like a comprehensive school in the UK)*
die Oberstufe — *sixth form, usually part of a Gymnasium*

## Talk about your extracurricular activities

Time to admit to all those weird and wonderful hobbies — or pretend you do something that's easy to say.

**Hast du Aktivitäten außerhalb des Stundenplans?** = Do you have extracurricular activities?

For more on hobbies, see pages 27-28.

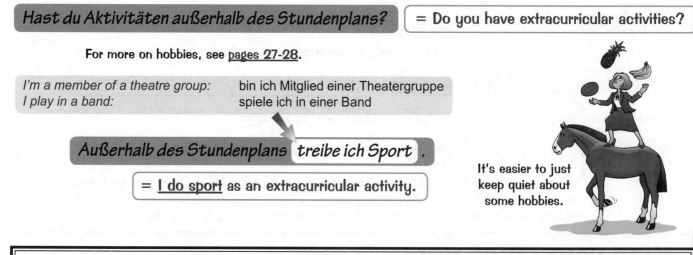

*I'm a member of a theatre group:* bin ich Mitglied einer Theatergruppe
*I play in a band:* spiele ich in einer Band

**Außerhalb des Stundenplans** treibe ich Sport .

= I do sport as an extracurricular activity.

It's easier to just keep quiet about some hobbies.

# Das Gymnasium — not a school for gymnasts...

Now, there's quite a bit of school-related vocab on this page, so make sure you learn it. It may be duller than a big dull thing, but if it comes up in an exam you'll be blummin' grateful for it.

# Problems at School

OK, it's time to get it all off your chest — in <u>German</u> of course. This page'll help you to pour out your <u>own</u> troubles as well as <u>listen</u> with a sympathetic ear to someone else's. Lovely jubbly.

## Wie geht es in der Schule? — How are things at school?

Es geht gut in der Schule, danke. = It's going well at school, thank you.

Eigentlich geht es nicht so gut. Ich habe einige Probleme... = Actually it's not going so well. I have a few problems...

Schule kann sehr stressig sein. = School can be very stressful.

## Was für Probleme gibt es in der Schule?
## — What sort of problems are there at school?

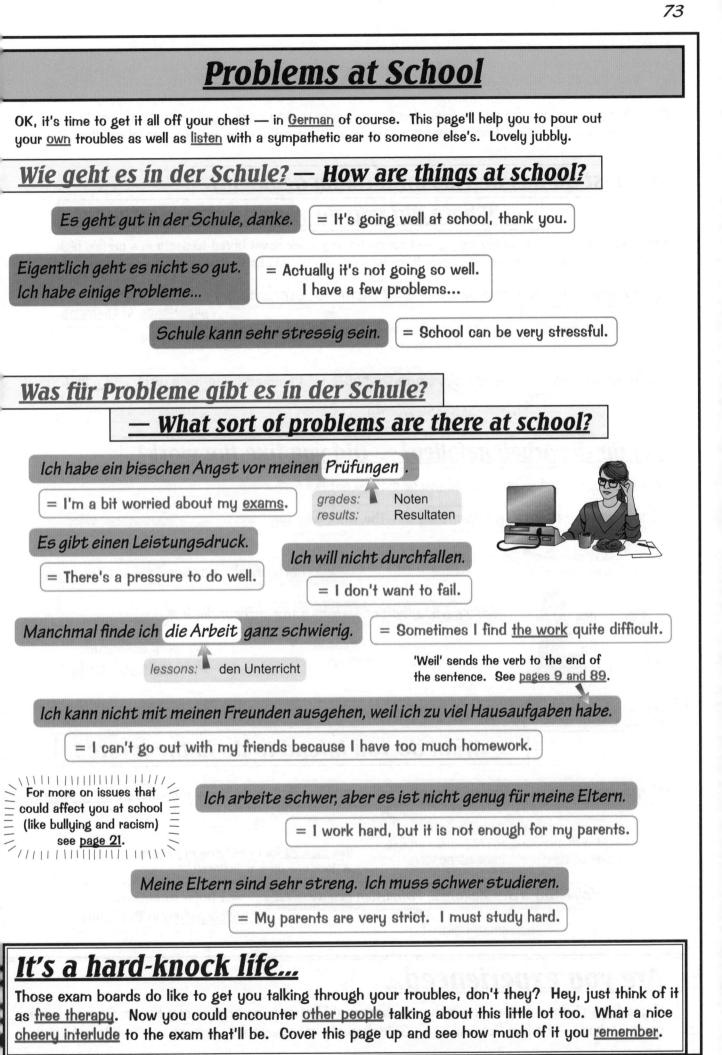

Ich habe ein bisschen Angst vor meinen Prüfungen.

= I'm a bit worried about my <u>exams</u>.

grades: Noten
results: Resultaten

Es gibt einen Leistungsdruck.

= There's a pressure to do well.

Ich will nicht durchfallen.

= I don't want to fail.

Manchmal finde ich die Arbeit ganz schwierig. = Sometimes I find <u>the work</u> quite difficult.

lessons: den Unterricht

'Weil' sends the verb to the end of the sentence. See <u>pages 9 and 89</u>.

Ich kann nicht mit meinen Freunden ausgehen, weil ich zu viel Hausaufgaben habe.

= I can't go out with my friends because I have too much homework.

For more on issues that could affect you at school (like bullying and racism) see <u>page 21</u>.

Ich arbeite schwer, aber es ist nicht genug für meine Eltern.

= I work hard, but it is not enough for my parents.

Meine Eltern sind sehr streng. Ich muss schwer studieren.

= My parents are very strict. I must study hard.

## It's a hard-knock life...

Those exam boards do like to get you talking through your troubles, don't they? Hey, just think of it as <u>free therapy</u>. Now you could encounter <u>other people</u> talking about this little lot too. What a nice <u>cheery interlude</u> to the exam that'll be. Cover this page up and see how much of it you <u>remember</u>.

# Work Experience

These two pages <u>encourage</u> you to think about your <u>future</u> in even more <u>detail</u> — heck, it's nearly a public service. If you can't quite manage to see your future without the aid of a crystal ball then get exercising your <u>imagination</u>.

## Wo hast du das Betriebspraktikum gemacht?
## — Where did you do your work experience?

Work experience is quite simply <u>joyous</u> — I remember my week spent bored to death in a certain high street bank. At least it helped me <u>decide</u> there was no way on this Earth that banking was for me.

Ich habe das Betriebspraktikum bei Siemens gemacht.

= I did my <u>work experience</u> at <u>Siemens</u>.

work experience: das Arbeitspraktikum
die Arbeitserfahrung

Put the place you worked in here.

Ich habe anderthalb Wochen dort gearbeitet.

= I worked there for <u>a week and a half</u>.

two weeks: zwei Wochen

## Hat dir die Arbeit gefallen? — Did you like the work?

More <u>opinions</u> wanted — own up, did you or did you not like it..?

Die Arbeit hat Spaß gemacht.

= The work <u>was fun</u>.

was stressful: war stressig
was interesting: war interessant

comfortable: wohl
at home: zu Hause

Ich fühlte mich einsam.

= I felt <u>lonely</u>.

Meine Mitarbeiter waren ganz unfreundlich.

very friendly: sehr freundlich
interesting: interessant

= My work colleagues were <u>quite unfriendly</u>.

## Was hast du vor, in der Zukunft zu machen?
## — What do you intend to do in the future ?

Ich möchte einen Beruf haben, wo ich Probleme löse.

= I'd like a job where I <u>solve problems</u>.

meet new people: neue Leute treffe
work with numbers: mit Nummern arbeite
travel abroad: ins Ausland fahre

See <u>page 76</u> for more types of jobs, or look one up in a dictionary.

Ich hoffe in der Zukunft Polizistin zu werden.

= I hope to become a <u>policewoman</u> in the future.

policeman: Polizist

# Are you experienced...

If you <u>haven't</u> done any work experience then you'd better <u>learn</u> how to say that in <u>German</u> in case you're asked — it's just 'ich habe <u>kein</u> Betriebspraktikum gemacht', in case you're interested.

# Plans for the Future

If you know what you're doing after school, great — if you haven't got a clue, <u>make it up</u>. Job's a good 'un.

## Was möchtest du nach der Schule machen?
## — What would you like to do after school?

This stuff could easily come up — so you'd be daft not to learn it, really.

*Abitur is the German equivalent of A-levels — except that they do more subjects than we do.*

Ich möchte das Abitur machen. = I would like to do 'A-levels'.

Ich möchte auf die Universität gehen. = I would like to go to university.

Ich möchte Geografie studieren. = I would like to study geography.

Ich möchte ein Jahr freinehmen. = I would like to take a year out.

Ich möchte Lehrer werden. = I would like to become a teacher.

## Give short, sharp reasons for your answers

Work out an explanation for the answer you've given above. Keep your explanations <u>short</u>, <u>clear</u> and <u>simple</u>. For example, 'I want to take a year out so that I can travel' — nice and concise.

Ich möchte das Abitur machen, weil ich später Biologie studieren will. = I would like to do 'A-levels', because I want to study <u>biology</u> afterwards.

chemistry: Chemie
music: Musik

For all the different school subjects see <u>page 68</u>.

Ich möchte Englisch studieren, weil ich später Journalist werden will. = I would like to study <u>English</u>, because I want to be <u>a journalist</u> afterwards.

a pharmacist: Apotheker(in)
a musician: Musiker(in)

*Use 'werden' (to become) to say what job you'd like to do.*

For other jobs, see <u>page 76</u>.

Ich möchte Arzt werden, weil der Job interessant wäre. = I would like to become a <u>doctor</u> because the job would be <u>interesting</u>.

easy: einfach   difficult: schwierig

## Future plans — I'd like to build a time machine...

Things like the stuff on this page come up <u>year after year</u> — so if you've learnt it all, you'll be laughing. Use words like '<u>weil</u>' for extra marks. Being able to explain <u>why</u> is dead <u>impressive</u>.

# Types of Job

There are more jobs here than you can shake a stick at — and you do need to be able to <u>recognise</u> <u>all</u> of them because any of the little blighters could pop up in your <u>listening</u> and <u>reading</u> exams.

## You usually add an '-in' to make a job feminine

### Masculine/Feminine
For most jobs, you add '-in' to the end to make it <u>feminine</u>. If the job ends in '-mann', change that to '-<u>frau</u>' for a woman. Watch out for exceptions like 'Friseur/ Friseuse', and for places where you have to add an <u>umlaut</u> as well as the <u>feminine ending</u>.

**Architekt (m)**  **Architektin (f)**  = architect

**Kaufmann (m)**  **Kauffrau (f)**  = businessman/woman

**Arzt (m)**  **Ärztin (f)**  = doctor

## The gender of a job depends on who's doing it...

You'll need to be able to <u>say</u> and <u>write</u> any of the jobs you and your family do — and <u>recognise</u> the rest when you see or hear them.

As you'd expect, the gender of the job is always masculine for a man and feminine for a woman.

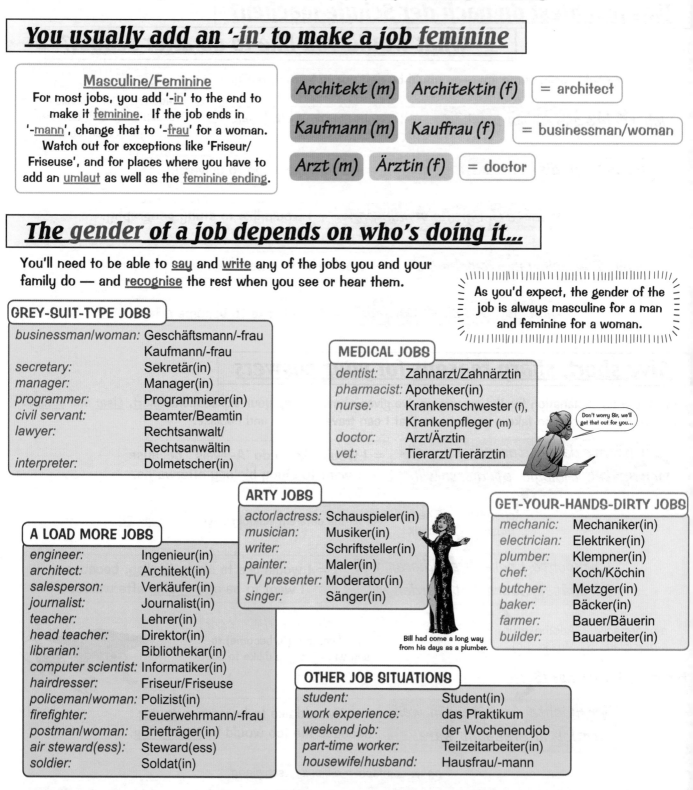

**GREY-SUIT-TYPE JOBS**

| | |
|---|---|
| businessman/woman: | Geschäftsmann/-frau |
| | Kaufmann/-frau |
| secretary: | Sekretär(in) |
| manager: | Manager(in) |
| programmer: | Programmierer(in) |
| civil servant: | Beamter/Beamtin |
| lawyer: | Rechtsanwalt/ |
| | Rechtsanwältin |
| interpreter: | Dolmetscher(in) |

**MEDICAL JOBS**

| | |
|---|---|
| dentist: | Zahnarzt/Zahnärztin |
| pharmacist: | Apotheker(in) |
| nurse: | Krankenschwester (f), |
| | Krankenpfleger (m) |
| doctor: | Arzt/Ärztin |
| vet: | Tierarzt/Tierärztin |

Don't worry Sir, we'll get that out for you...

**ARTY JOBS**

| | |
|---|---|
| actor/actress: | Schauspieler(in) |
| musician: | Musiker(in) |
| writer: | Schriftsteller(in) |
| painter: | Maler(in) |
| TV presenter: | Moderator(in) |
| singer: | Sänger(in) |

Bill had come a long way from his days as a plumber.

**A LOAD MORE JOBS**

| | |
|---|---|
| engineer: | Ingenieur(in) |
| architect: | Architekt(in) |
| salesperson: | Verkäufer(in) |
| journalist: | Journalist(in) |
| teacher: | Lehrer(in) |
| head teacher: | Direktor(in) |
| librarian: | Bibliothekar(in) |
| computer scientist: | Informatiker(in) |
| hairdresser: | Friseur/Friseuse |
| policeman/woman: | Polizist(in) |
| firefighter: | Feuerwehrmann/-frau |
| postman/woman: | Briefträger(in) |
| air steward(ess): | Steward(ess) |
| soldier: | Soldat(in) |

**GET-YOUR-HANDS-DIRTY JOBS**

| | |
|---|---|
| mechanic: | Mechaniker(in) |
| electrician: | Elektriker(in) |
| plumber: | Klempner(in) |
| chef: | Koch/Köchin |
| butcher: | Metzger(in) |
| baker: | Bäcker(in) |
| farmer: | Bauer/Bäuerin |
| builder: | Bauarbeiter(in) |

**OTHER JOB SITUATIONS**

| | |
|---|---|
| student: | Student(in) |
| work experience: | das Praktikum |
| weekend job: | der Wochenendjob |
| part-time worker: | Teilzeitarbeiter(in) |
| housewife/husband: | Hausfrau/-mann |

# Ingenieur — quite a job to pronounce...

<u>Don't</u> be put off by the long lists. Start off with the jobs you find <u>easiest</u>, and remember that you'll only need to <u>say</u> the ones people in your family do — but you should <u>understand</u> the rest. Make sure you know the <u>female</u> version of each job title — and watch out for those odd ones.

# Jobs: Advantages and Disadvantages

Pretty self-explanatory this, really. You have to be able to talk about the pros and cons of different jobs, what you would or wouldn't like to do in the future and why, that sort of thing. So let's get cracking...

## Was für Beruf möchtest du?

### — What sort of job would you like?

Ich will **im Freien** arbeiten. | = I want to work outdoors.

Ich möchte selbständig sein.

= I'd like to be self-employed.

with animals: mit Tieren
with the public: mit der Öffentlichkeit
in a hospital: in einem Krankenhaus

Ich will nicht **in einem Büro** arbeiten. | = I don't want to work in an office.

with children: mit Kindern

## Ich möchte nicht gern... — I wouldn't like...

OK, so what don't you want to do?

a soldier: Soldat     a policeman: Polizist

Ich möchte nicht gern **Rechtsanwalt** sein... | = I wouldn't like to be a lawyer...

...obwohl das Gehalt ganz gut ist. | = ... although the pay is quite good.

'Obwohl' affects word order — see page 89 for more info.

Die Arbeit wäre zu **schwierig** . | = The work would be too hard.

stressful: stressig
boring: langweilig

Die Arbeitszeit wäre zu lang. | = The working hours would be too long.

## Ich bin lieber... — I'd prefer to be...

Ich möchte einen Beruf, der **interessanter** ist. | = I'd like a job that's more interesting.

more creative: kreativer
not so stressful: nicht so stressig

For more jobs, see page 76. If you're a girl, you'll need to use the feminine form.

Ich bin lieber **Architekt** . | = I'd prefer to be an architect.

a doctor: Arzt
a musician: Musiker

# Advantage one: will be able to afford new trainers...

This page kinda relies on you having an opinion. The more interesting things you can think of to say, the more marks you'll get. Which is really the whole point after all. So get your thinking-cap on...

# Working Abroad

Working abroad is the perfect opportunity to put all your finely-honed German skills to use.
And a little jaunt in a Berlin Bäckerei will jazz up your CV nicely...

## Arbeiten im Ausland... — Working abroad...

For more about work experience, see page 74.

First up, a mite of work experience...

*Nächstes Jahr, möchte ich ein Betriebspraktikum in Deutschland machen.*

= Next year, I would like to do a work experience placement in Germany.

*Ich würde gern mein Deutsch verbessern.*

= I would like to improve my German.

*Ich werde in einer Tierarztpraxis arbeiten.*
*Ich interessiere mich für Tiere.*

= I will work at a veterinary practice.
I'm interested in animals.

## Möchtest du im Ausland arbeiten?

### — Would you like to work abroad?

Me? Work abroad? With all that sun, sand and sea? No thank you.
But just in case that appeals to you, here's how to tell people all about your plans...

For more on plans for the future, see page 75.

Austria:      nach Österreich
Switzerland: in die Schweiz

See page 43 for more countries.

*Nach meinem Abitur werde ich* nach Deutschland *fahren.*

= After my 'A-levels', I will go to Germany.

You know, I think we're a little overdressed for the office.

*Ich möchte ...*

= I would like ...

... to work in a ski resort:      in einem Skiurlaubsort arbeiten
... to work in a hotel:      in einem Hotel arbeiten
... to be an au pair:      Au-pair sein
... to travel and meet people:      reisen und Leute kennen lernen

*Ich möchte ein Jahr freinehmen, um ein Jahr in Europa zu verbringen.*

= I would like to take a gap year in order to spend a year in Europe.

*Es wird ein tolles Erlebnis sein.*

= It will be a great experience.

## Mind the gap...

Obviously you need to know what to say if someone asks you whether you'd like to work abroad, but this is the sort of thing that crops up in reading and listening exams all the time, so you're likely to get to hear about other people's opinions on the matter too. You have been warned. Learn it.

# Getting a Job

Everybody needs a job. This page is all about how to nab yourself one.
Don't say you never learn anything useful...

## Stellenangebote... — Job vacancies...

You might see (and be asked questions about) adverts like these in the reading exam...

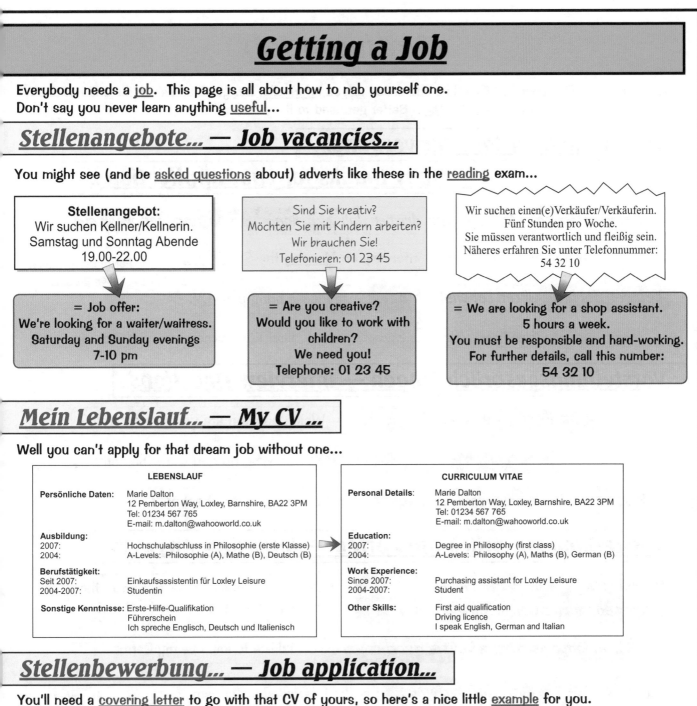

**Stellenangebot:**
Wir suchen Kellner/Kellnerin.
Samstag und Sonntag Abende
19.00-22.00

Sind Sie kreativ?
Möchten Sie mit Kindern arbeiten?
Wir brauchen Sie!
Telefonieren: 01 23 45

Wir suchen einen(e)Verkäufer/Verkäuferin.
Fünf Stunden pro Woche.
Sie müssen verantwortlich und fleißig sein.
Näheres erfahren Sie unter Telefonnummer:
54 32 10

= Job offer:
We're looking for a waiter/waitress.
Saturday and Sunday evenings
7-10 pm

= Are you creative?
Would you like to work with children?
We need you!
Telephone: 01 23 45

= We are looking for a shop assistant.
5 hours a week.
You must be responsible and hard-working.
For further details, call this number:
54 32 10

## Mein Lebenslauf... — My CV ...

Well you can't apply for that dream job without one...

**LEBENSLAUF**

| | |
|---|---|
| **Persönliche Daten:** | Marie Dalton<br>12 Pemberton Way, Loxley, Barnshire, BA22 3PM<br>Tel: 01234 567 765<br>E-mail: m.dalton@wahooworld.co.uk |
| **Ausbildung:**<br>2007:<br>2004: | <br>Hochschulabschluss in Philosophie (erste Klasse)<br>A-Levels: Philosophie (A), Mathe (B), Deutsch (B) |
| **Berufstätigkeit:**<br>Seit 2007:<br>2004-2007: | <br>Einkaufsassistentin für Loxley Leisure<br>Studentin |
| **Sonstige Kenntnisse:** | Erste-Hilfe-Qualifikation<br>Führerschein<br>Ich spreche Englisch, Deutsch und Italienisch |

**CURRICULUM VITAE**

| | |
|---|---|
| **Personal Details:** | Marie Dalton<br>12 Pemberton Way, Loxley, Barnshire, BA22 3PM<br>Tel: 01234 567 765<br>E-mail: m.dalton@wahooworld.co.uk |
| **Education:**<br>2007:<br>2004: | <br>Degree in Philosophy (first class)<br>A-Levels: Philosophy (A), Maths (B), German (B) |
| **Work Experience:**<br>Since 2007:<br>2004-2007: | <br>Purchasing assistant for Loxley Leisure<br>Student |
| **Other Skills:** | First aid qualification<br>Driving licence<br>I speak English, German and Italian |

## Stellenbewerbung... — Job application...

You'll need a covering letter to go with that CV of yours, so here's a nice little example for you.
For more on writing formal letters, see page 11.

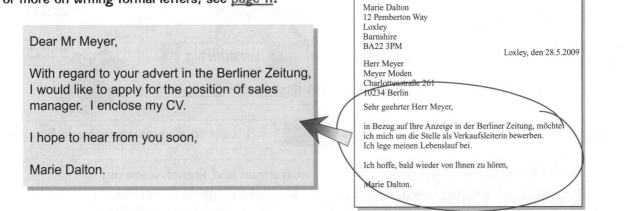

Dear Mr Meyer,

With regard to your advert in the Berliner Zeitung, I would like to apply for the position of sales manager. I enclose my CV.

I hope to hear from you soon,

Marie Dalton.

Marie Dalton
12 Pemberton Way
Loxley
Barnshire
BA22 3PM

Loxley, den 28.5.2009

Herr Meyer
Meyer Moden
Charlottenstraße 261
10234 Berlin

Sehr geehrter Herr Meyer,

in Bezug auf Ihre Anzeige in der Berliner Zeitung, möchte ich mich um die Stelle als Verkaufsleiterin bewerben. Ich lege meinen Lebenslauf bei.

Ich hoffe, bald wieder von Ihnen zu hören,

Marie Dalton.

## Wanted: chocolate taster, no experience necessary...

This page is pretty darn important, so make sure you're familiar with it. You could get given this sort of thing in the reading exam, or you might have to write something similar yourself.

# Getting a Job

A lot of the stuff in your GCSEs will be addressed to you <u>informally</u>, i.e. you'll be called 'du' and not 'Sie'. In an <u>interview</u> you would always be '<u>Sie</u>'. Better get used to it.

## Vielen Dank für Ihre Berwerbung...

### — Many thanks for your application...

Wir laden Sie am Montag , den dritten Juli , zu einem Vorstellungsgespräch ein.

= We invite you to come for an interview on <u>Monday</u> the <u>3rd of July</u>.

*For more on dates, see page 3.*

Bringen Sie bitte Ihren Lebenslauf mit.    = Please bring <u>your CV</u>.

*your passport:* Ihren Pass     *your driving licence:*   Ihren Führerschein     *a photo:* ein Foto

## Vorstellungsgespräch Fragen — Interview Questions

Für welche Stelle interessieren Sie sich?    = Which position are you interested in?

Warum möchten Sie diese Stelle?    = Why do you want this job?

Was haben Sie in der Schule gemacht?    = What did you do at school?

## Vorstellungsgespräch Antworten — Interview Answers

Ich möchte gern als Helfer bei der Touristeninformation in Münster arbeiten.    = I'd like to work as an assistant in the tourist information office in Münster.

Ich möchte gern mein Deutsch verbessern.    = I'd like to improve my German.

Ich interessiere mich für Tourismus.    = I'm interested in tourism.

*For more personality traits, see page 19.*

*qualifications:* Qualifikationen     *responsible:* verantwortlich     *hard-working:* fleißig

Ich habe die nötige Erfahrung . Ich bin flexibel und vernünftig.

= I have the necessary <u>experience</u>. I'm <u>flexible</u> and <u>sensible</u>.

*So, as you can see, I'm pretty flexible...*

Ich habe eine Gesamtschule in Fareham besucht.    = I went to a comprehensive in Fareham.

In der Schule waren Deutsch und Französisch meine Lieblingsfächer.    = German and French were my favourite subjects at school.

## "Selling Yourself" — sounds dodgy...

Most of this stuff isn't new, but get used to dealing with it in this <u>context</u>. There's loads of <u>clever stuff</u> to say here and you can use a lot of it when you're <u>writing</u> job applications too (see <u>page 79</u>).

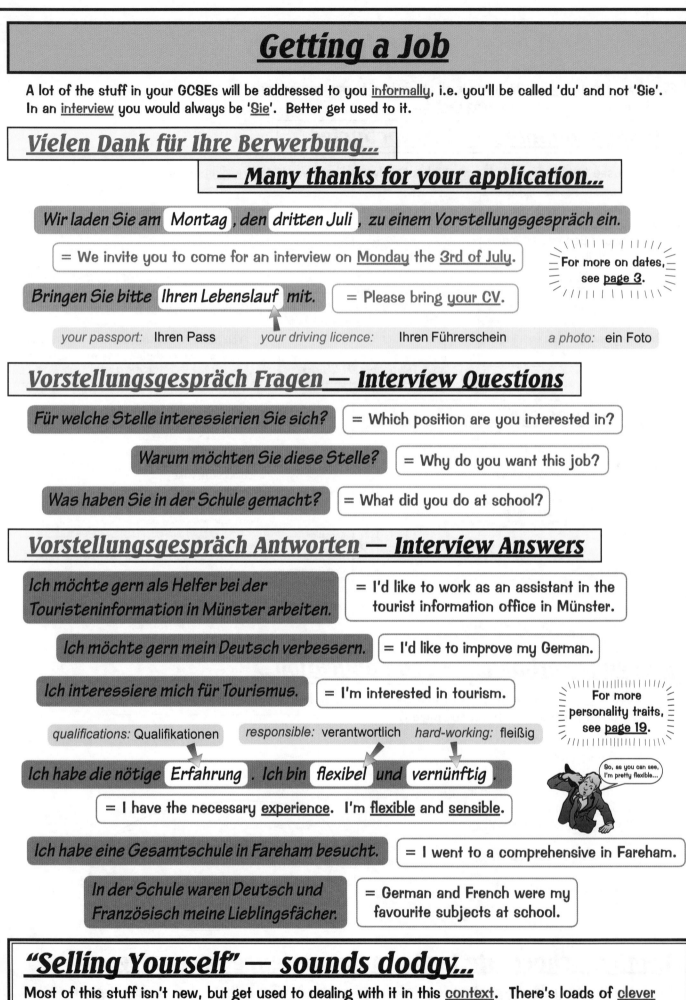

# Telephones

Phone calls come up <u>all the time</u>. So make sure you <u>learn</u> this page. You need to know what to say when you <u>call</u> someone, how to <u>answer</u> the phone, and about passing a <u>message</u> on.

## Telefonieren — *Telephoning*

**Was ist deine Telefonnummer?** = What is <u>your</u> telephone number?

Use '<u>deine</u>' for someone you know well. If you need to be more formal, use '<u>Ihre</u>'.

**Meine Telefonnummer ist achtundzwanzig, neunzehn, zwoundfünfzig.**

See <u>page 1</u> for more numbers.

= My telephone number is <u>281952</u>. German phone numbers are usually given in pairs like this. The number 2, 'zwei', is sometimes said as 'zwo' on the phone.

*Please call me (informal):* Rufst du mich an, bitte. → **Rufen Sie mich an, bitte.** = Please call me (formal).

## Hallo, ist Lisa da? — *Hello, is Lisa there?*

Say this when you <u>answer</u> the phone: **Hallo! Reginald am Apparat.** = Hello! <u>Reginald</u> speaking.

These are for when <u>you</u> phone someone:

**Hallo! Hier spricht Andreas.** = Hello! Andreas speaking.

**Kann ich mit Lisa sprechen?** = Can I speak to Lisa?

## Der Anrufbeantworter — *The answering machine*

You have to understand phone <u>messages</u>, and be able to leave one. This is your <u>bog-standard</u> phone message:

**Hallo, hier spricht Gabriele. Meine Telefonnummer ist neunundfünfzig, neunzehn, sechsundfünfzig. Kann Bob mich um 20 Uhr zurückrufen? Danke. Auf Wiederhören.**

= Hello, Gabriele speaking. My phone number is 59 19 56. Can Bob call me back at 8 pm? Thanks, bye.

You say 'Auf Wieder<u>hören</u>' not 'Auf Wieder<u>sehen</u>' when you're on the phone.

## Ich höre zu... — *I'm listening...*

More stuff you might hear on the phone...

**Warten Sie einen Moment, ich verbinde Sie.** = Wait a moment, I'll put you through.

**Augenblick, ich bin gleich wieder da.** = Just a moment, I'll be right back.

**Darf ich etwas ausrichten?** = May I take a message?

**Sie haben die falsche Nummer.** = You've got the wrong number.

*Sorry, wrong number.:* Es tut mir Leid, falsch verbunden.

# Telefonieren — what a load of phoney rubbish...

Whether you end up having to <u>talk</u> on the phone in a <u>speaking assessment</u>, or <u>listen</u> to a phone conversation in your <u>listening exam</u>, this stuff is pretty <u>crucial</u>. Get learning those set phrases.

82

# The Business World

This page covers all those little consumer-y type problems you might find yourself with.  Which is nice.

## Können Sie mir helfen, bitte? — Can you help me please?

Here's how to ask for information:

**Entschuldigung, wo kann ich einen Klempner finden?**

= Excuse me, where can I find a plumber?

| | |
|---|---|
| a hairdresser: | einen Friseur |
| a dentist: | einen Zahnarzt |
| a chemist: | einen Drogist |

**Sie sollten im Telefonbuch suchen.**   = You should look in the phone book.

| | |
|---|---|
| on the internet: | im Internet |
| in the post office: | in der Post |
| in the tourist information office: | im Verkehrsamt |

## Es gibt ein Problem mit meiner Bestellung...
## — There's a problem with my order...

Here's an example of a phone conversation between a vendor and a customer:

Verkäuferin:

'Hallo, ComputerWelt.  Erika am Apparat.'
*Hello, ComputerWelt.  Erika speaking.*

'Also, kann ich Ihren Namen haben, bitte?'
*OK, can I have your name please?*

'Danke schön.  Ich habe Ihre Bestellung gefunden.
Was für ein Problem gibt es?'
*Thank you.  I've found your order.  What's the problem?*

'Es tut mir Leid, mein Herr.  Morgen früh werden wir
Ihnen die Tastatur schicken.'
*I'm sorry sir.  We'll send the keyboard to you tomorrow
morning.'*

'Bitte schön.  Sonst noch etwas?'
*You're welcome.  Will there be anything else?*

'Auf Wiederhören.'
*Good bye.*

Kunde:

'Hallo.  Letzte Woche habe ich einen Computer bestellt,
aber es gibt ein Problem mit der Bestellung.'
*Hello.  I ordered a computer last week, but there's a
problem with the order.*

'Ja.  Mein Name ist Hans Klaus.'
*Yes.  My name is Hans Klaus.*

'Sie haben den Computer und den Bildschirm geschickt,
aber die Tastatur ist noch nicht angekommen.'
*You've sent the computer and the monitor, but the
keyboard hasn't arrived yet.*

'Das ist toll.  Danke schön.'
*That's great.  Thank you.*

For more computer vocab, see page 33.

'Nein danke, das ist alles.  Auf Wiederhören.'
*No thanks, that's everything.  Good bye.*

## Business World — Britain's least exciting theme park...

The phone conversation above is the sort of thing you might have to listen to in an exam.
Obviously there are loads of different possible scenarios, but they'll all use vocab you should already
be familiar with.  The important thing is not to get thrown by hearing it in a different context.

*Section 6 — Education and Work*

# _Revision Summary_

You really need to <u>know</u> this stuff. Go through these questions — if you can answer them all without looking anything up, then give yourself a pat on the back and <u>smile widely</u>. If there are some you can't do, <u>look them up</u>. Then try again. And again. Keep going till you can do 'em all.

1) Say what all your GCSE subjects are in German (or as many as possible).
   I guess one of them will be Deutsch...

2) Roland goes to school by bike, but Sonia goes by car.
   How would each of them tell the other in German how they get to school?

3) How would you say in German that your lunch break begins at 12:45 pm and lasts one hour?

4) Marie wants to know what your school is like.
   Tell her in German there's an assembly hall, a canteen, a library and a large sports field.

5) Your teacher has just said a long sentence in German and you don't understand.
   How would you ask her to repeat it?

6) How do you say in German that you've been learning French for five years and German
   for four years?

7) Your German friend Michael is looking a bit down. You ask him if he has any problems at
   school and he tells you that he sometimes finds the work a bit difficult and he's worried
   about his exams. Write down what he's told you in German.

8) Write a full German sentence explaining where you did your work experience.
   If you haven't done work experience then write that down.

9) Write the German for whether you liked your work experience and why,
   or say whether you would like to do work experience and where.

10) Monika wants to study physics.
    How does she say that she wants to do the Abitur so that she can go to university?
    How does she say her favourite subjects are maths, physics and chemistry?

11) Write down the German names of four occupations that you might possibly do in the future and
    four that you would never ever want to do. Say why you wouldn't want to do one of the jobs.

12) You have two German pen friends, Nadja and Karl. Nadja wants to have a job where she works
    with animals and Karl wants to take a gap year in Europe. How would each of them say that?

13) How would you write a reply in German to a job advert for an assistant in a bookshop?
    Explain why you want the job and why you think you're suitable.

14) A friend of your brother's calls.
    Write down a message in German for your brother, saying his friend can't go out tonight.

CASES: NOMINATIVE
AND ACCUSATIVE
# The Wonderful Truth About Cases

Cases are a pain in the neck. They can seem pretty <u>nasty</u>, but if you get the <u>four</u> cases <u>clear</u> in your head, it'll make the <u>rest</u> of this grammar stuff a lot <u>easier</u>. And that could make a <u>real</u> difference to your <u>marks</u>.

## 'Cases' mean you have to change words to fit

The <u>only</u> reason you need to <u>know</u> about cases is that some words have to be <u>spelt differently</u> depending on what case they're in.

**EXAMPLE:** *Der rote Hund* *folgt* *dem roten Hund* . = <u>The red dog</u> follows <u>the red dog</u>.

<u>Both</u> these bits <u>mean</u> the <u>same</u> thing ('the red dog') but some of the <u>letters</u> in the words have <u>changed</u>, because the second bit is in a <u>different case</u> from the first bit.

This page and the next page are about <u>when</u> you use the different cases.
<u>How</u> you <u>change the words</u> to fit the case is on <u>pages 85-86</u>, <u>90-92</u> & <u>96-99</u>.

Excuse me sir, I've think you've got the wrong case...

## The most often-used cases are

## the nominative and the accusative

<u>What case</u> a bit of the sentence is <u>depends</u> on what the words are <u>doing</u> in the sentence:

*Hermann* *isst* *Eis* . = <u>Hermann</u> eats <u>ice cream</u>.

...this bit of the sentence is <u>who is doing it</u>...
(<u>Hermann</u> — or Harold, or Henry or the Queen of Sheba or whoever — is eating ice cream.)

This bit of the sentence is <u>what is going on</u>... it's the <u>verb</u>. (Hermann is <u>eating</u> ice cream, or buying it, or drinking it or whatever.)

...and this bit of the sentence is <u>who or what it is done to</u>. (Hermann is eating <u>ice cream</u>, or biscuits, or toast or whatever.)

### = NOMINATIVE CASE

This is kind of the <u>normal common-or-garden</u> case. If you look up a word in the <u>dictionary</u>, it'll tell you what it is in the <u>nominative</u> case.

### = ACCUSATIVE CASE

Oh how lovely — an ice cream. Don't mind if I do...

Her Majesty the Queen of Sheba

That's the secret of all this <u>mysterious-sounding</u> 'nominative' and 'accusative' cases business. Or, in <u>two lines</u>...

### The Golden Rules
#### <u>NOMINATIVE</u> = who (or what) is <u>DOING</u> it
#### <u>ACCUSATIVE</u> = who (or what) it's <u>DONE TO</u>

*For grammar fans — the <u>subject</u> of the verb is in the <u>nominative</u> case. The <u>object</u> of the verb is in the <u>accusative</u> case.*

## I learnt German grammar — just in case...

<u>Cases</u> are one of the <u>trickiest</u> things about GCSE German, so get this stuff <u>learnt</u> and you're well on your way to success. The <u>nominative</u> and <u>accusative</u> cases are an <u>absolute must</u> — go over this page till you can write down those <u>golden rules</u> from <u>memory</u>. For top marks, read on...

# More Cases and Noun Endings

Top Tip Number 1 in a series of 1 — read page 84 before you tackle this page.
The genitive and the dative cases sound hard, but they're just as easy (☺) as the accusative.

## The genitive case — things like Bob's, Sue's...

When you want to say things like Bob's, the milkman's, my mum's... you use the genitive case.

Der Wagen  meines Vaters .

= My father's car.
(The car of my father.)        = GENITIVE CASE

Hermann isst das Eis  des Mädchens .

= Hermann eats the girl's ice cream.
(Hermann eats the ice cream of the girl.)        = GENITIVE CASE

NB: Stuff like 'my dad's a doctor' isn't in the genitive — it's short for 'my dad is a doctor',
which has got nothing to do with a doctor belonging to your dad.

## The dative case — to Bob, from Bob...

Make sure you totally understand the accusative case (see page 84), then look at these sentences:

Hermann schreibt  einen Brief .

= Hermann writes a letter.        = ACCUSATIVE CASE

Hermann schreibt  einem Freund .

= Hermann writes to a friend.        = DATIVE CASE

1. These sentences are different. The friend is not being written — he's being written to.
   So the letter is more directly involved in the action than the friend is. That's why they're in different cases.

2. Usually when you've got a word like 'on', 'at', 'from', 'of', 'for', 'in', 'by', 'with', 'to'...
   in the English translation, that's when you need to use the dative in the German.
   (Sometimes you need to use the accusative with words like this though — see page 96.)

"Dear Jane,
It's not you,
it's me..."

3. There are a few sneaky exceptions that
   don't have one of those words, but are in
   the dative case anyway — see page 97.

   For grammar fans — the indirect object
   of the verb is in the dative case.

## Nouns get these endings to fit the case

Words for people and objects (nouns — see page 86) sometimes have to change, depending
on what case they're in. You change them by adding on the right ending from this table.

You don't have to change them very often — that's why the table is mostly blank.

EXAMPLE:
Normally, 'apples' =
'Äpfel', but in the
dative plural it's 'Äpfeln'.

Ich singe den Äpfeln.

= I sing to the apples.

NB: If it already ends in 'n', you don't add an
extra 'n'. For example, streets = Straßen,
and in the plural dative it's still Straßen.

Watch out though. Some words don't follow this pattern
— if you've learnt some different endings for a word,
then make sure you use those instead.

| Endings for nouns in different cases | | | |
|---|---|---|---|
| | Masculine | Feminine | Neuter | Plural |
| Nominative | – | – | – | – |
| Accusative | – | – | – | – |
| Genitive | -s | – | -s | – |
| Dative | – | – | – | -n |

There are quite a few words where you have to add '-es' rather than
'-s' in the genitive — they tend to end in '-s', '-ß', '-x' or '-z'.

---

# To Bob, Happy Birthday, from Bob...

Not my idea of fun, but you need to learn about the genitive and dative cases to know when to
change the endings on things like nouns and describing words. Make sure you know that table too.

| NOUNS | **Words for People and Objects** |

Scary — it looks like there's a lot on this page, but it's all <u>pretty simple</u> stuff about words for <u>people</u> and <u>objects</u> — nouns. Just about <u>every</u> sentence has a noun in it, so this is <u>dead important</u>.

## Every German noun starts with a capital letter

In English, words like Richard, London and January always have capital letters.
In German <u>absolutely every noun</u> (<u>object</u>, <u>person</u> or <u>place</u>) has a capital letter.

**EXAMPLE:**   *apple:* der <u>A</u>pfel   *elephant:* der <u>E</u>lefant   *cow:* die <u>K</u>uh   *baby:* das <u>B</u>aby

I said USE A CAPITAL!!

## Every German noun is masculine, feminine or neuter

It's no good just knowing the German words for things — you have to know whether each one's <u>masculine</u>, <u>feminine</u> or <u>neuter</u> too.

**DER, DIE AND DAS**

A <u>DER</u> in front means it's <u>masculine</u> (in the <u>nominative</u> case).

<u>DIE</u> in front = <u>feminine</u> (or a plural).

<u>DAS</u> in front = <u>neuter</u>.

**The Golden Rule**
Each time you <u>learn</u> a <u>word</u>, remember a <u>der</u>, <u>die</u> or <u>das</u> to go with it — don't think 'cow = Kuh', think 'cow = <u>die</u> Kuh'.

Whether a word is <u>masculine</u>, <u>feminine</u> or <u>neuter</u> affects loads of stuff. You have to use different words for 'the' and 'a', and you have to change adjectives (like big, red, shiny) to fit the word.

**EXAMPLE:**   *a big apple:* <u>ein</u> großer Apfel (masculine)
*a big cow:*   <u>eine</u> große Kuh (feminine)

See pages 90-91 for more on this.

## These rules help you guess what a word is

If you have to guess if a word is <u>masculine</u>, <u>feminine</u> or <u>neuter</u>, these are good rules of thumb.

### Rules of Thumb for Masculine, Feminine and Neuter Nouns

| MASCULINE NOUNS: | FEMININE NOUNS: | NEUTER NOUNS: |
|---|---|---|
| nouns that end: | nouns that end: | nouns that end: |
| -el   -us   -ling | -ie   -heit   -tion | -chen   -um   -lein   -ment |
| -ismus   -er | -ei   -keit   -sion | also: infinitives of verbs used as nouns, |
| also: male people, days, | -ung   -schaft   -tät | e.g. das Turnen (gymnastics) |
| months, seasons | also: most female people | |

## Weak nouns have weird endings

Some <u>masculine nouns</u> take <u>different endings</u> to the ones at the bottom of <u>page 85</u>.
They're called <u>weak nouns</u> and most of them are words for <u>people or animals</u>.
As long as you learn which nouns they are, it's not too tricky — the endings are actually <u>dead simple</u>.

1) There's <u>no ending</u> to add for the <u>nominative singular case</u>.
2) For <u>most</u> weak nouns, the ending in <u>all other cases</u> is '<u>-n</u>' (if the noun ends in '<u>-e</u>') or '<u>-en</u>' (for all others). E.g. 'der Junge' → 'den Junge<u>n</u>' in the accusative, 'der Mensch' → 'dem Mensch<u>en</u>' in the dative.
3) There are just a couple of <u>sneaky exceptions</u> — a few weak nouns take the ending '<u>-ns</u>' in the <u>genitive singular</u> instead of '-n'. The only ones like this that you're likely to meet at GCSE are '<u>der Name</u>' (name), '<u>der Buchstabe</u>' (letter), '<u>der Glaube</u>' (belief) and '<u>der Gedanke</u>' (thought).
4) Oh, and '<u>der Herr</u>' is a bit of a rascal too — it's got the ending '<u>-n</u>' instead of '<u>-en</u>' in the singular accusative, dative and genitive.

## I didn't know about this gender thing — it's neuter me...

Blimey. This page is pretty full of stuff, but it <u>all</u> boils down to this — <u>every time</u> you learn a word in German, you <u>have</u> to learn whether it's <u>der</u>, <u>die</u> or <u>das</u>, and you have to learn what its <u>plural</u> is...

# Words for People and Objects

The stuff on page 86 is fine if you've only got one of something. But if you've got more than one then it's not going to be much help to you. That's why you also need to know about plurals...

## When you learn a German word, learn the plural too

In English you generally add an 's' to make things plural, e.g. boy + s = boys.
German is much trickier — there are nine main ways to make something plural. Yuck.

### Nine Ways To Make Something Plural

No change, *der Metzger → die Metzger (butchers)*.
Add an umlaut to the stressed syllable, *der Apfel → die Äpfel (apples)*
Add an 'e' on the end, *der Tag → die Tage (days)*.
Add an umlaut and an 'e' on the end, *die Hand → die Hände (hands)*.
Add an 'er' on the end, *das Lied → die Lieder (songs)*.
Add an umlaut and an 'er' on the end, *das Haus → die Häuser (houses)*.
Add an 's' on the end, *das Sofa → die Sofas (sofas)*.
Add an 'n' on the end, *die Straße → die Straßen (streets)*.
Add an 'en' on the end, *das Bett → die Betten (beds)*.

Most feminine nouns do one of these two things.

Whatever gender a noun is, its plural is always a 'die' word (in the nominative and accusative cases, anyway).

Top tip for plurals: Each time you learn a word, learn how to make it into a plural too.

1. When you look them up in a dictionary, you get the plural in brackets like this: 'Bett (-en)', which means 'Betten', or 'Hand (¨e)', which means 'Hände'.

2. A compound noun is a noun made up of two or more words stuck together. When you add an umlaut, it goes on the stressed syllable of the 'root word' (the last bit of the compound noun). E.g. the plural of 'die Bratwurst' is 'die Bratwürste', not 'die Brätwurste'.

## Some adjectives can be used as nouns

In English you can use some adjectives (see pages 91-92) as nouns — e.g. the good, the bad and the ugly. Well, it's the same in German...

A noun is an object, person or place.

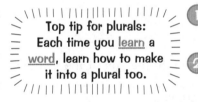 **Der Deutsche** *ist sehr freundlich.*

The old man: Der Alte
The pretty girl: Die Hübsche

= The German (man) is very friendly.

You can do this with any adjective.

Because the adjective is now a noun, it has to have a capital letter.

You don't always have to say whether you're talking about a man or a woman in German, because it's clear from whether you use der (for a man) or die (for a woman).

The noun has the same ending that it would have if it was still an adjective (see page 91 for the tables of endings).

## Nouns the time to get those plurals learnt...

Nouns, nouns, nouns — you just can't move for them, they're absolutely everywhere. It's a pain, but if you can get your head round them now then you're on to a winner. You know what to do...

# Word Order

You need to write proper sentences — so I'm going to tell you where to stick your words...

## The five commandments for German word order

### 1 Put the verb second

The verb (the action word) almost always goes second in a German sentence.

E.g. | Ich spiele Fußball. | = I play football. |

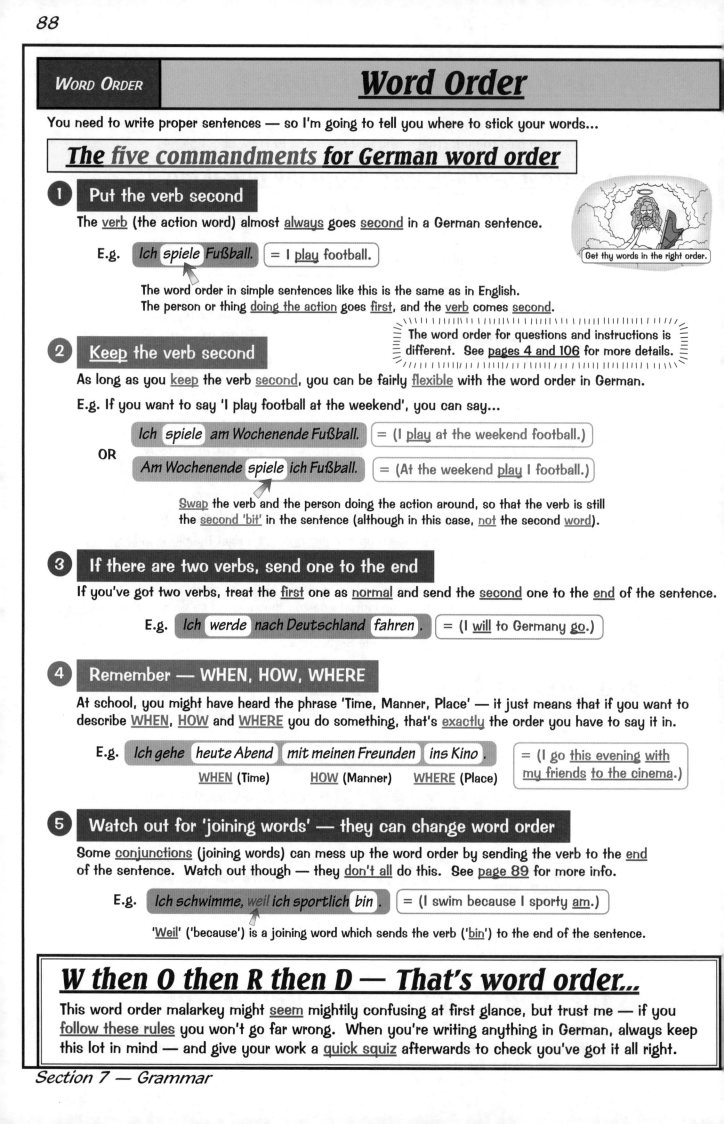
Get thy words in the right order.

The word order in simple sentences like this is the same as in English.
The person or thing doing the action goes first, and the verb comes second.

The word order for questions and instructions is different. See pages 4 and 106 for more details.

### 2 Keep the verb second

As long as you keep the verb second, you can be fairly flexible with the word order in German.

E.g. If you want to say 'I play football at the weekend', you can say...

Ich spiele am Wochenende Fußball. | = (I play at the weekend football.)

OR

Am Wochenende spiele ich Fußball. | = (At the weekend play I football.)

Swap the verb and the person doing the action around, so that the verb is still the second 'bit' in the sentence (although in this case, not the second word).

### 3 If there are two verbs, send one to the end

If you've got two verbs, treat the first one as normal and send the second one to the end of the sentence.

E.g. | Ich werde nach Deutschland fahren. | = (I will to Germany go.)

### 4 Remember — WHEN, HOW, WHERE

At school, you might have heard the phrase 'Time, Manner, Place' — it just means that if you want to describe WHEN, HOW and WHERE you do something, that's exactly the order you have to say it in.

E.g. | Ich gehe heute Abend mit meinen Freunden ins Kino. | = (I go this evening with my friends to the cinema.)
WHEN (Time)     HOW (Manner)     WHERE (Place)

### 5 Watch out for 'joining words' — they can change word order

Some conjunctions (joining words) can mess up the word order by sending the verb to the end of the sentence. Watch out though — they don't all do this. See page 89 for more info.

E.g. | Ich schwimme, weil ich sportlich bin. | = (I swim because I sporty am.)

'Weil' ('because') is a joining word which sends the verb ('bin') to the end of the sentence.

## W then O then R then D — That's word order...

This word order malarkey might seem mightily confusing at first glance, but trust me — if you follow these rules you won't go far wrong. When you're writing anything in German, always keep this lot in mind — and give your work a quick squiz afterwards to check you've got it all right.

# Words to Join Up Phrases

**CONJUNCTIONS**

These words help you to join phrases together to make more interesting sentences.
The examiners will be looking for things like this — show them how clever you are.

## Und = And

Ich spiele gern Fußball.   **AND**   Ich spiele gern Rugby.   **=**   Ich spiele gern Fußball und Rugby.

= I like playing football.     = I like playing rugby.     = I like playing football and rugby.

ANOTHER EXAMPLE:   Ich habe einen Bruder und eine Schwester.   = I have a brother and a sister.

## Oder = Or

Er spielt jeden Tag Fußball.   **OR**   Er spielt jeden Tag Rugby.   **=**   Er spielt jeden Tag Fußball oder Rugby.

= He plays football every day.     = He plays rugby every day.

= He plays football or rugby every day.

ANOTHER EXAMPLE:   Ich möchte Ärztin oder Polizistin werden.

= I would like to become a doctor or a policewoman.

## Aber = But

Ich spiele gern Fußball.   **BUT**   Ich spiele nicht gern Rugby.   **=**   Ich spiele gern Fußball, aber ich spiele nicht gern Rugby.

= I like playing football.     = I don't like playing rugby.

= I like playing football but I don't like playing rugby.

ANOTHER EXAMPLE:   Ich will Tennis spielen, aber es regnet.

= I want to play tennis, but it's raining.

## These joining words affect the word order

The words below work in the same way as the stuff above, but with one difference — if there's
a verb (see page 100) after them, then that verb gets sent to the end of the sentence.

Weil = Because

Bob geht ins Kino, weil Hermann geht ins Kino geht.

= Bob is going to the cinema, because Hermann is going to the cinema.

Während = While

Es regnet, während ich spiele Hockey spiele.

= It rains while I play hockey.

All these joining words (and 'aber' above) need a comma before them in a sentence.

This one doesn't send the verb to the end.

**MORE JOINING WORDS**

| | |
|---|---|
| *if/when:* | wenn |
| *after:* | nachdem |
| *so that:* | damit |
| *before:* | bevor |
| *until:* | bis |
| *when:* | als |
| *whether:* | ob |
| *although:* | obwohl |
| *that:* | dass |
| *because:* | denn |

## I can do joined-up letters, but joined-up phrases?

At last, a fairly easy page.  You use 'and', 'or' and 'but' all the time when you're speaking English
— if you don't use them when you speak German, you'll sound a bit weird.  Which no-one wants.

## ARTICLES ## 'The' and 'A'

'The' and 'a' are really important words — you use them all the time.
They're tricky in German, because there are different ones for <u>masculine</u>, <u>feminine</u> or <u>neuter</u> words
(see <u>page 86</u>), and for different <u>cases</u> (nominative, accusative or whatever — see <u>pages 84-85</u>).

## 'The' — start by learning der, die, das, die

1) In English there's just <u>one</u> word for 'the' — simple.
2) In German, you need to know whether you want the <u>masculine</u>, <u>feminine</u> or <u>neuter</u>, and what <u>case</u> you want (<u>nominative</u>, <u>accusative</u>, <u>genitive</u> or <u>dative</u>).
3) Start by learning the <u>first line</u> — <u>der</u>, <u>die</u>, <u>das</u>, <u>die</u>. You <u>absolutely</u> have to know those ones.

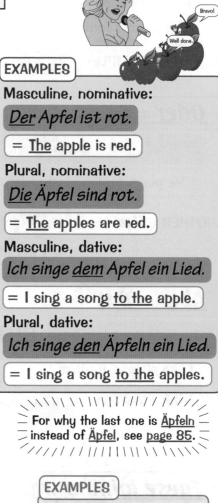

**EXAMPLES**

Masculine, nominative:

*Der Apfel ist rot.*

= <u>The</u> apple is red.

Plural, nominative:

*Die Äpfel sind rot.*

= <u>The</u> apples are red.

Masculine, dative:

*Ich singe dem Apfel ein Lied.*

= I sing a song <u>to the</u> apple.

Plural, dative:

*Ich singe den Äpfeln ein Lied.*

= I sing a song <u>to the</u> apples.

For why the last one is <u>Äpfeln</u> instead of <u>Äpfel</u>, see <u>page 85</u>.

Table of the German words for 'THE'

|  | masculine | feminine | neuter | plural |
|---|---|---|---|---|
| nominative | der | die | das | die |
| accusative | den | die | das | die |
| genitive | des | der | des | der |
| dative | dem | der | dem | den |

This table is pretty scary, but you <u>have</u> to know it <u>all</u> to get everything right in your writing tasks. Cover the page, and <u>write</u> the table out. When you can get it <u>right</u> every time, you'll <u>know</u> which word to use when you're <u>writing</u> or <u>speaking</u> in German.

## 'A' — start by learning ein, eine, ein

1) Like the German for 'the', the word for 'a' is different for <u>masculine</u>, <u>feminine</u> or <u>neuter</u>, and for different <u>cases</u> (<u>nominative</u>, <u>accusative</u>, <u>genitive</u> or <u>dative</u>).
2) Start by learning the <u>first line</u> — <u>ein</u>, <u>eine</u>, <u>ein</u>. When you've got that sorted, move on to the other ones.

Table of the German words for 'A'

|  | masculine | feminine | neuter |
|---|---|---|---|
| nominative | ein | eine | ein |
| accusative | einen | eine | ein |
| genitive | eines | einer | eines |
| dative | einem | einer | einem |

**EXAMPLES**

Masculine, nominative:
*Ein Hund.* = <u>A</u> dog.

Feminine, nominative:
*Eine Katze.* = <u>A</u> cat.

Masculine, accusative:
*Ich habe einen Hund.*
= I have <u>a</u> dog.

Feminine, accusative:
*Ich habe eine Katze.*
= I have <u>a</u> cat.

# Der-die-das — sounds like German trainers...

It's stuff like this that makes me glad I speak English — just one word for 'the', and one word* for 'a'... But there's no getting round it, you <u>need</u> all this stuff to be able to write in <u>German</u>. You have to be able to <u>cover up</u> the page and write out <u>both tables</u> — keep on practising till you can.

\* Well, two words actually — let's not forget about 'an'.

# *Words to Describe Things*

Make your sentences a lot more interesting (which means more marks) with some describing words (adjectives).

## Adjectives that go after the noun don't change

When the describing word (the adjective — e.g. red) is somewhere after the word it's describing (e.g. apple), it doesn't change at all.

**Der Apfel ist rot.** = The apple is red.

**Das Haus ist rot.** = The house is red.

**Die Lampe ist rot.** = The lamp is red.

For how to add things like 'very' and 'almost', see page 93.

You just use the basic describing word, without any endings.

## Endings for when the adjective comes before the noun

In the sentences below, red comes before apples, so you have to give it the right ending from this table:

Plural, accusative: **Ich habe rote Äpfel.** = I have red apples.

You also have to use these endings if the describing word comes after a number bigger than one, or after viele (many), wenige (few), einige (some), etwas (something), or nichts (nothing).

Plural, nominative: **Zwei rote Äpfel.** = Two red apples.

**Ich habe viele große Äpfel.** = I have many big apples.

| Endings for adjectives before the noun | | | |
|---|---|---|---|
| | masculine | feminine | neuter | plural |
| nominative | roter | rote | rotes | rote |
| accusative | roten | rote | rotes | rote |
| genitive | roten | roter | roten | roter |
| dative | rotem | roter | rotem | roten |

You almost never need to use the ones shaded in grey.

*If you love grammar — these endings are for when there's no article before the adjective.*

## There are special endings after 'the'

You've got to add these endings if the describing word comes after 'the' (der, die, das etc.), 'dieser' (this), 'jeder' (each/every), 'beide' (both), 'welcher' (which) and alle (all).

Masculine, nominative:

**Der rote Apfel.** = The red apple.

**Dieser kleine Apfel ist gut.** = This small apple is good.

| Endings for adjectives after definite articles | | | |
|---|---|---|---|
| | masculine | feminine | neuter | plural |
| nominative | rote | rote | rote | roten |
| accusative | roten | rote | rote | roten |
| genitive | roten | roten | roten | roten |
| dative | roten | roten | roten | roten |

*If you love grammar — these endings are for when it's after a definite article or a demonstrative adjective.*

## There are special endings after 'a' and belonging words

You need these endings when the describing word comes after ein (a, or one) or kein (no, or none), or after belonging words like mein, dein, sein, ihr...

Masculine, nominative:

**Der rote Apfel.** = The red apple.

**Mein roter Apfel ist gut.** = My red apple is good.

| Endings for adjectives after indefinite articles | | | |
|---|---|---|---|
| | masculine | feminine | neuter | plural |
| nominative | roter | rote | rotes | roten |
| accusative | roten | rote | rotes | roten |
| genitive | roten | roten | roten | roten |
| dative | roten | roten | roten | roten |

*If you love grammar — these endings are for when it's after an indefinite article or a possessive adjective.*

## This is a roten way to spend an evening...

But at least with this stuff, once you know it, you know it. And lots of the words end in '-en', which makes it easier. Learn the nominative and accusative part of each table first — they're the ones you'll need most often.

| ADJECTIVES | # Words to Describe Things |
|---|---|

Here are 21 <u>describing words</u> to whet your appetite. You need to know how to say <u>my</u>, <u>his</u>, <u>your</u>... too.

**21 TOP DESCRIBING WORDS**

| | | | | | | | |
|---|---|---|---|---|---|---|---|
| *big/tall:* | groß | *easy:* | einfach | *ugly:* | hässlich | *interesting:* | interessant |
| *small/short:* | klein | *difficult:* | schwierig | *old:* | alt | *boring:* | langweilig |
| *long:* | lang | *good:* | gut | *young:* | jung | *strange:* | seltsam |
| *wide:* | breit | *bad:* | schlecht | *new:* | neu | *normal:* | normal |
| *happy:* | glücklich | | (or schlimm) | *fast:* | schnell | | |
| *sad:* | traurig | *beautiful:* | schön | *slow:* | langsam | | |

*See page 38 for colours.*

## My, your, our — words for who it belongs to

You have to be able to <u>use</u> and <u>understand</u> these words to say that something <u>belongs</u> to someone:

But <u>watch out</u> — they need the right <u>ending</u> to go with the <u>object</u> you're talking about (they're the same as the ein/eine/ein table — see <u>page 90</u> — except there's an extra 'plurals' column):

**THE POSSESSIVE ADJECTIVES**

| | | | |
|---|---|---|---|
| **mein:** | *my* | **unser:** | *our* |
| **dein:** | *your (informal singular)* | **euer:** | *your (informal plural)* |
| **sein:** | *his* | **Ihr:** | *your (formal singular & plural)* |
| **ihr:** | *her* | | |
| **sein:** | *its* | **ihr:** | *their* |

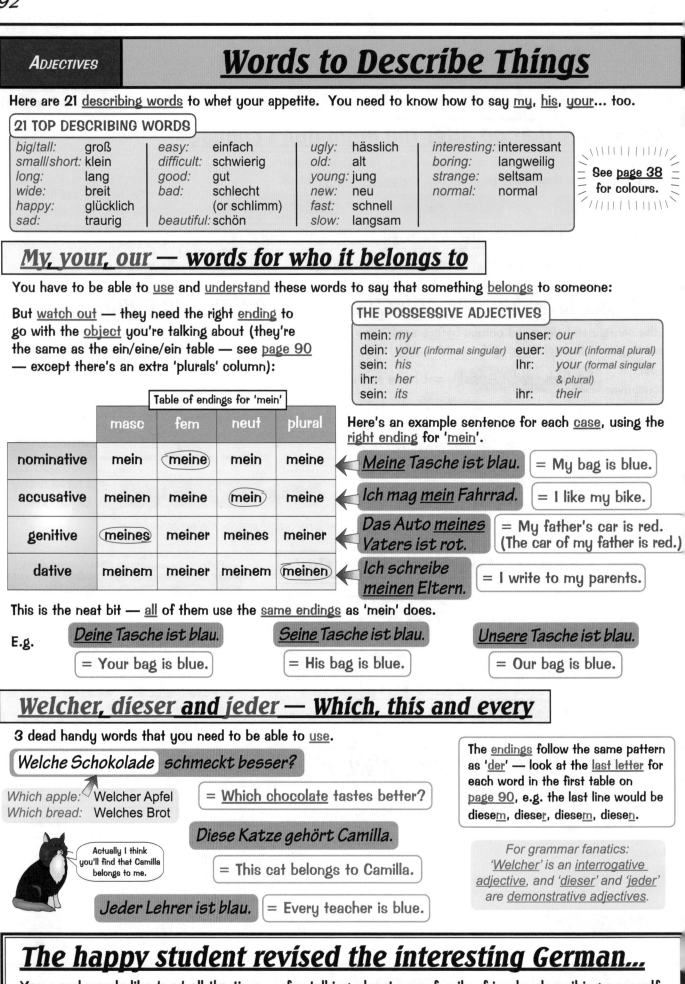

**Table of endings for 'mein'**

| | masc | fem | neut | plural |
|---|---|---|---|---|
| nominative | mein | (meine) | mein | meine |
| accusative | meinen | meine | (mein) | meine |
| genitive | (meines) | meiner | meines | meiner |
| dative | meinem | meiner | meinem | (meinen) |

Here's an example sentence for each <u>case</u>, using the <u>right ending</u> for '<u>mein</u>'.

*Meine Tasche ist blau.* ← = My bag is blue.

*Ich mag mein Fahrrad.* ← = I like my bike.

*Das Auto meines Vaters ist rot.* ← = My father's car is red. (The car of my father is red.)

*Ich schreibe meinen Eltern.* ← = I write to my parents.

This is the neat bit — <u>all</u> of them use the <u>same endings</u> as 'mein' does.

E.g.

*Deine Tasche ist blau.*
= Your bag is blue.

*Seine Tasche ist blau.*
= His bag is blue.

*Unsere Tasche ist blau.*
= Our bag is blue.

## Welcher, dieser and jeder — Which, this and every

3 dead handy words that you need to be able to <u>use</u>.

*Welche Schokolade schmeckt besser?*

Which apple: Welcher Apfel
Which bread: Welches Brot

= <u>Which chocolate</u> tastes better?

The <u>endings</u> follow the same pattern as '<u>der</u>' — look at the <u>last letter</u> for each word in the first table on <u>page 90</u>, e.g. the last line would be diese<u>m</u>, diese<u>r</u>, diese<u>m</u>, diese<u>n</u>.

*Diese Katze gehört Camilla.*

= This cat belongs to Camilla.

Actually I think you'll find that Camilla belongs to me.

For grammar fanatics: '*Welcher*' is an <u>interrogative adjective</u>, and '*dieser*' and '*jeder*' are <u>demonstrative adjectives</u>.

*Jeder Lehrer ist blau.* = Every teacher is blue.

## The happy student revised the interesting German...

You need words like '<u>my</u>' all the time — for talking about your family, friends, describing yourself... The 21 top <u>describing words</u> are a good start, but you'll need loads more — <u>learn</u> each new one you come across. And remember, '<u>welcher</u>' = which, '<u>dieser</u>' = this and '<u>jeder</u>' =each or every.

93

# Making Sentences More Interesting — *ADVERBS*

The two pages before this are about describing <u>objects</u> e.g. 'the <u>red</u> bus'. This page is about describing things you <u>do</u>, e.g. 'I speak German <u>perfectly</u>', and about adding <u>more info</u>, e.g. 'I speak German <u>almost</u> perfectly'.

## Make your sentences better by saying how you do things

In <u>English</u>, you don't say 'We speak strange' — you <u>add</u> an '<u>ly</u>' onto the end to say 'We speak strange<u>ly</u>'.
In <u>German</u>, you <u>don't</u> have to do anything — you just stick the describing word in <u>as it is</u>.

EXAMPLE:

Ich fahre langsam . = I drive <u>slowly</u> (slow).

badly (bad): schlecht
quickly (fast): schnell

'Langsam' is just the German word for 'slow' — you can use any other suitable describing word here.

Ich singe. = I sing.

Ich singe laut. = I sing loudly.

Ich singe schlecht. = I sing badly.

La la la laAAAA

## Use one of these words to give even more detail

Stick one of these words in <u>front</u> of the <u>describing word</u> in a sentence to add detail and impress your teacher:

You can use them for sentences saying <u>how something is done</u>...

...and for sentences about <u>what something is like</u>.

Ich fahre sehr langsam.

= I drive <u>very</u> slowly.

| | |
|---|---|
| quite: | ganz/ziemlich |
| slightly: | etwas/ein wenig |
| a bit: | ein bisschen |
| almost: | fast |
| too: | zu |
| a lot: | viel |

Bob ist ganz glücklich.

= Bob is <u>quite</u> happy.

## These words give extra detail about time and place

You'll get even more marks if you can add information about <u>when</u> you do something...

| now and then: | ab und zu |
| now and then: | dann und wann |
| as soon as possible: | so bald wie möglich |
| last week: | letzte Woche |
| next weekend: | nächstes Wochenende |

Ich gehe oft ins Kino. = I <u>often</u> go to the cinema.

Manchmal isst sie Birnen. = <u>Sometimes</u> she eats pears.

The word order changes because the <u>verb</u> has to <u>come second</u>. See <u>page 88</u>.

...and <u>where</u> it is.

Ich wohne hier . = I live <u>here</u>.

Ich wohne nicht gern dort . = I don't like living <u>there</u>.

## I speak German good (but English less good)...

For once, saying something in German is <u>easier</u> than saying it in English. To say how you <u>do</u> something, you <u>just</u> stick in a <u>describing word</u> — <u>no</u> endings, <u>no</u> faffing, brilliant. <u>Practise</u> taking a few German sentences and adding extra detail... then use 'em in the assessments.

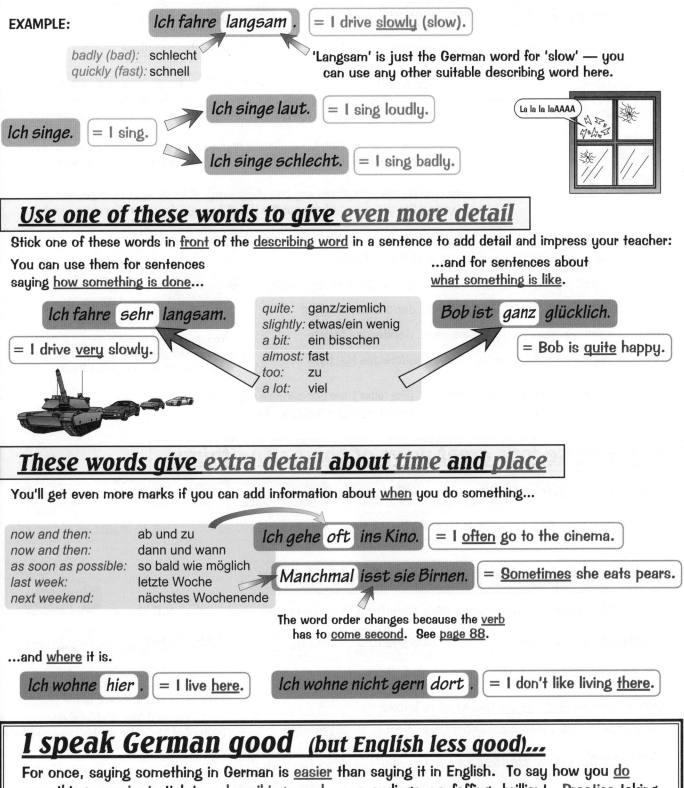

**COMPARATIVES AND SUPERLATIVES**

# Comparing Things

A lot of the time you don't just want to say that something is <u>big</u>, or <u>red</u> or whatever, you want to say that it's the <u>biggest</u>, or <u>bigger than</u> someone else's...

## How to say smaller, smallest

In <u>English</u> you say small, small<u>er</u>, small<u>est</u>.
It's <u>almost</u> the <u>same</u> in German:

So here the adjective acts as the <u>noun</u>, just like in English — and of course all German nouns get a <u>capital letter</u>.

**Anna ist** `klein` .

= Anna is <u>small</u>.

**Hermann ist** `kleiner` .

= Hermann is <u>smaller</u>.

**Sina ist** `der Kleinste` .

= Sina is the <u>smallest</u>.

| *Stem* | | *Stem + '-er'* | | *Stem + 'der', 'die' or 'das' and '-(e)ste'* |
|---|---|---|---|---|
| old: | alt | older: | <u>älter</u> | oldest: | der/die/das <u>Älteste</u> |
| interesting: | interessant | more interesting: | interessant<u>er</u> | most interesting: | der/die/das Interessant<u>este</u> |

For most words, '-ste' is added, but sometimes it's '-<u>e</u>ste', to make it easier to pronounce.
(You <u>can't</u> miss out the <u>der</u>, <u>die</u> or <u>das</u> — you <u>CAN'T</u> say 'Ethel ist Interessanteste'.)

You can do this with almost any <u>describing word</u>. A lot of <u>short</u> ones get an added <u>umlaut</u> like 'alt' does. Check out the top of <u>page 92</u> for more describing words.

Anna   Hermann   Sina

Just like in English, there are <u>odd ones out</u> — for example, you <u>don't</u> say good, gooder, goodest...

*good:* gut ➡ *better:* <u>besser</u> ➡ *the best:* der/die/das <u>Beste</u>

*big (or tall):* groß ➡ *bigger:* <u>größer</u> ➡ *the biggest:* der/die/das Größ<u>te</u> ➡ **Liz ist** `die Größte` .

= Liz is <u>the tallest</u>.

*high:* hoch ➡ *higher:* <u>höher</u> ➡ *the highest:* der/die/das <u>Höchste</u>

*much/a lot:* viel ➡ *more:* <u>mehr</u> ➡ *the most:* der/die/das <u>Meiste</u>

*near:* nah ➡ *nearer:* <u>näher</u> ➡ *the nearest:* der/die/das <u>Nächste</u>

You <u>don't</u> need to use a <u>capital</u> if the adjective goes <u>before</u> a noun e.g. 'the tallest tree' would be 'der größte Baum'.

Describing words that end in '-er' (like 'älter') are <u>comparative adjectives</u>.
If you use them <u>before</u> a noun, they need <u>adjective endings</u>, like on <u>page 91</u>.

## Learn these four great ways of comparing things

**Jo ist älter** `als` **Ed.**

= Jo is older <u>than</u> Ed.

**Jo ist** `weniger` **alt** `als` **Ed.**

= Jo is <u>less</u> old <u>than</u> Ed.

**Jo ist** `so` **alt** `wie` **Ed.**

= Jo is <u>as</u> old <u>as</u> Ed.

**Jo ist** `ebenso` **alt** `wie` **Ed.**

= Jo is <u>just as</u> old <u>as</u> Ed.

## You can compare how people do things

It's all relative you know...

If you're talking about how someone <u>does</u> something, it's almost <u>the same</u> as the stuff above:

**Einstein fährt** `schnell` .

= Einstein drives <u>quickly</u>.

**Bob fährt** `schneller` .

= Bob drives <u>more quickly</u>.

**Ethel fährt** `am schnellsten` .

= Ethel drives <u>the quickest</u>.

The bit that's different is the <u>last one</u>.
You add '<u>am</u>' and '<u>-(e)sten</u>'.
(Instead of 'der', 'die' or 'das', and '-(e)ste'.)

Here's one more <u>odd one out</u> you need to know:

*willingly:* gern ➡ *preferably:* <u>lieber</u> ➡ *best of all:* <u>am liebsten</u>

**Ich spreche** `lieber` **Deutsch.**   = I <u>prefer</u> speaking German.

'Best' is also slightly different: To say someone does something <u>best</u>, it's '<u>am besten</u>'.

# Sneaky Wee Words

This stuff looks horrendous, but you've got to learn it if you want good marks.

## TO — zu, or nach

Where we use 'to', German speakers often use 'zu':

(zum = zu dem — see page 96)

**Komm zu mir.** = Come to me.   **zum Bahnhof gehen** = to go to the station

For 'the train to London' (and other towns), it's 'nach':

For things like to go, to do, use the infinitive — see page 100. E.g. gehen = to go, machen = to make.

**der Zug nach London** = the train to London

They sometimes use 'an', 'auf' or 'in' too.

## AT — an, bei, um or zu

Where we use 'at', in German it's usually 'an':   **an der Universität** = at university

Sometimes 'bei' is used: **bei einer Party** = at a party

For 'at home', it's 'zu': **zu Hause** = at home      For times it's 'um': **um acht Uhr** = at 8 o'clock

## ON — an, auf

Where we use 'on', in German it tends to be 'an':

**an der Wand** = on the wall      **am Montag** = on Monday

am = an dem — see page 96.

For 'on foot', it's 'zu': **zu Fuß** = on foot

Die Katze ist auf dem Elch.

For on top of something, it's 'auf': **Das Buch ist auf dem Tisch.** = The book is on the table.

## FROM — von or aus

When we use 'from' in English, they usually use 'von' in German, including for where someone/thing has come from recently:

**Der Zug ist von London gekommen.** = The train has come from London.

For where someone/thing is from originally, it's 'aus': **Ich komme aus England.** = I come from England.

For 'made from' — see 'made of' on page 96.

## IN — in or an

Where we use 'in', German speakers also tend to use 'in':

**in Deutschland** = in Germany      **im Bett** = in bed   (im = in dem — see page 96)

For in the morning/evening, it's 'an': **am Morgen** = in the morning   (am = an dem — see page 96)

# This page is a gift to you, from me...

It may seem like a pain in the neck having to remember where and when to use all these little words, but trust me — if you get it right, it'll bag you loads of lovely marks in your writing assessment.

**PREPOSITIONS**

# Sneaky Wee Words

Yep, more sneaky wee words (or <u>prepositions</u> as they're known by grammar fanatics).
Make sure you learn <u>which</u> words to use and <u>where</u> — it's not always obvious from the English.

## OF — 'von', 'aus' or left out

Where we use 'of', the German is usually '<u>von</u>':

> ein Freund von mir    = a friend of mine

For 'made of', it's '<u>aus</u>':

> aus Wolle    = made of wool

*Es besteht aus Wolle.*

You <u>leave it out</u> of dates:   der erste März    = the first of March   See <u>page 3</u> for more on dates.

It's often <u>left out</u> in <u>genitive</u> sentences too:   einer der Besten    = one of the best

## FOR — für, or seit

Where we use 'for', German speakers usually use '<u>für</u>':

> ein Geschenk für mich    = a present for me

For time amounts in the past, it's '<u>seit</u>':

> Ich habe sie seit zwei Jahren nicht gesehen.    = I haven't seen her for two years.

## An dem ➔ am — short forms

Some of the words on these two pages get <u>shortened</u> when they go with dem, das or der. For example:

> an dem ersten Januar ➔ am ersten Januar
> = on the first of January

**SHORT FORMS**

| | |
|---|---|
| an dem = am | bei dem = beim |
| an das = ans | von dem = vom |
| in dem = im | zu der = zur |
| in das = ins | zu dem = zum |

## To be 100% right, you have to use the right case

When they're in a sentence, these words <u>change the case</u> (<u>pages 84-85</u>) of the stuff that comes <u>after</u> them. To be sure <u>what case</u> to use, you have to <u>learn</u> these lists.

**ACCUSATIVE**
bis = *till, by*
durch = *through*
für = *for*
gegen = *against, about*
ohne = *without*
um = *round, around, at*

**DATIVE**
aus = *from, out of, made of*
bei = *at, near*
gegenüber = *opposite, facing*
mit = *with*
nach = *to, after*
seit = *since, for*
von = *from, of*
zu = *to, at*

**GENITIVE**
außerhalb = *outside of*
statt = *instead of*
trotz = *despite*
während = *during, while*
wegen = *because of*

**DATIVE OR ACCUSATIVE**
an = *to, on, in, at*
auf = *on, to, at*
entlang = *along*
hinter = *after, behind*
in = *in, to*
neben = *next to, beside*
über = *via, above, over*
unter = *under, among*
vor = *before, ago, in front of*

For prepositions which use <u>either</u> the dative <u>or</u> accusative case, use the <u>accusative</u> when what you're talking about is <u>moving</u> and the <u>dative</u> if there's <u>no movement</u>.

E.g.   Die Katze schläft hinter *dem* Sofa.    = The cat sleeps behind <u>the</u> (dative) sofa. ◀ The cat <u>isn't</u> moving.

Die Katze läuft hinter *das* Sofa.    = The cat runs behind <u>the</u> (accusative) sofa. ◀ The cat <u>is</u> moving.

## In, out, shake it all about...

The <u>take-home message</u> here? To get the most marks, you have to use the <u>right case</u>. If you're not sure about cases, go and <u>look them up</u> (on <u>pages 84-85</u>) — they're pretty darned important.

# I, You, Him, Them...

Dead handy page, this. Pronouns are everywhere, and they can make your German sound much more natural.

## Pronouns replace nouns

Pronouns are words like 'you', 'she' or 'them'.          'He' is a pronoun. It means you don't have to say 'Dave' again.

> Dave has a new job at the poodle parlour. (He) likes shaving poodles.

You use different sets of pronouns for different cases.
If you're not sure about this case stuff, look at pages 84-85.

## You use ich (I) in the nominative case

You need 'I', 'you', 'he', etc. the most often — for the main person/thing in a sentence (the subject).
Learn them all, or you'll be totally scuppered in the exams.

**THE NOMINATIVE CASE**

| I: | ich | we: | wir |
|---|---|---|---|
| you (informal sing.): | du | you (inf. plu.): | ihr |
| he: | er | you | |
| she: | sie | (formal sing. & plu.): | Sie |
| it: | es | they: | sie |

> Der Hund beißt den Kamm. = The dog bites the comb.
> (Er) beißt den Kamm. = He bites the comb.

The nominative case is explained on page 84.

Remember — in English there's only one word for 'you', but in German there are loads.

The nominative words for you are:
du = you (informal singular) — for talking to one person you know well, or another young person
ihr = you (informal plural) — the same as 'du' but for talking to more than one person
Sie = you (formal singular and plural) — for talking to one or more older people who you don't know well or who you should be polite to

## You use mich (me) in the accusative case

These are for the person/thing in a sentence that's having the action done to it (the direct object).
This is the accusative case.

**THE ACCUSATIVE CASE**

| me: | mich | us: | uns |
|---|---|---|---|
| you (informal sing.): | dich | you (inf. plu.): | euch |
| him: | ihn | you (formal | |
| her: | sie | sing. & plu.): | Sie |
| it: | es | them: | sie |

> Dave kitzelt den Hund. = Dave tickles the dog.
> Dave kitzelt (ihn). = Dave tickles him.

Accusative case — see page 84.

## There are special words for to me, to her, to them

For things that need 'to', 'by', 'with' or 'from' — like writing to someone — you use the dative case.

> Der Hund gibt Dave den Kamm. = The dog gives the comb to Dave.

**THE DATIVE CASE**

| to me: | mir | to us: | uns |
|---|---|---|---|
| to you (inf. sing.): | dir | to you (inf. plu.): | euch |
| to him: | ihm | to you (formal sing. & plu.): | Ihnen |
| to her: | ihr | to them: | ihnen |
| to it: | ihm | | |

> Der Hund gibt (ihm) den Kamm. = The dog gives the comb to him.

See page 85 for more on the dative case.

Grammar spotters call these indirect object pronouns.

## These examiners are really taking the mich now...

So, grammar's no fun — big deal. Think the examiners care? You're the one who wants to get through your GCSE, so it's you who has to learn this stuff — there's no escape.
Shut the book, write down each lot of pronouns, then write a German sentence using each one.

| PRONOUNS | **Someone, No One, Who? & What?** |

You need to know things like 'one' or 'someone' and ask questions like 'who?' or 'what?'.
So you'd better get stuck in. <u>This bit's dead easy</u>, so don't whinge — just do it.

## The German word 'man' means 'one', not 'man'

Get this in your skull now — '<u>man</u>' means '<u>one</u>'. It <u>doesn't</u> mean the English word 'man'.
The Germans use 'man' more than we use 'one' in English — it isn't posh at all.

*Wie sagt* man *das auf Deutsch?*  = How does <u>one</u> say that in German?
(How do you say that in German?)

In English, we usually say 'you' instead of 'one' in everyday conversation.

## Someone, anyone — <u>jemand</u>

The word for '<u>someone</u>' is the same as for '<u>anyone</u>' — '<u>jemand</u>'.

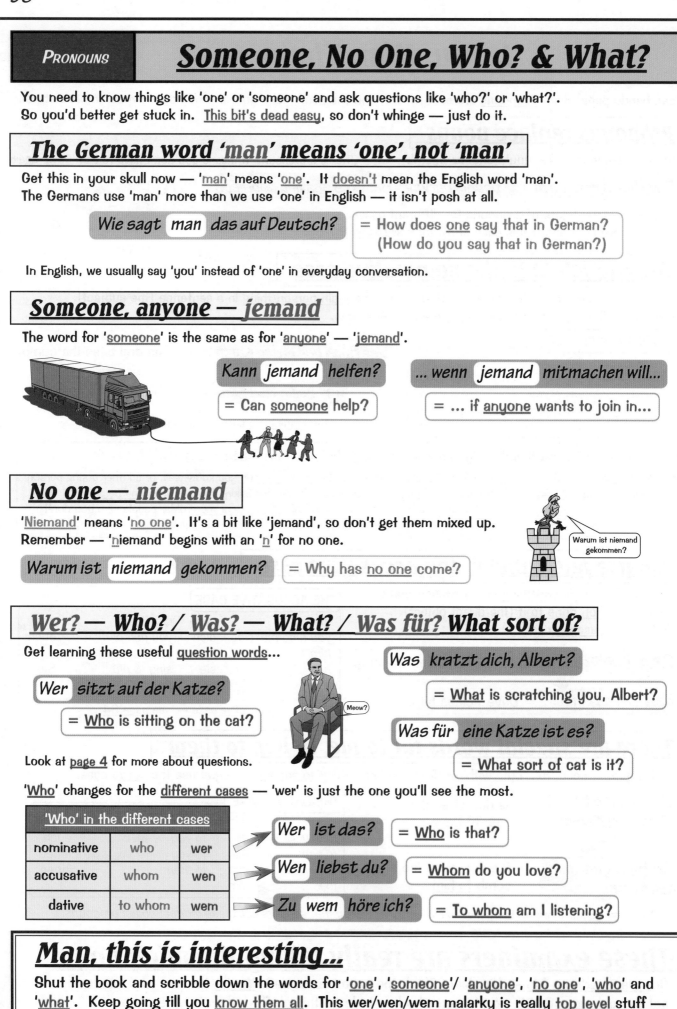

*Kann* jemand *helfen?*  = Can <u>someone</u> help?

*... wenn* jemand *mitmachen will...*  = ... if <u>anyone</u> wants to join in...

## No one — <u>niemand</u>

'<u>Niemand</u>' means '<u>no one</u>'. It's a bit like 'jemand', so don't get them mixed up.
Remember — '<u>n</u>iemand' begins with an '<u>n</u>' for no one.

*Warum ist* niemand *gekommen?*  = Why has <u>no one</u> come?

Warum ist niemand gekommen?

## Wer? — Who? / Was? — What? / Was für? What sort of?

Get learning these useful <u>question words</u>...

*Was kratzt dich, Albert?*  = <u>What</u> is scratching you, Albert?

*Wer sitzt auf der Katze?*  = <u>Who</u> is sitting on the cat?

Meow?

*Was für eine Katze ist es?*  = <u>What sort of</u> cat is it?

Look at <u>page 4</u> for more about questions.

'<u>Who</u>' changes for the <u>different cases</u> — 'wer' is just the one you'll see the most.

| 'Who' in the different cases | | |
|---|---|---|
| nominative | who | wer |
| accusative | whom | wen |
| dative | to whom | wem |

*Wer ist das?*  = <u>Who</u> is that?
*Wen liebst du?*  = <u>Whom</u> do you love?
*Zu wem höre ich?*  = <u>To whom</u> am I listening?

## Man, this is interesting...

Shut the book and scribble down the words for '<u>one</u>', '<u>someone</u>'/'<u>anyone</u>', '<u>no one</u>', '<u>who</u>' and
'<u>what</u>'. Keep going till you <u>know them all</u>. This wer/wen/wem malarky is really <u>top level</u> stuff —
but if you can use them in a sentence and get it <u>right</u>, you'll sound <u>dead impressive</u>. Wunderbar.

# 'That', 'Which', 'Whom' & 'Whose'

Tricky stuff this, but <u>learn it</u> and you'll nab yourself loads of <u>juicy marks</u>.

## Relative pronouns — 'that', 'which', 'whom', 'whose'

You need to understand all these words — and if you're after <u>top marks</u>, you need to be able to <u>use them yourself</u>. Words like '<u>that</u>', '<u>which</u>', '<u>whom</u>' and '<u>whose</u>' are relative pronouns — they relate back to the thing you're talking about. This is the kind of thing I mean:

The dog, which had dug up my sprouts, looked guilty.

The 'which' refers back to the dog.

In German the <u>relative clause</u> (the bit with the <u>relative pronoun</u> in) is separated from the rest of the sentence by <u>commas</u>.

Relative pronouns <u>change</u> the <u>word order</u>. They send the <u>verb</u> to the <u>end</u> of the <u>relative clause</u> (the bit <u>inside</u> the <u>commas</u>).

The <u>pronoun</u> refers to '<u>der Mann</u>'.     The <u>verb</u> goes to the <u>end</u> of the <u>clause</u>.

Der Mann, der in der Ecke sitzt, ist ganz klein.

= The man who sits in the corner is quite small.

## You've got to use the right one...

These are the German equivalents — yuk. It's a bit tricky working out which one you need to use, but as you'd probably expect, it just depends on the noun (page 86) and its case (pages 84-85).

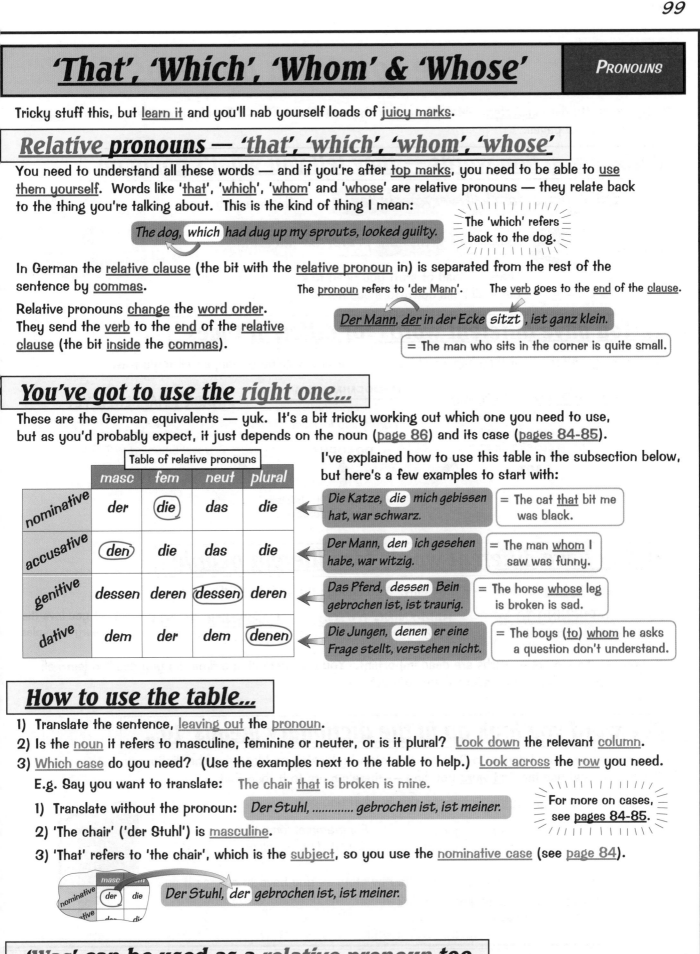

| Table of relative pronouns | masc | fem | neut | plural |
|---|---|---|---|---|
| nominative | der | die | das | die |
| accusative | den | die | das | die |
| genitive | dessen | deren | dessen | deren |
| dative | dem | der | dem | denen |

I've explained how to use this table in the subsection below, but here's a few examples to start with:

Die Katze, die mich gebissen hat, war schwarz.
= The cat that bit me was black.

Der Mann, den ich gesehen habe, war witzig.
= The man whom I saw was funny.

Das Pferd, dessen Bein gebrochen ist, ist traurig.
= The horse whose leg is broken is sad.

Die Jungen, denen er eine Frage stellt, verstehen nicht.
= The boys (to) whom he asks a question don't understand.

## How to use the table...

1) Translate the sentence, <u>leaving out</u> the <u>pronoun</u>.
2) Is the <u>noun</u> it refers to masculine, feminine or neuter, or is it plural? <u>Look down</u> the relevant <u>column</u>.
3) <u>Which case</u> do you need? (Use the examples next to the table to help.) <u>Look across</u> the <u>row</u> you need.

E.g. Say you want to translate:   The chair <u>that</u> is broken is mine.

1) Translate without the pronoun:  Der Stuhl, ............ gebrochen ist, ist meiner.

2) 'The chair' ('der Stuhl') is <u>masculine</u>.

3) 'That' refers to 'the chair', which is the <u>subject</u>, so you use the <u>nominative case</u> (see <u>page 84</u>).

For more on cases, see <u>pages 84-85</u>.

Der Stuhl, der gebrochen ist, ist meiner.

## 'Was' can be used as a relative pronoun too

'<u>Was</u>' can be used as a relative pronoun — for example, you use it after '<u>alles</u>', '<u>nichts</u>', '<u>etwas</u>' '<u>vieles</u>' and '<u>weniges</u>'.

E.g.   Alles, was der Lehrer sagte, war interessant.

= Everything <u>that</u> the teacher said was interesting.

# The Lowdown on Verbs

<u>Verbs</u> are pretty darn <u>important</u>.  Make sure you know all this stuff — it'll make your life a whole lot <u>easier</u> over the next few pages.

## <u>Verbs <u>are</u> action words — they tell you what's going on</u>

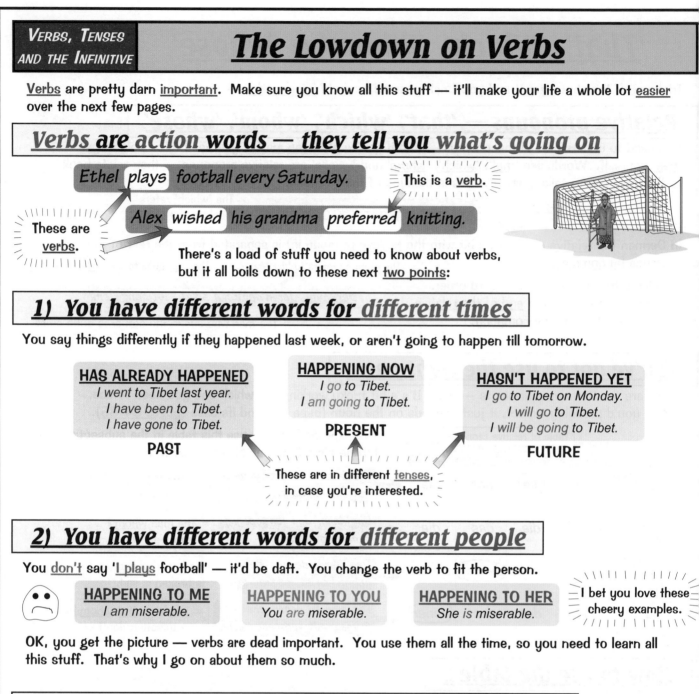

Ethel <u>plays</u> football every Saturday.

This is a <u>verb</u>.

Alex <u>wished</u> his grandma <u>preferred</u> knitting.

These are <u>verbs</u>.

There's a load of stuff you need to know about verbs, but it all boils down to these next <u>two points</u>:

## 1) You have different words for <u>different times</u>

You say things differently if they happened last week, or aren't going to happen till tomorrow.

**HAS ALREADY HAPPENED**
*I went to Tibet last year.*
*I have been to Tibet.*
*I have gone to Tibet.*

**PAST**

**HAPPENING NOW**
*I go to Tibet.*
*I am going to Tibet.*

**PRESENT**

**HASN'T HAPPENED YET**
*I go to Tibet on Monday.*
*I will go to Tibet.*
*I will be going to Tibet.*

**FUTURE**

These are in different <u>tenses</u>, in case you're interested.

## 2) You have different words for <u>different people</u>

You <u>don't</u> say '<u>I plays</u> football' — it'd be daft.  You change the verb to fit the person.

**HAPPENING TO ME**
*I am miserable.*

**HAPPENING TO YOU**
*You are miserable.*

**HAPPENING TO HER**
*She is miserable.*

I bet you love these cheery examples.

OK, you get the picture — verbs are dead important.  You use them all the time, so you need to learn all this stuff.  That's why I go on about them so much.

## <u>The word you look up in the <u>dictionary</u> means 'to...'</u>

When you want to say '<u>I dance</u>' in German, you start by looking up '<u>dance</u>' in the dictionary.  But you can't just use the <u>first word</u> you find — there's more to it than that...

When you look up a verb <u>in the dictionary</u>, this is what you get:

*to go:* gehen
*to dance:* tanzen

*For grammar fans, this is called the <u>infinitive</u>.*

You're <u>not supposed</u> to just use the verb in its <u>raw state</u> — you have to <u>change</u> it so it's right for the <u>person</u> and <u>time</u> you're talking about.  The different verb forms are covered on the next few pages.

## Action words round the edge — a verbacious border...

I'm not kidding — this is <u>mega-important</u> stuff.  Over the next few pages I've given you <u>loads of stuff</u> on verbs because there's loads you <u>need to know</u>.  Some of it's easy, some of it's tricky — but if you <u>don't understand</u> the things on <u>this page</u> before you start, you'll have <u>no chance</u>.

# Verbs in the Present Tense

If you want <u>loads of marks</u>, you've got to make your German sound <u>natural</u>. One <u>sure-fire way</u> to lose marks is to say something <u>daft</u> like '<u>I likes to gone swimming</u>.' Here's how you can avoid it...

## The present tense is what's happening now

The <u>present tense</u> is the <u>easy</u> one — and you use it more than anything else, so it's <u>dead important</u>. The <u>endings are the same</u> for all <u>regular verbs</u>. 'Machen' is regular, so here it is with its endings...

The first bit ('<u>mach</u>') doesn't change.

**MACHEN = TO DO OR MAKE**

| | |
|---|---|
| *I make =* | ich mach**e** |
| *you (inf. sing.) make =* | du mach**st** |
| *he makes =* | er mach**t** |
| *she makes =* | sie mach**t** |
| *it makes =* | es mach**t** |
| *we make =* | wir mach**en** |
| *you (inf. plu.) make =* | ihr mach**t** |
| *you (frml. sing. & plu.)* | |
| *make =* | Sie mach**en** |
| *they make =* | sie mach**en** |

*inf.* = informal
*frml.* = formal
*sing.* = singular
*plu.* = plural

So if you want to say something like 'He <u>makes</u> me happy', it's dead easy:

1) Start by <u>knocking off</u> the '<u>-en</u>':  mache~~n~~

2) Then <u>add on</u> the <u>new ending</u>:  mach<u>t</u>

3) And — <u>ta da</u>...

> *Er macht mich glücklich.*

> = He makes me happy.

Here are some more <u>regular verbs</u> — these verbs all follow the same pattern as '<u>machen</u>'. Learn it and you've learnt them all.

| | | | | | |
|---|---|---|---|---|---|
| *to ask:* | fragen | *to book:* | buchen | *to explain:* | erklären |
| *to believe:* | glauben | *to buy:* | kaufen | *to dance:* | tanzen |

## Watch out — There's a catch...

Some regular verbs don't end in '-en' — they end in '<u>-rn</u>' or '<u>-ln</u>'.
Still, it's no problem — they follow nearly the same rules. Just watch out for missing '-e's.

**'-rn' verbs:**

You <u>miss</u> out the '<u>-e</u>' before the '-r' for ich.

**FEIERN = TO CELEBRATE**

| ich | feire | wir | feiern |
|---|---|---|---|
| du | feierst | ihr | feiert |
| er | feiert | Sie | feiern |
| sie | feiert | sie | feiern |
| es | feiert | | |

You only add '<u>-n</u>' instead of '-en' for wir, Sie and sie.

**'-ln' verbs:**

<u>Lose</u> the '<u>-e</u>' before the 'l' for ich.

**SEGELN = TO SAIL**

| ich | segle | wir | segeln |
|---|---|---|---|
| du | segelst | ihr | segelt |
| er | segelt | Sie | segeln |
| sie | segelt | sie | segeln |
| es | segelt | | |

Add '<u>-n</u>' not '-en' for wir, Sie and sie.

Just learn one of these types, and you can use the same rules for the other. Great stuff.

## Instead of 'I go swimming', say 'I go to swim'

You sometimes need to say '<u>I go swimming</u>' rather than just 'I swim' — so you need <u>two</u> verbs. For the <u>first</u> verb, you need to put it in the <u>right form</u> for the <u>person</u>, but for the <u>second</u>, you just need the <u>infinitive</u>.

to swim = *schwimmen*

I <u>go</u> = *Ich gehe*

*Ich gehe schwimmen .*

= I go <u>swimming</u>.

| | | | | | | | |
|---|---|---|---|---|---|---|---|
| *bowling:* | kegeln | *jogging:* | joggen | *dancing:* | tanzen | *camping:* | zelten |
| *hiking:* | wandern | *running:* | laufen | *fishing:* | angeln | *skiing:* | Ski fahren / Ski laufen |

## Great, I love presents...

OK, this is pretty easy stuff. <u>Learn the endings</u> for normal, regular '<u>en</u>' verbs, and remember that they go a <u>bit weird</u> for '<u>-rn</u>' and '<u>-ln</u>' ones. And when you say '<u>I go swimming</u>', the '<u>go</u>' works like normal and the '<u>swimming</u>' part needs to be the <u>infinitive</u> (the one you look up <u>in the dictionary</u>).

# Verbs in the Present Tense

You could be conned into thinking nearly all verbs are regular (see page 101). But in fact, loads aren't.

## Sein, haben, fahren and essen are irregular

Verbs that don't follow the same pattern as regular verbs are called 'irregular verbs' (how original). Most of the really useful verbs are irregular — d'oh. Anyway, here are four that you'll need most...

inf. = informal
frml. = formal
sing. = singular
plu. = plural

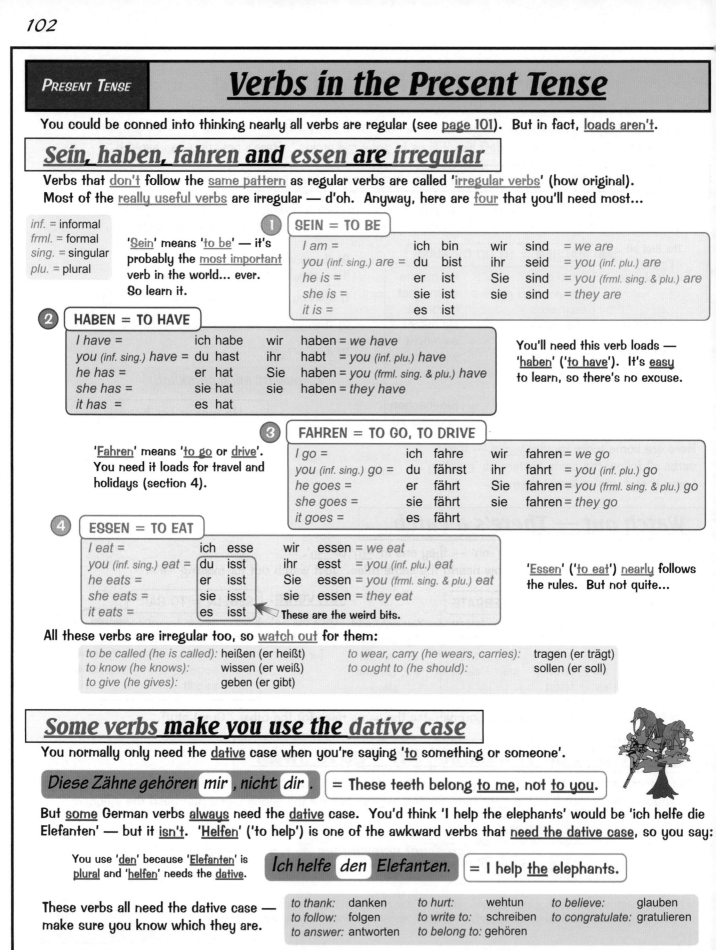

'Sein' means 'to be' — it's probably the most important verb in the world... ever. So learn it.

**① SEIN = TO BE**

| I am = | ich | bin | wir | sind | = we are |
| you (inf. sing.) are = | du | bist | ihr | seid | = you (inf. plu.) are |
| he is = | er | ist | Sie | sind | = you (frml. sing. & plu.) are |
| she is = | sie | ist | sie | sind | = they are |
| it is = | es | ist | | | |

**② HABEN = TO HAVE**

| I have = | ich habe | wir | haben | = we have |
| you (inf. sing.) have = | du hast | ihr | habt | = you (inf. plu.) have |
| he has = | er hat | Sie | haben | = you (frml. sing. & plu.) have |
| she has = | sie hat | sie | haben | = they have |
| it has = | es hat | | | |

You'll need this verb loads — 'haben' ('to have'). It's easy to learn, so there's no excuse.

'Fahren' means 'to go or drive'. You need it loads for travel and holidays (section 4).

**③ FAHREN = TO GO, TO DRIVE**

| I go = | ich | fahre | wir | fahren | = we go |
| you (inf. sing.) go = | du | fährst | ihr | fahrt | = you (inf. plu.) go |
| he goes = | er | fährt | Sie | fahren | = you (frml. sing. & plu.) go |
| she goes = | sie | fährt | sie | fahren | = they go |
| it goes = | es | fährt | | | |

**④ ESSEN = TO EAT**

| I eat = | ich | esse | wir | essen | = we eat |
| you (inf. sing.) eat = | du | isst | ihr | esst | = you (inf. plu.) eat |
| he eats = | er | isst | Sie | essen | = you (frml. sing. & plu.) eat |
| she eats = | sie | isst | sie | essen | = they eat |
| it eats = | es | isst | | | |

These are the weird bits.

'Essen' ('to eat') nearly follows the rules. But not quite...

All these verbs are irregular too, so watch out for them:

| to be called (he is called): heißen (er heißt) | to wear, carry (he wears, carries): tragen (er trägt) |
| to know (he knows): wissen (er weiß) | to ought to (he should): sollen (er soll) |
| to give (he gives): geben (er gibt) | |

## Some verbs make you use the dative case

You normally only need the dative case when you're saying 'to something or someone'.

**Diese Zähne gehören mir, nicht dir.** = These teeth belong to me, not to you.

But some German verbs always need the dative case. You'd think 'I help the elephants' would be 'ich helfe die Elefanten' — but it isn't. 'Helfen' ('to help') is one of the awkward verbs that need the dative case, so you say:

You use 'den' because 'Elefanten' is plural and 'helfen' needs the dative.

**Ich helfe den Elefanten.** = I help the elephants.

These verbs all need the dative case — make sure you know which they are.

| to thank: danken | to hurt: wehtun | to believe: glauben |
| to follow: folgen | to write to: schreiben | to congratulate: gratulieren |
| to answer: antworten | to belong to: gehören | |

## No fahrt jokes please...

People talk about German being easy, because it's got loads of rules to follow. But it's a right pain that loads of words don't follow the rules. And of course it's all the really important stuff that doesn't — how typical. (So the only way forward is simply to learn all this stuff. Sorry.)

# Talking About the Future

You'll need to talk about things that are going to happen at some point in the future. There are two ways you can do it — and the first one's a piece of cake, so I'd learn that first if I were you.

## 1) You can use the present tense to talk about the future

Wahey — an easy bit. All you need to do to say something is going to happen in the future, is to say it does happen and then say when it's going to happen. Brilliant.

HAPPENING NOW ▷ **Ich fahre nach Wales.** = I am going to Wales.

GOING TO HAPPEN ▷ **Ich fahre nächstes Jahr nach Wales.** = I am going to Wales next year.

This tells you when it's going to happen.

You can stick the time bit anywhere in the sentence, as long as you don't break the rules of word order — see page 88.

See pages 101-102 for all the stuff on the present tense.

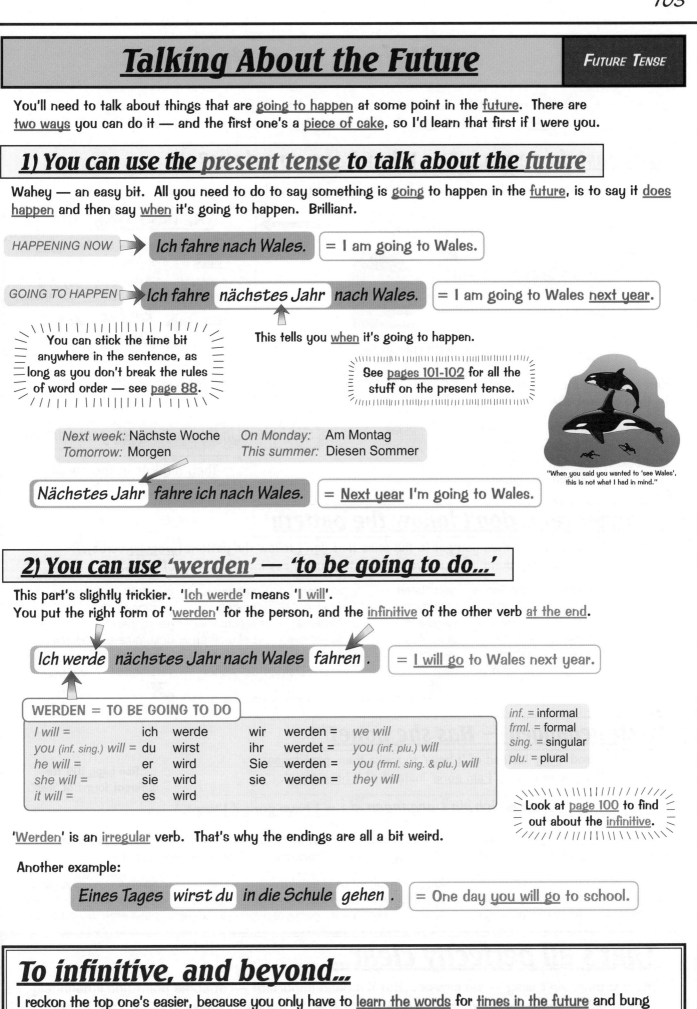

"When you said you wanted to 'see Wales', this is not what I had in mind."

| | | | |
|---|---|---|---|
| *Next week:* Nächste Woche | *On Monday:* Am Montag | | |
| *Tomorrow:* Morgen | *This summer:* Diesen Sommer | | |

**Nächstes Jahr fahre ich nach Wales.** = Next year I'm going to Wales.

## 2) You can use 'werden' — 'to be going to do...'

This part's slightly trickier. 'Ich werde' means 'I will'.
You put the right form of 'werden' for the person, and the infinitive of the other verb at the end.

**Ich werde nächstes Jahr nach Wales fahren.** = I will go to Wales next year.

### WERDEN = TO BE GOING TO DO

| I will = | ich | werde | wir | werden = | *we will* |
|---|---|---|---|---|---|
| *you (inf. sing.) will* = | du | wirst | ihr | werdet = | *you (inf. plu.) will* |
| *he will* = | er | wird | Sie | werden = | *you (frml. sing. & plu.) will* |
| *she will* = | sie | wird | sie | werden = | *they will* |
| *it will* = | es | wird | | | |

*inf.* = informal
*frml.* = formal
*sing.* = singular
*plu.* = plural

Look at page 100 to find out about the infinitive.

'Werden' is an irregular verb. That's why the endings are all a bit weird.

Another example:

**Eines Tages wirst du in die Schule gehen.** = One day you will go to school.

# To infinitive, and beyond...

I reckon the top one's easier, because you only have to learn the words for times in the future and bung them in a bog-standard sentence. 'Werden' is a bit trickier, but you should be able to use that too.

| PERFECT TENSE | # Talking About the Past |
|---|---|

Sometimes they'll want you to talk about stuff that's <u>already happened</u> — so you need to say '<u>I have done</u>...' or '<u>I did</u>...', instead of '<u>I do</u>...'. (It's the <u>perfect</u> tense, if you're interested.)

## Was hast du gemacht? — What have you done?

The past tense looks a bit fiddly, I agree, but it's easy once you've learnt the basics.

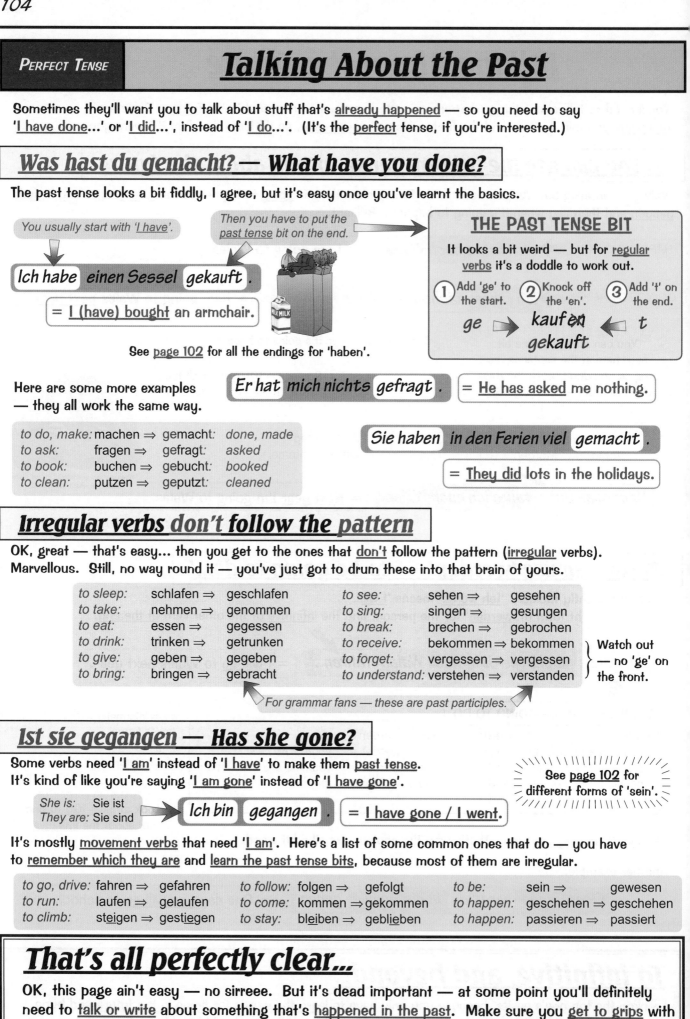

*You usually start with '<u>I have</u>'.*

*Then you have to put the <u>past tense</u> bit on the end.*

**THE PAST TENSE BIT**

It looks a bit weird — but for <u>regular verbs</u> it's a doddle to work out.

① Add 'ge' to the start. ② Knock off the 'en'. ③ Add 't' on the end.

ge ⇒ kaufen ⇐ t
gekauft

Ich habe einen Sessel gekauft .

= <u>I (have) bought</u> an armchair.

See <u>page 102</u> for all the endings for 'haben'.

Here are some more examples — they all work the same way.

Er hat mich nichts gefragt .

= <u>He has asked</u> me nothing.

| to do, make: | machen ⇒ | gemacht: | *done, made* |
| to ask: | fragen ⇒ | gefragt: | *asked* |
| to book: | buchen ⇒ | gebucht: | *booked* |
| to clean: | putzen ⇒ | geputzt: | *cleaned* |

Sie haben in den Ferien viel gemacht .

= <u>They did</u> lots in the holidays.

## Irregular verbs don't follow the pattern

OK, great — that's easy... then you get to the ones that <u>don't</u> follow the pattern (<u>irregular</u> verbs). Marvellous. Still, no way round it — you've just got to drum these into that brain of yours.

| to sleep: | schlafen ⇒ | geschlafen | | to see: | sehen ⇒ | gesehen |
|---|---|---|---|---|---|---|
| to take: | nehmen ⇒ | genommen | | to sing: | singen ⇒ | gesungen |
| to eat: | essen ⇒ | gegessen | | to break: | brechen ⇒ | gebrochen |
| to drink: | trinken ⇒ | getrunken | | to receive: | bekommen ⇒ | bekommen |
| to give: | geben ⇒ | gegeben | | to forget: | vergessen ⇒ | vergessen |
| to bring: | bringen ⇒ | gebracht | | to understand: | verstehen ⇒ | verstanden |

} Watch out — no 'ge' on the front.

*For grammar fans — these are past participles.*

## Ist sie gegangen — Has she gone?

Some verbs need '<u>I am</u>' instead of '<u>I have</u>' to make them <u>past tense</u>. It's kind of like you're saying '<u>I am gone</u>' instead of '<u>I have gone</u>'.

See <u>page 102</u> for different forms of 'sein'.

*She is:* Sie ist
*They are:* Sie sind

Ich bin gegangen .

= <u>I have gone / I went</u>.

It's mostly <u>movement verbs</u> that need '<u>I am</u>'. Here's a list of some common ones that do — you have to <u>remember which they are</u> and <u>learn the past tense bits</u>, because most of them are irregular.

| to go, drive: | fahren ⇒ | gefahren | | to follow: | folgen ⇒ | gefolgt | | to be: | sein ⇒ | gewesen |
|---|---|---|---|---|---|---|---|---|---|---|
| to run: | laufen ⇒ | gelaufen | | to come: | kommen ⇒ | gekommen | | to happen: | geschehen ⇒ | geschehen |
| to climb: | steigen ⇒ | gestiegen | | to stay: | bleiben ⇒ | geblieben | | to happen: | passieren ⇒ | passiert |

# That's all perfectly clear...

OK, this page ain't easy — no sirreee. But it's dead important — at some point you'll definitely need to <u>talk or write</u> about something that's <u>happened in the past</u>. Make sure you <u>get to grips</u> with the <u>easy stuff</u> at the top, then you won't find the tricky stuff anywhere near as bad. Honest.

# Talking About the Past

Fed up of the past tense yet? Yep, me too. But this stuff is really handy, so it's worth the pain.

## Ich hatte — I had / Ich war — I was

These little words are absolute gold dust — you'll soon find yourself using them all the time.

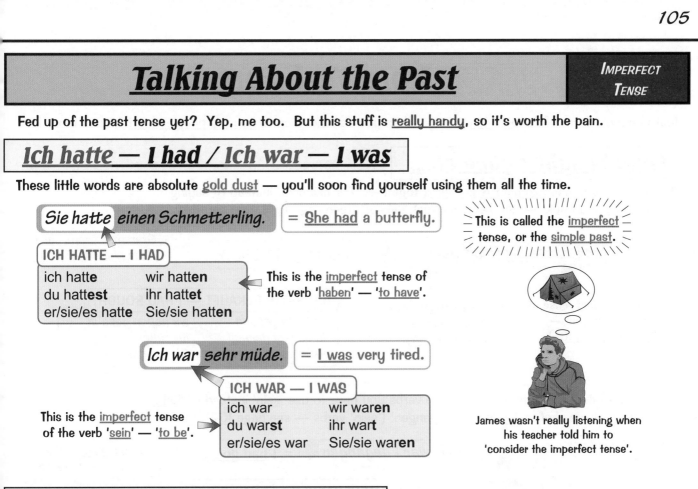

Sie hatte einen Schmetterling. = She had a butterfly.

This is called the imperfect tense, or the simple past.

**ICH HATTE — I HAD**

| | |
|---|---|
| ich hatte | wir hatten |
| du hattest | ihr hattet |
| er/sie/es hatte | Sie/sie hatten |

This is the imperfect tense of the verb 'haben' — 'to have'.

Ich war sehr müde. = I was very tired.

**ICH WAR — I WAS**

| | |
|---|---|
| ich war | wir waren |
| du warst | ihr wart |
| er/sie/es war | Sie/sie waren |

This is the imperfect tense of the verb 'sein' — 'to be'.

James wasn't really listening when his teacher told him to 'consider the imperfect tense'.

## More verbs in the imperfect tense

You use this when you're talking about things that happened in the past, without using 'haben' or 'sein' (that would be the perfect tense, see page 104). So, you use it to say things like 'I drank' or 'they jumped'.

All regular verbs take these endings (in bold):

Look for the extra 't' in the middle of a verb — that's your clue that it's the imperfect tense.

**ICH MACHTE — I MADE**

| | |
|---|---|
| ich machte | wir machten |
| du machtest | ihr machtet |
| er/sie/es machte | Sie/sie machten |

Was machtest du?

= What did you do?

These are the most common irregular verbs. They use the same endings as 'war' in the box above. It looks really good if you can use them in your writing assessment.

| Verb | Imperfect | English | | | | | | |
|---|---|---|---|---|---|---|---|---|
| kommen | ich kam | I came | essen | ich aß | I ate | laufen | ich lief | I ran |
| denken | ich dachte | I thought | trinken | ich trank | I drank | springen | ich sprang | I jumped |
| fahren | ich fuhr | I drove | sehen | ich sah | I saw | ziehen | ich zog | I pulled |
| gehen | ich ging | I went | werden | ich wurde | I became | sein | ich war | I was |
| helfen | ich half | I helped | bringen | ich brachte | I brought | haben | ich hatte | I had |
| schreiben | ich schrieb | I wrote | nehmen | ich nahm | I took | geben | ich gab | I gave |
| | | | singen | ich sang | I sang | | | |

You can use the imperfect tense with 'seit' to talk about things that started in the past, and carried on until more recently. Sounds confusing, but it's quite simple really...

Ich sang seit fünf Jahren. = I had been singing for five years.

## Past tense? I'm always tense...

I'm not just telling you about this because of some strange whim of mine — if you don't know this stuff, then you won't be able to say things like 'I won the lottery' or 'I had eaten lots'. And that'd be a terrible shame, because they're great things to say. So cover the page and get learning.

# More Verb Forms

Just one more form of the past tense to go, then you can move on to bossing people about. Much more fun.

## I had bought / gone etc...

This is when you use two past tense verbs together. For example, instead of saying 'I have bought a book' — 'Ich habe ein Buch gekauft' (see page 104), you say this:

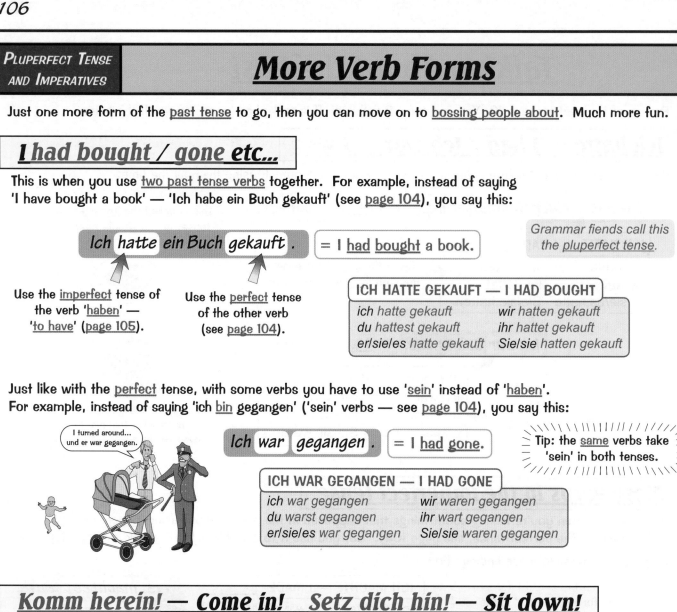

Ich hatte ein Buch gekauft .    = I had bought a book.

*Grammar fiends call this the pluperfect tense.*

Use the imperfect tense of the verb 'haben' — 'to have' (page 105).

Use the perfect tense of the other verb (see page 104).

**ICH HATTE GEKAUFT — I HAD BOUGHT**

| | |
|---|---|
| ich hatte gekauft | wir hatten gekauft |
| du hattest gekauft | ihr hattet gekauft |
| er/sie/es hatte gekauft | Sie/sie hatten gekauft |

Just like with the perfect tense, with some verbs you have to use 'sein' instead of 'haben'. For example, instead of saying 'ich bin gegangen' ('sein' verbs — see page 104), you say this:

I turned around... und er war gegangen.

Ich war gegangen .    = I had gone.

*Tip: the same verbs take 'sein' in both tenses.*

**ICH WAR GEGANGEN — I HAD GONE**

| | |
|---|---|
| ich war gegangen | wir waren gegangen |
| du warst gegangen | ihr wart gegangen |
| er/sie/es war gegangen | Sie/sie waren gegangen |

## Komm herein! — Come in!   Setz dich hin! — Sit down!

This is known as the imperative. It's used to give instructions and is really useful when you're bossing people about. Here's how to turn a verb into an imperative:

**EXAMPLE — TELLING PEOPLE TO GO:**

| Verb | Imperative | English |
|---|---|---|
| du gehst | Geh! | Go! (informal, singular) |
| ihr geht | Geht! | Go! (informal, plural) |
| Sie gehen | Gehen Sie! | Go! (formal, sing. & plu.) |
| wir gehen | Gehen wir! | Let's go! |

You can use these endings for most verbs. Luckily, the only form that ends differently from the normal present tense is the 'du' form. It loses its ending (the '-st').

Some verbs lose the '-st' in the 'du' form, but gain an '-e'.

Just go!

The 2nd column shows what you turn the verb into to get the imperative.

Make sure you learn these:

| | |
|---|---|
| Come in! | Komm herein! |
| Help me! | Hilf mir! |
| Take the book. | Nimm das Buch! |
| Bring the dog along. | Bring den Hund mit! |
| Ask the man there. | Frag den Mann da! |
| Sit down. | Setz dich hin! |

You'd normally end an imperative sentence in German with an exclamation mark — even if you wouldn't even for the same sentence in English.

## Revise!

The pluperfect tense looks like a nightmare, but if you know the imperfect and the perfect then it's not too tricky at all. The bottom half of this page is dead important too — you need to know this stuff because they'll expect you to understand things like signs and instructions.

# Myself, Yourself, etc.

REFLEXIVE VERBS

This page tells you how to say 'myself', 'yourself', 'themselves', etc. It's dead important that you learn all this stuff, because some verbs just don't make sense without them.

## Talking about yourself — 'sich'

'Sich' means 'oneself'. All the different ways to say 'self' are in the box on the right.

You can tell which verbs need 'self' by checking in the dictionary. If you look up 'to wash oneself', it'll say 'sich waschen'.

**SICH = ONESELF**

| | | | |
|---|---|---|---|
| myself: | mich | ourselves: | uns |
| yourself (informal): | dich | yourselves (informal plural): | euch |
| himself: | sich | yourself, yourselves (formal): | sich |
| herself: | sich | themselves, each other: | sich |
| itself: | sich | | |

## Ich wasche mich — I wash myself

You need to talk about your 'daily routine'. So if you don't know how to say 'I wash myself', everyone'll think you smell.

*Grammar fans call these reflexive verbs.*

*Remember — these verbs don't make sense without the 'sich' bit.*

**SICH WASCHEN = TO WASH ONESELF**

| | | | |
|---|---|---|---|
| I wash myself = | ich wasche mich | | |
| you wash yourself (informal) = | du wäschst dich | wir waschen uns = | we wash ourselves |
| he washes himself = | er wäscht sich | ihr wascht euch = | you wash yourselves (informal) |
| she washes herself = | sie wäscht sich | Sie waschen sich = | you wash yourself, yourselves (formal) |
| it washes itself = | es wäscht sich | sie waschen sich = | they wash themselves |

There are lots of these verbs, but here are a few of the most useful ones. Learn these:

| | | | |
|---|---|---|---|
| to dress oneself: | sich anziehen | to excuse oneself: | sich entschuldigen |
| to feel: | sich fühlen | to sit oneself down: | sich setzen |
| to get changed: | sich umziehen | to sun oneself: | sich sonnen |

*inf.* = informal
*frml.* = formal
*sing.* = singular
*plu.* = plural

... and learn how they work: **Ich fühle mich schlecht.** = I feel bad (ill).

The 'mich' goes straight after the verb.

**Ich ziehe mich an.** = I dress myself.

With separable verbs (page 108), 'mich' goes straight after the main verb.

## Ich putze mir die Zähne — I clean my teeth

Some verbs need you to use 'to myself' or 'to yourself'. This is the dative case, by the way. These are the three most important ones:

| | |
|---|---|
| to clean one's teeth: | sich die Zähne putzen |
| to want/wish for ... : | sich ... wünschen |
| to imagine ... : | sich ... vorstellen |

**MIR = TO MYSELF**

| | | | |
|---|---|---|---|
| to myself: | mir | to ourselves: | uns |
| to yourself (inf.): | dir | to yourselves (informal): | euch |
| to him/her/itself: | sich | to yourself, yourselves (frml.): | sich |
| | | to themselves: | sich |

This is how you put them in a sentence...

**Ich wünsche mir ein Pferd.** = I want a horse.

These are the bits you change for each person.

## Ich habe mich gewaschen — I have washed myself

The perfect tense of these verbs is pretty much the same as normal (see page 104) except they all go with 'haben', not 'sein'.

**Sie hat sich schlecht gefühlt.** = She felt bad (ill).

Put the 'sich' straight after 'haben'.

## That's enough — I'm sich of talking about myself...

Learn how to say 'I wash myself', 'you wash yourself', etc. for each person — once you've got that, it's the same for almost all 'sich' verbs. Keep at it till it's firmly planted in that brain. Then have a go at the same thing for 'I clean my teeth'. Sorted. Then it's probably time to have a biscuit.

## Separable Verbs

# Separable verbs are made up of two bits

Some verbs are made up of two bits: the main verb and a bit stuck on the front, that can split off.

**abfahren** = to depart

Ignore 'ab' for now and use 'fahren' as a normal verb — then send 'ab' to the end of the sentence:

**Ich fahre um neun Uhr ab.** = I depart at 9 o'clock.

When you come across one of these verbs, think of it as two separate words. It's much easier.

**Sie nimmt ihre Katze ins Kino mit.** = She takes her cat into the cinema with her.

Here are some more of them — I've underlined the bits that split off.

| | | | |
|---|---|---|---|
| to wash up: | abwaschen | to take with you: | mitnehmen |
| to arrive: | ankommen | to check: | nachsehen |
| to stop: | aufhören | to happen: | vorkommen |
| to go out: | ausgehen | to go out/away: | weggehen |
| to show: | darstellen | to look at: | zuschauen |
| to enter: | eintreten | to give back: | zurückgeben |

Sometimes you get two bits added on — like 'herauskommen' ('to come out'). The two added bits stay together as if they were just one bit.

# The past tense is a bit weird with these verbs

To make the past (perfect) tense of a separable verb, you split it up then put it back together. You leave the front bit as it is, then turn the main bit into the past tense.

**aufhören** = to stop ➡ **aufgehört** = stopped

So you end up with the 'ge' in the middle of the word.

You put the 'haben' (or 'sein') bit in the normal place, then shove the past tense bit at the end.

Here's an example: **Er hat endlich aufgehört.** = He has finally stopped.

# Here's how to spot separable verbs anywhere

In your reading or listening paper, you've got to be able to spot these verbs, so you know what's going on. Check each sentence to see if there are two bits of a separable verb hiding in there. Watch out though — they could be the wrong way round. Here are a few examples with 'zurückfahren' ('to go back'):

**Er will zurückfahren.** = He wants to go back.

**Wenn er zurückfährt, werde ich weinen.** = If he goes back, I will cry.

**Sie fuhr nach Berlin zurück.** = She went back to Berlin.

This is the past (imperfect) tense of 'fahren'. There's more about this on page 105.

**Morgen fahre ich zurück.** = Tomorrow, I go back.

**Ich werde morgen zurückfahren.** = I will go back tomorrow.

These are talking about the future — see page 103.

# I love my verbs — we're inseparable...

The best way to remember this is that a separable verb is really just two separate words. They're usually split up in the present tense, and you only make them into one word if they're right next to each other. Learn this page, then cover it up and test yourself by writing (in German) 'I arrive at 9:00'.

# How to Say 'No', 'Not' and 'Nobody'

This is one of those bits where if you <u>learn</u> just a <u>couple of things</u>, you can <u>say loads more</u>.

## Nicht — Not

This stuff is <u>pretty easy</u>. And it's bound to come up somewhere in the <u>exam</u>.

*I shan't and I won't. You can't make me.*

**Der Vogel wollte nicht singen.** = The bird did not want to sing.

**NEGATIVE WORDS:**

| | |
|---|---|
| *not:* | nicht |
| *no longer:* | nicht mehr |
| *not even:* | nicht einmal |
| *never:* | nie |
| *not yet:* | noch nicht |
| *nowhere:* | nirgendwo |

**Ich lese nie Bücher.** = I never read books.

*I just don't do that sort of thing any more.*

**Das mache ich nicht mehr.** = I don't do that any more.

If you want to say a joke is <u>neither</u> clever <u>nor</u> funny, then it's a bit different: *neither ... nor:* weder ... noch

**Ihre Haare sind weder blond noch braun.** = Her hair is <u>neither</u> blonde <u>nor</u> brown.

## Ich habe keine Bratkartoffeln — I have no roast potatoes

'<u>Kein</u>' means '<u>no</u>' — as in '<u>I have no roast potatoes</u>'. When you use it in the singular, you need to change the ending depending on the gender, but in the plural (and the nominative case) it's just '<u>keine</u>' for <u>all the genders</u>.

*I beg to differ...*

**Ich habe keinen Kartoffelsalat.** = I have no potato salad.

**Keine Hunde sind grün.** = No dogs are green.

*'Kein' also has other forms for different cases. In fact it takes exactly the same endings as 'mein' — see page 92.*

## Niemand — Nobody...

You need to be able to say '<u>nobody</u>' and '<u>nothing</u>'. It's not much to learn, so there's no excuse.

**Ich habe niemand gesehen.** = I've seen <u>nobody</u>.

*This is ridiculous. I can't see anything.*

*nothing:* nichts

**SOME HANDY VARIATIONS:**

| | |
|---|---|
| *nothing yet:* | noch nichts |
| *nothing left/nothing more:* | nichts mehr |
| *nobody yet:* | noch niemand |
| *nobody else/nobody any more:* | niemand mehr |

**Ich sehe gar nichts.** = I see <u>nothing at all</u>.

You can put '<u>gar</u>' in front of '<u>nicht</u>' or '<u>nichts</u>' to emphasise it — like saying '<u>nothing at all</u>'.

# You need to be able to say 'nothing' — sounds easy...

This stuff <u>doubles</u> what you can say — for anything you could already say, you can now say the <u>opposite</u>. '<u>Nicht</u>', '<u>nichts</u>', '<u>niemand</u>' and '<u>kein</u>' are really basic essential words, but if you want a decent mark, learn the others too. Cover the page, scribble them down, and see what you know.

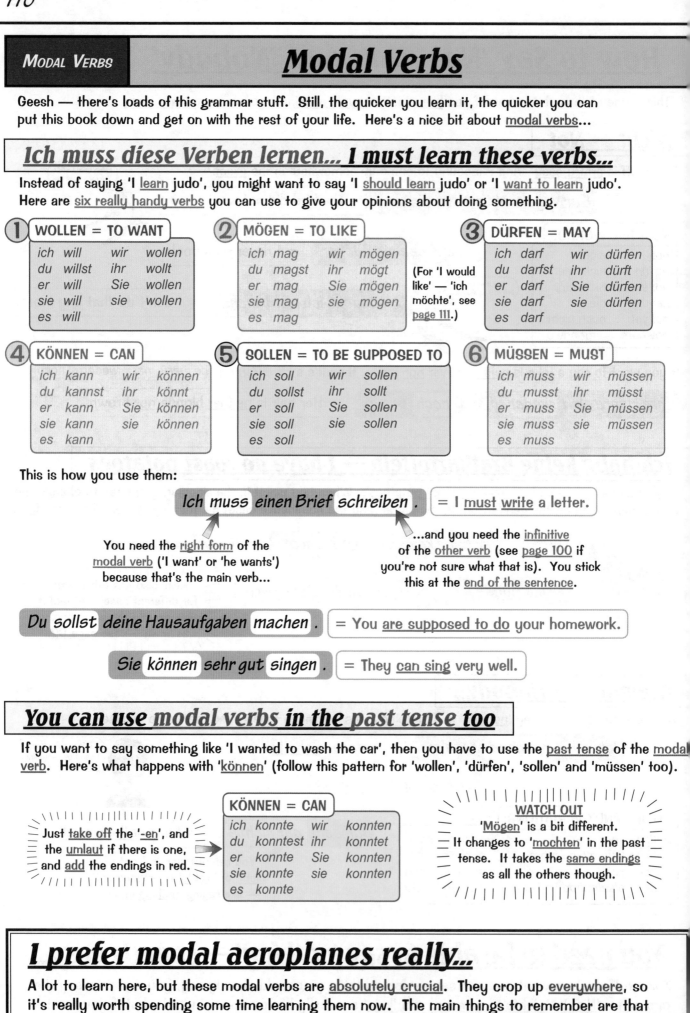

**MODAL VERBS**

# Modal Verbs

Geesh — there's loads of this grammar stuff. Still, the quicker you learn it, the quicker you can put this book down and get on with the rest of your life. Here's a nice bit about modal verbs...

## Ich muss diese Verben lernen... I must learn these verbs...

Instead of saying 'I learn judo', you might want to say 'I should learn judo' or 'I want to learn judo'. Here are six really handy verbs you can use to give your opinions about doing something.

**① WOLLEN = TO WANT**

| | | | |
|---|---|---|---|
| ich | will | wir | wollen |
| du | willst | ihr | wollt |
| er | will | Sie | wollen |
| sie | will | sie | wollen |
| es | will | | |

**② MÖGEN = TO LIKE**

| | | | |
|---|---|---|---|
| ich | mag | wir | mögen |
| du | magst | ihr | mögt |
| er | mag | Sie | mögen |
| sie | mag | sie | mögen |
| es | mag | | |

(For 'I would like' — 'ich möchte', see page 111.)

**③ DÜRFEN = MAY**

| | | | |
|---|---|---|---|
| ich | darf | wir | dürfen |
| du | darfst | ihr | dürft |
| er | darf | Sie | dürfen |
| sie | darf | sie | dürfen |
| es | darf | | |

**④ KÖNNEN = CAN**

| | | | |
|---|---|---|---|
| ich | kann | wir | können |
| du | kannst | ihr | könnt |
| er | kann | Sie | können |
| sie | kann | sie | können |
| es | kann | | |

**⑤ SOLLEN = TO BE SUPPOSED TO**

| | | | |
|---|---|---|---|
| ich | soll | wir | sollen |
| du | sollst | ihr | sollt |
| er | soll | Sie | sollen |
| sie | soll | sie | sollen |
| es | soll | | |

**⑥ MÜSSEN = MUST**

| | | | |
|---|---|---|---|
| ich | muss | wir | müssen |
| du | musst | ihr | müsst |
| er | muss | Sie | müssen |
| sie | muss | sie | müssen |
| es | muss | | |

This is how you use them:

Ich **muss** einen Brief **schreiben**. = I must write a letter.

You need the right form of the modal verb ('I want' or 'he wants') because that's the main verb...

...and you need the infinitive of the other verb (see page 100 if you're not sure what that is). You stick this at the end of the sentence.

Du **sollst** deine Hausaufgaben **machen**. = You are supposed to do your homework.

Sie **können** sehr gut **singen**. = They can sing very well.

## You can use modal verbs in the past tense too

If you want to say something like 'I wanted to wash the car', then you have to use the past tense of the modal verb. Here's what happens with 'können' (follow this pattern for 'wollen', 'dürfen', 'sollen' and 'müssen' too).

Just take off the '-en', and the umlaut if there is one, and add the endings in red.

**KÖNNEN = CAN**

| | | | |
|---|---|---|---|
| ich | konnte | wir | konnten |
| du | konntest | ihr | konntet |
| er | konnte | Sie | konnten |
| sie | konnte | sie | konnten |
| es | konnte | | |

**WATCH OUT**
'Mögen' is a bit different. It changes to 'mochten' in the past tense. It takes the same endings as all the others though.

## I prefer modal aeroplanes really...

A lot to learn here, but these modal verbs are absolutely crucial. They crop up everywhere, so it's really worth spending some time learning them now. The main things to remember are that the other verb has to be in the infinitive, and it has to go to the end of the sentence.

# 'Would' and 'Would Like'

OK, I'll admit it. This is tricky. But it is important, so if you want top marks you need to learn it.

## Ich würde — I would

The word for 'would' in German is 'würden'.

This is the conditional. You use it to talk about something that hasn't happened.

| ICH WÜRDE — I WOULD: | |
|---|---|
| ich würde | wir würden |
| du würdest | ihr würdet |
| er/sie/es würde | Sie/sie würden |

Ich würde Chinesisch lernen, aber ich kann es nicht.

= I would learn Chinese, but I can't.

'Würden' works like a modal verb (page 110), so the other verb has to be in the infinitive, and go at the end.

## Ich möchte — I would like

Dead useful verb, this, so get it learnt.

For grammatical types, this is the imperfect subjunctive of 'mögen' — 'to like' (page 110).

Ich möchte fünfzig Tassen Tee, bitte.

= I would like fifty cups of tea, please.

| ICH MÖCHTE — I WOULD LIKE | | | |
|---|---|---|---|
| ich | möchte | wir | möchten |
| du | möchtest | ihr | möchtet |
| er/sie/es | möchte | Sie/sie | möchten |

Ich möchte Chinesisch lernen.

= I would like to learn Chinese.

(There are. I promise.)

The other verb has to be in the infinitive, and go at the end.

I know this is pretty complicated grammar, but you should already be familiar with 'möchten' — it's part of the basic shopping vocab (see page 36).

## Ich könnte — I could    Ich sollte — I should

You need to know 'could' (könnten) and 'should' (sollten), too.

| ICH KÖNNTE — I COULD: | |
|---|---|
| ich könnte | wir könnten |
| du könntest | ihr könntet |
| er/sie/es könnte | Sie/sie könnten |

| ICH SOLLTE — I SHOULD: | |
|---|---|
| ich sollte | wir sollten |
| du solltest | ihr solltet |
| er/sie/es sollte | Sie/sie sollten |

Ich sollte essen.

= I should eat.

'Ich könnte' means 'I could' as in 'I would be able' — as opposed to 'ich konnte', which means 'I was able' (see page 110).

## Ich wäre — I would be    Ich hätte — I would have

Wenn ich fünf Million Euro hätte, wäre ich sehr reich.

= If I had 5 million euros, I would be very rich.

Here's how you say 'would be' and 'would have' for all the different people:

| ICH WÄRE = I WOULD BE | | | | ICH HÄTTE = I WOULD HAVE | | |
|---|---|---|---|---|---|---|
| ich | wäre | wir | wären | ich | hätte | wir | hätten |
| du | wärest | ihr | wäret | du | hättest | ihr | hättet |
| er | wäre | Sie | wären | er | hätte | Sie | hätten |
| sie | wäre | sie | wären | sie | hätte | sie | hätten |
| es | wäre | | | es | hätte | | |

This is also the imperfect subjunctive, but you use it to talk about something unreal that's unlikely to happen.

# What's the conditional — I würden know...

Get all this stuff right in your writing assessments and you'll be in Marksville, Arizona. ☺
Same goes for the speaking assessments actually...

# Odds and Ends

With some verbs you have to stick an '<u>es</u>' (which means 'it') in.
1) Whatever is <u>doing</u> the action becomes something that's <u>having something done</u> to it.
2) So instead of saying something like 'I don't feel good' you'd say: 'It feels to me not good'. Crazy stuff.

## Wie geht es dir? — How are you?

It looks strange, but you <u>have</u> to learn it — and <u>never</u> say 'ich bin gut' for 'I'm fine'.

Mir geht's gut.  = I'm fine.      Es geht mir nicht so gut.  = I don't feel so good.

This is just short for 'geht es'.

## Other useful phrases that use 'es'

Here are some more of these awkward phrases. They're <u>easy</u> once you've <u>learnt</u> them <u>properly</u>.

Ist es dir zu warm?  = Is it too warm for you?   But: say '<u>Mir ist warm</u>' for 'I'm warm' (i.e. not 'Es ist mir warm').

Es regnet.  = It's raining.   This'll come in handy for talking about the weather — see <u>pages 54 and 56</u>.      Es tut weh.  = It hurts.

Es gibt viel zu tun.  = <u>There is</u> lots to do.     Es gefällt mir in München.  = <u>I like it</u> in Munich.

(more literally, 'it gives lots to do')      (literal translation: 'it pleases to me')

Es tut mir Leid, aber heute bin ich nicht frei.  = <u>I'm sorry</u>, but I'm not free today.

(literally, 'it does sorrow to me')

Here are a few more miscellaneous things that you really need to <u>know</u>...

## Um... zu — in order to, ohne ... zu — without

Here are some handy ways of saying '<u>in order to</u>' and '<u>without</u>'.

Um diesen Satz zu verstehen, muss man Deutsch sprechen können.

= <u>In order to understand</u> this sentence, you must be able to speak German.

Sie kann nicht verlassen ohne ihn zu küssen.  = She can't leave <u>without kissing</u> him.

The verb that's in the infinitive comes <u>after</u> the 'zu'.

## Ignore 'zu' before a verb if there's no 'um'

When verbs <u>link</u> with an infinitive in the sentence, you sometimes find '<u>zu</u>' before the infinitive.
Basically, if the first verb is a <u>modal verb</u> (see <u>page 110</u>), you <u>don't</u> need the 'zu' — if not, you <u>do</u>.

Ich versuche den besten Satz in der Welt zu schreiben.  = I'm <u>trying to write</u> the best sentence in the world.

If this is a <u>modal verb</u> (e.g. 'ich kann'), then you <u>don't</u> need this 'zu'.

Die Stunde beginnt langweilig zu werden.  = The lesson is <u>beginning to get</u> boring.

## Wie geht es dir? Not bad thanks, ducky...

This grammar stuff can be seriously scary. But if you <u>learn</u> all the phrases on these pages, it becomes <u>a lot easier</u>. And don't worry too much about all the weirdy grammar names. Sorted.

# Revision Summary

The stuff in this section really helps you to put words together to say what you want. The way to make sure you've learnt it is to check you can do <u>all these questions</u>. Try them all, and look up any you can't do. Then try them all again. And keep doing that until you can answer <u>every single one</u>.

1) In the sentence 'Lucas isst ein Eis' — Lucas eats an ice cream, is 'Lucas' in:
   a) the nominative  b) the accusative?

2) When do you use the genitive case?

3) Which part of this sentence is in the dative case?
   'Ich spreche zu meiner Schwester' — I speak to my sister

4) How do you say  It is sunny (sonnig) but not warm (warm) in German?

5) Rearrange the order of this sentence so it's correct:
   'Ich bin müde, weil ich hatte keinen Schlaf' — I am tired because I haven't had any sleep.

6) What are the words for 'the' and 'a' that go with each of these words in the nominative case?
   a) Käse (masculine)    b) Baumwolle (feminine)    c) Messer (neuter)

7) What are the words for 'the' and 'a' that go with the words in Q6 in the accusative case?

8) How do you say this sentence in German:  I have an ugly (hässlich) cat (Katze)?

9) What are the German words for:   a) my    b) his    c) your (informal plural)?
   For each answer, give the nominative for each gender.

10) How do you say Now and then I am very funny (lustig) in German?

11) How do you say I am nearer than Lotte in German?  How do you say I am the nearest?

12) What do these words mean in English?  a) nach    b) bei    c) seit

13) Which case do these prepositions take?  a) für    b) mit    c) wegen

14) What are the German words for 'I', 'you' (informal singular), 'he', 'she', 'it', 'we', 'you' (formal)
    and 'they' in:  a) the nominative   b) the accusative   c) the dative?

15) How do you say 'who' in German?  What about 'whom' and 'to whom'?

16) Translate this sentence and pick out the relative clause:
    'Der Mann, der sehr dick ist, isst einen Kuchen.'

17) How do you say each of these in German?
    a) he is  b) they are  c) you (informal singular) have  d) I drive  e) you (informal plural) eat

18) How do you say I will go to the shops in German?

19) How do you say these sentences in German?  Use the perfect tense.
    a) They made a cake   b) He booked a room    c) We drank coffee    d) They ran quickly

20) How do you say these sentences in German?  Use the imperfect tense.
    a) She had four dogs  b) They were friends  c) I ate a banana

21) How do you say these sentences in German?  Use the pluperfect tense.
    a) I had bought a skirt    b) She had been shopping

22) Translate these phrases into English:
    a) Geh!    b) Komm herein!       c) Nimm das Buch!      d) Setz dich hin!

23) How do you say these phrases in German?
    a) I wash myself  b) He excuses himself  c) They clean their teeth  d) You washed yourself

24) What do these words mean in English?
    a) nicht einmal    b) kein    c) niemand    d) gar nichts

25) How do you say these phrases in German?
    a) I must eat vegetables    b) He can    c) They are supposed to go    d) I wanted

26) How do you say these phrases in German?
    a) I would wash up  b) I would like to drive the car  c) I should watch TV  d) I would be tired

27) How do you say these phrases in German?
    a) I don't feel so good     b) There's lots to do

28) What does this sentence mean in English?   'Ich gehe in die Stadt, um meinen Freund zu sehen.'

# Do Well in Your Exam

Here are some <u>handy hints</u> to help you in your exams.  And not a <u>smidgen</u> of learning in sight.  Ahh.

## Read **the Questions carefully**

<u>Don't</u> go losing <u>easy marks</u> — it'll break my heart.
Make sure you <u>definitely</u> do the things on this list:

1) <u>Read all the instructions</u> properly.
2) <u>Read the question</u> properly.
3) <u>Answer the question</u> — don't waffle.

## Don't **give up if you don't** Understand

If you don't understand, <u>don't panic</u>.  The <u>key thing</u> to remember is that you
can still <u>do well</u> in the exam, even if you <u>don't understand</u> every German word
that comes up.  Just use one of the <u>two methods</u> below:

If you're reading or listening — look for lookalikes

1)   Some words <u>look</u> or <u>sound</u> the <u>same</u> in German and English.

2)   These words are <u>great</u> because you'll recognise them when you see or hear them.

3)   Be careful though — there are some <u>exceptions</u> you need to watch out for.  Here are just a few
     examples of German words that <u>look</u> like an English word but have a totally <u>different meaning</u>:

| | | | | | |
|---|---|---|---|---|---|
| sensibel: | *sensitive* | also: | *so* | der Fotograf: | *photographer* |
| groß: | *big/tall* | sympathisch: | *nice* | das Rezept: | *prescription* |
| fast: | *almost* | die Fabrik: | *factory* | der Roman: | *novel* |
| bald: | *soon* | die Marmelade: | *jam* | die Wand: | *wall* |
| aktuell: | *current* | das Gymnasium: | *grammar school* | Ich will...: | *I want...* |

Words like these are called 'falsche Freunde' — false friends.

## Make use of the Context

You'll likely come across the odd word that you don't know, especially in the <u>reading exam</u>.
Often you'll be able to find some <u>clues</u> telling you what the text is all about.

1)   The <u>type of text</u>, e.g. newspaper article, advertisement, website
2)   The <u>title</u> of the text
3)   Any <u>pictures</u>
4)   The <u>verbal context</u>

Say you see the following in the reading exam, and don't know what any of these words mean:

"...die Kleidung aus Polyester , aus Wolle , aus Baumwolle und aus Seide ."

1)   Well, the fact that this is a list of things, all starting with '<u>aus ...</u>' coming after the German word for
     '<u>clothes</u>' suggests they're all <u>things</u> that <u>clothes</u> can be <u>made out of</u>.

2)   You can guess that '<u>Polyester</u>' means '<u>polyester</u>', and '<u>Wolle</u>' means '<u>wool</u>'.

3)   So it's a pretty good guess that the two words you don't know are different types of <u>fabric</u>.
     (In fact, '<u>Seide</u>' means '<u>silk</u>' and '<u>Baumwolle</u>' means '<u>cotton</u>'.)

4)   Often the questions <u>won't</u> depend on you understanding these more difficult words.
     It's important to be able to understand the <u>gist</u> though, and not let these words <u>throw</u> you.

## Darn that Roman — I thought he was my friend...

I can't emphasise enough how <u>important</u> it is to <u>read</u> the questions and instructions through <u>properly</u>.
It might seem <u>obvious</u> now, but it's amazing how many people get caught out in the exam...

# Do Well in Your Exam

More ways to improve your marks and still not a drop of learning on the horizon...
It's almost as good as free cake.

## Look for the Verb...

Here are a few tips to help you out if you're struggling with sentences in the reading exam.

1) The verb (or 'doing word') is probably going to give you the biggest clue as to what the sentence is about. Word order in German isn't always the same as it is in English, so you might have to go looking for one...

First verb, 'have to', is the second idea in the sentence.

*Nach der Schule* **muss** *ich mit meiner Mutter meine Großeltern* **besuchen**.

= After school, I have to visit my grandparents with my mother.

The second verb, 'to visit', is sent to the end of the sentence.

2) German is full of scarily long words. Don't be put off if you don't understand one at first glance though — they're often 'compounds' made up of two or three smaller words stuck together. Try breaking a word up to get at its meaning...

A compound verb

| zusammenkommen: | 'zusammen' = *together*, 'kommen' = *to come*: | → | *to meet* |
| der Tiefkühlschrank: | 'tief' = *deep*, 'kühl' = *cool*, 'der Schrank' = *cupboard*: | → | *freezer* |

A compound noun

There is no need to resort to violence when breaking up words.

3) Don't ignore the little words — they can often make a big difference to the meaning of a sentence...

*Ich spiele gern Sport,* **besonders** *Tennis.* = I like playing sport, especially Tennis.

*Ich spiele gern Sport* **außer** *Tennis.* = I like playing sport, except Tennis.

4) Don't panic if you don't understand absolutely everything. Often, the important thing is to get the gist of what you're reading (or even listening to).

## Take notes in the listening exam

1) You'll have 5 minutes at the start of the exam to have a quick look through the paper. This'll give you a chance to see how many questions there are, and you might get a few clues from the questions about what topics they're on, so it won't be a horrible surprise when the tape starts running.

2) You'll hear each extract twice. Different people have different strategies, but it's a good idea to jot down a few details that you think might come up in the questions, especially things like:

Dates    Numbers        Spelt-out names

3) But... don't forget to keep listening to the gist of the recording while you're making notes.

## Are you taking notes?

Despite what some people might say, exams aren't meant to be easy. There are bound to be a few tricky bits, but you stand a good chance of working them out if you use your noggin. Don't leave blank spaces — at the end of the day a guess (preferably educated) is better than nothing.

# How to Use Dictionaries

You're allowed to use a dictionary to help you in your writing task. 'Yippee!' I hear you cry — but using a dictionary isn't as easy as it seems. Finding the right word can be dead tricky, so here are some tips to help you make the most of one. And remember: if it doesn't make sense, you've got the wrong word.

## Don't translate word for word — it DOESN'T work

Turn each word of this phrase into English, and you get rubbish.

Wie heißt du? ⟩✕⟩ How called you?

It's the same the other way round — turn English into German word by word, and you get gibberish — don't do it.

What are you called? ⟩✕⟩ Was bist du geheißen?

**NO!**

## If it doesn't make sense, you've got it wrong

Some words have several meanings — don't just pick the first one you see. Look at the meanings listed and suss out which one is what you're looking for.

If you read this... Ich finde es sehr schwer, Deutsch zu sprechen.

...you might look up 'schwer' and find this:

schwer

a heavy; (schwierig) difficult, hard; (schlimm) serious, bad // ad (sehr) very (much); (verletzt etc.) seriously, badly; S-arbeiter m manual labourer; S-e f weight, heaviness; (PHYS) gravity; schwerelos a weightless

So the sentence could mean:

I find it very heavy to speak German. ✗

I find it very difficult to speak German. ✓

I find it very serious to speak German. ✗

This is the only one that makes sense.

Ich finde es sehr schwer, Deutsch zu sprechen.

I think you're doing it wrong.

## Look up bits of long words

Not all long German words are in all dictionaries. But you can look up parts of these words.

Say you need to know what Wetterbericht means...

1) If you tried to look up 'Wetterbericht', you might only find the word 'Wetter': weather.
2) So the whole word might be 'weather something'.
3) Look up the rest of it ('Bericht') and it turns out it means 'report'.
4) So 'Wetterbericht' means 'weather report'.

Here's another example: 'Fachsprache'. If you try to look it up, you might not find it, but you do find 'Fach-' (which means technical or expert). So try to find the rest of the word — look up 'Sprache' (which means language). 'Fachsprache' means 'technical language'.

## The right words — 'food', 'TV', 'sleep'...

A word to the wise: don't go mad on the dictionary front or it'll all go horribly wrong. Instead of writing long complicated sentences where you have to look up every word, try to use the German you already know. Dictionaries can be really helpful — just make sure you can use them properly.

# Hints for Writing

Here are a few general hints about how you should approach the writing tasks.

## Write about what you know

1) You won't be asked to write about obscure German poetry.

2) You will need to cover certain specific things that the question asks you to, but there'll be plenty of scope to be imaginative.

3) Usually the writing tasks will give you some flexibility so you can base your answer on something you know about.

## Examiners like to know When and Why...

1) Saying when and how often you did things gets you big bonus marks. Learn times and dates carefully (see pages 2-3).

2) Make sure you write about what you've done in the past (see pages 104-106) or what you will do in the future (page 103).

3) Give descriptions where possible, but keep things accurate — a short description in perfect German is better than a longer paragraph of nonsense.

4) Examiners also love opinions (see pages 7-9). Try to vary them as much as possible.

So where were you on the night of the 21st?

Er... Gestern war ich im Kino mit...

Johnny was having flashbacks to GCSE German.

## ...and Where and Who With...

The examiners really are quite nosy, and love as many details as you can give. It's a good idea to ask yourself all these 'wh-' questions, and write the bits that show your German off in the best light. Also, it doesn't matter if what you're writing isn't strictly true — as long as it's believable.

## Vocab and grammar make you look good

1) The more correct grammar and vocab you can include, the better. But a correct simple sentence is much better than something complicated that doesn't make sense.

2) Your grammar doesn't have to be perfect — don't panic if you write something and then realise that it wasn't quite right. But if you want to get really good marks, you need to get your grammar sorted.

3) Make sure you pay attention to things like word order and adjective endings. There's a special grammar section in this book (see pages 84-113) to help you out.

## Use your dictionary, but sparingly

1) DON'T try to use the dictionary to learn a completely new, fancy way of saying something.

2) Use it to look up a particular word that you've forgotten — a word that, when you see it, you'll know it's right.

3) Use it to check genders of nouns — that's whether words are masculine, feminine or neuter.

4) Check any spellings you're unsure of.

Most importantly, don't use the dictionary to delve into the unknown. If you stick to what you know, you're far less likely to go wrong.

## 1) If right-handed, use right hand...

One of the most important things you can do when it comes to the writing task is plan ahead. Think about what you're going to write first and how you're going to cover all the points in the task. Then think about how you can show off your German. This could actually be fun you know...

*Do Well in Your Exam*

# Hints for Writing

<u>Accuracy</u> is really important in the writing assessment. Without it, your work will look like <u>sloppy custard</u>.

## Start with the <u>Verb</u>

1) Verbs really are the <u>cornerstone</u> of any sentence.
   If you get the verb right, everything else should <u>fall into place</u>.

**EXAMPLE:**

> Last weekend, I played badminton with my friends.

You need '<u>haben</u>', '<u>to have</u>', as well as the past participle of the verb '<u>spielen</u>', '<u>to play</u>':

> Letztes Wochenende habe ich Badminton mit meinen Freunden gespielt.

You also need to think about <u>word order</u> and where the verbs appear in the sentence.

2) Be careful to get the <u>whole expression</u> that uses the verb, not just the verb itself.

**EXAMPLE:**

> It was fun.

You don't use '<u>war</u>' here. Germans literally say '<u>it makes fun</u>' rather than '<u>it is fun</u>'.

> Es hat Spaß gemacht.

## Check <u>and</u> re-check

No matter how careful you think you're being, <u>mistakes</u> can easily creep into your work.
Go through the <u>checklist</u> below for every sentence <u>straight after</u> you've written it.

1) Are the <u>ENDINGS</u> of the verbs right?
   Er <u>spiele</u> Tennis. ✘ | Er <u>spielt</u> Tennis. ✓

2) Is the <u>WORD ORDER</u> right?
   Heute <u>ich gehe</u> ins Kino. ✘ | Heute <u>gehe ich</u> ins Kino. ✓

3) Have you got the correct <u>GENDERS</u> for things?
   <u>Die</u> Kleid. ✘ | <u>Das</u> Kleid. ✓

4) Is everything in the right <u>CASE</u>?
   Ich esse <u>der</u> Apfel. ✘ | Ich esse <u>den</u> Apfel. ✓

5) Do your adjectives <u>AGREE</u>?
   Der <u>groß</u> Hund. ✘ | Der <u>große</u> Hund. ✓

6) Have all your nouns got <u>CAPITALS</u>?
   Ich wohne in einer <u>stadt</u>. ✘ | Ich wohne in einer <u>Stadt</u>. ✓

Then when you've finished the whole piece of work, have <u>another</u> read through with <u>fresh eyes</u>.
You're bound to pick up one or two more mistakes.

## Check please...

<u>Grammar</u>. It might seem boring, but you've just <u>got</u> to know it. The more <u>correct</u> vocab and grammar you include in your work, the more <u>lovely marks</u> will fly your way. So get <u>learning</u> it.

# Hints for Speaking

The speaking assessment fills many a student with <u>dread</u>. Remember though — it's your chance to show what you can <u>do</u>. It won't be nearly as bad as you think it's going to be. <u>Honest</u>.

## Be Imaginative

There are two tricky things about the speaking assessment — one is <u>what to say</u>, and two is <u>how to say it</u>. No matter how good your German is, it won't shine through if you can't think of anything to say.

Say you're asked to talk about your <u>daily routine</u> (or to imagine someone else's daily routine). It would be easy to give a list of things you do when you get in from school:

> *"Ich mache meine Hausaufgaben. Ich sehe fern. Ich esse. Ich gehe ins Bett."*

> = I do my homework. I watch television. I eat. I go to bed.

It makes sense, but the problem is, it's all a bit <u>samey</u>...

1) Try to think of when this <u>isn't</u> the case, and put it into a <u>DIFFERENT TENSE</u>:

> *"Morgen werde ich Fußball nach der Schule spielen."*

> = Tomorrow I will play football after school.

2) Don't just talk about yourself. Talk about <u>OTHER PEOPLE</u> — even if you have to imagine them.

> *"Manchmal sehe ich mit meiner Schwester fern, aber sie mag Zeichentrickfilme und ich sehe lieber die Nachrichten."*

> = Sometimes I watch TV with my sister, but she likes cartoons and I prefer to watch the news.

Imaginary friends are for speaking assessments — not real life.

3) Give loads of <u>OPINIONS</u> and <u>REASONS</u> for your opinions.

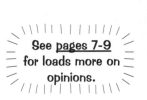
See pages 7-9 for loads more on opinions.

> *"Ich mache meine Hausaufgaben vor dem Abendessen. Dann kann ich mich später entspannen."*

> = I do my homework before dinner. Then I can relax later on.

## A couple of 'DON'T's...

1) <u>DON'T</u> try to <u>avoid</u> a topic if you find it difficult — that'll mean you won't get <u>any</u> marks at all for that bit of the assessment. You'll be surprised what you can muster up if you stay calm and concentrate on what you <u>do</u> know how to say.

2) <u>DON'T</u> make up a word in the hope that it exists in German unless you're really, really stuck (and you've tried all the other tricks on these pages). If it's your <u>last resort</u>, it's worth a try.

## Once upon a time in a land far, far away...

... lived a little girl with a golden unicorn, and she... Er, OK, you don't have to be that imaginative. But <u>do</u> make sure you get plenty of <u>opinions</u>, <u>tenses</u> and <u>what-not</u> in there. It's about <u>showing off</u>.

# Hints for Speaking

Even with all that <u>careful planning</u>, sometimes things can still go a bit <u>wonky</u>.
Never fear though — here's how to come out the other side <u>smiling</u>...

## Try to find _another way_ of saying it

There may be a particular word or phrase that trips you up. There's always a <u>way round it</u> though.

1) If you can't <u>remember</u> a German word, use an <u>alternative</u> word or try <u>describing it</u> instead.

2) E.g. if you can't remember that '<u>strawberries</u>' are '<u>die Erdbeeren</u>' and you really need to say it, then describe them as 'small red fruit', or 'kleines rotes Obst'.

3) You can <u>fib</u> to avoid words you can't remember — if you can't remember the word for '<u>dog</u>' then just say you've got a <u>cat</u> instead. Make sure what you're saying makes <u>sense</u> though — saying you've got a <u>pet radio</u> isn't going to get you any marks, trust me.

4) If you can't remember the word for a <u>cup</u> (die Tasse) in your speaking assessment, you could say '<u>glass</u>' (das Glas) instead — you'll still make yourself <u>understood</u>.

## You may just need to _buy_ yourself some _time_

If you get a bit <u>stuck</u> for what to say, there's always a <u>way out</u>.

1) If you can't think of a way around it, you <u>can</u> ask for help in the speaking assessment — as long as you ask for it in <u>German</u>.

2) If you can't remember what a chair is, ask your examiner: "Wie sagt man 'chair' auf Deutsch?" It's <u>better</u> than wasting time trying to think of the word.

3) If you just need some <u>thinking time</u> in your speaking assessment or you want to check something then you can use these useful sentences to help you out:

| | | | |
|---|---|---|---|
| Also... | _So..._ | Können Sie das bitte wiederholen? | _Can you repeat that please?_ |
| Ach so! | _Oh, I see!_ | Ich verstehe nicht. | _I don't understand._ |
| Ja, natürlich... | _Yes, of course..._ | Können Sie das erklären? | _Can you explain that?_ |
| Ich bin nicht sicher. | _I'm not sure._ | | |

The added bonus of using phrases like these is that they make you sound more like a real German.

## Have Confidence

1) Believe it or not, the teacher isn't trying to catch you out.
He or she <u>wants</u> you to do <u>well</u>, and to be dazzled by all the excellent German you've learnt.

2) Speaking assessments can be pretty <u>daunting</u>. But remember it's the same for <u>everyone</u>.

3) <u>Nothing horrendous</u> is going to happen if you make a few slip-ups.
Just try and focus on showing the teacher how much you've <u>learnt</u>.

4) Don't be afraid to make mistakes — even native German speakers make 'em.
Don't let a silly error shake your <u>concentration</u> for the rest of the assessment.

# Most importantly — DON'T PANIC...

That's easy for me to say I know, but seriously, <u>stay calm</u> and you stand a far better chance of <u>navigating</u> the bumpy bits. Well, that's it for now folks. Make sure you take this lot <u>on board</u> and <u>soar</u> through the assessments like a flying trapeze... <u>Viel Glück</u> — not that you'll need it of course.

## :EY

/f/n/pl: a masculine, feminine, neuter or plural noun — see p86/87
ı), (-e) etc.: add whatever is in the brackets to make the plural
: plural is the same as singular (add nothing)
ı: put an umlaut on the stressed vowel to make the plural, e.g. Apfel → Äpfel
a verb — see p100
sep: separable verb — splits into two words in the present and some other tenses — see p108 (all verbs not labelled 'sep' are inseparable)
ir: irregular verb (its forms are irregular in some tenses and persons, e.g. sein: ich bin)
dj: adjective — see p91/92 (has to agree with the noun it describes)
dv: adverb — see p93 (describes a verb or adjective)
ep: preposition — see p95/96 (connects the verb to a place, thing or person: 'to', 'for', 'with' etc.)
on: pronoun — see p97-99 (replaces noun: e.g. 'he', 'me')
onj: conjunction — see p89 (connects two parts of a sentence, e.g. 'but')

rep + dat *from*
nd zu *from time to time*
estellen v sep *to cancel*
nd m (-e) *evening*
ndessen n (-) *dinner, evening meal*
nds adv *in the evening*
nteuerfilm m (-e) *adventure film*
r conj *but, however*
hren v sep ir *depart*
ahrt f (-en) *departure*
all m (no pl) *rubbish*
alleimer m (-) *rubbish bin*
egen v sep ir *to take off (plane)*
ug m (¨e) *take-off, departure*
ase n pl *exhaust gases, emissions*
esehen von adv *apart from*
ängen von v sep ir *to depend on (something/one)*
ängig adj *dependent*
olen v sep *to collect, to meet*
ur n *equivalent of A-level(s)*
urient/in m/f (-en/-nen) *A-level student*
chließen v sep ir *to shut/lock, to end (studies)*
chluss m (¨e) *end, final exams*
chlusszeugnis n (-se) *school leaving certificate*
pülen v sep *to wash up*
eil n (-e) *compartment*
eilung f (-en) *department, section*
rocknen v sep *to dry up*
vaschen v sep ir *to wash up*
er m (¨) *field*
AC (= Allgemeiner Deutscher Automobil-Club) m *German version of AA/RAC*
er f (-n) *blood vessel*
esse f (-n) *address*
obics machen *to do aerobics*
m (-n) *monkey*
ka n *Africa*
kaner/in m/f (-/-nen) *African person*
kanisch adj *African*
(= Aktiengesellschaft) f *PLC/Ltd.*
ression f (-en) *aggression*
lich adj *similar*
ıung f (-en) *idea, suspicion, hunch*
S n *AIDS*
e f (-n) *file, record*
entasche f (-n) *briefcase*
v adj *active*
ivität f (-en) *activity*
ıell adj *current*
eptieren v *accept*
ohol m (-e) *alcohol*
oholfrei adj *non-alcoholic*
oholiker/in m/f (-/-nen) *alcoholic*
oholisch adj *alcoholic*
oholismus m *alcoholism*
pron *all, everyone*
ee f (-n) *avenue*
in adj *alone*
s Gute *all the best*
emein adj *general*
en f pl *the Alps*
conj *as, than, when*
ob *as if, as though*
o conj *so, therefore*
adj *old*
enheim n (-e) *old people's home*
er n (-) *age*
er adj *older*
nodisch adj *old-fashioned*

Altpapier n *waste paper*
am Anfang *at the start*
am Apparat *speaking! (on telephone)*
Amerika n *America*
Amerikaner/in m/f (-/-nen) *American*
amerikanisch adj *American*
Ampel f (-n) *traffic lights*
amüsant adj *entertaining, amusing*
amüsieren sich v *to be amused, to have fun*
an prep + acc/dat *at, to, by*
an Bord m *aboard*
Ananas f (-/-se) *pineapple*
anbauen v sep *to build on, to grow*
anbieten v sep ir *to offer*
andere/r/s adj *other*
anders adj/adv *different(ly)*
anderswo adv *somewhere else*
anderthalb adj *one and a half*
Anfang m (¨e) *beginning*
anfangen v sep ir *to begin, to start*
Angebot n (-e) *offer*
angeln v *to fish*
Angelrute f (-n) *fishing rod*
angenehm adj *pleasant, enjoyable*
angenommen dass *assuming that*
Angestellte(r) *employee*
Angst haben *to be frightened*
ängstlich adj *anxious*
anhalten v sep ir *to stop (vehicles)*
anklopfen v sep *to knock*
ankommen v sep ir *to arrive*
Ankunft f (¨e) *arrival*
anmachen v sep *to put on / turn on*
Anmeldung f (-en) *reception (room)*
annehmen v sep ir *to accept, to suppose*
anonym adj *anonymous*
anprobieren v sep *try on (clothes)*
Anrufbeantworter m (-) *answerphone*
anrufen v sep ir *to phone*
anschauen v sep *to look at / watch*
ansehen v sep ir *to look at*
Ansichtskarte f (-n) *picture postcard*
Anspitzer m (-) *sharpener*
anspringen v sep ir *to start (cars)*
Antwort f (-en) *answer*
antworten v *to answer*
Anzeige f (-n) *advert (written)*
anziehen sich v sep ir *to put on, to get dressed*
Anzug m (¨e) *(men's) suit*
Apfel m (¨) *apple*
Apfelsine f (-n) *orange*
Apotheke f (-n) *pharmacy*
Apotheker/in m/f (-/-nen) *pharmacist*
Apparat m (-e) *machine, telephone*
Appetit m (-e) *appetite*
Aprikose f (-n) *apricot*
April m *April*
Arbeit f (-en) *work*
arbeiten v *to work*
Arbeiter/in m/f (-/-nen) *worker*
Arbeitgeber m (-) *employer*
Arbeitsbedingungen f pl *terms of employment*
Arbeitserfahrung f (-en) *work experience*
arbeitslos adj *unemployed*
Arbeitslosigkeit f *unemployment*
Arbeitspraktikum n *work experience*
Arbeitszeit f (-en) *working hours*
Arbeitszimmer n (-) *study*
Architekt/in m/f (-en/-nen) *architect*

ARD *German television company*
ärgerlich adj *annoying (thing/event)*
ärgern sich v *to get angry*
arm adj *poor*
Armband n (¨er) *bracelet*
Armbanduhr f (-en) *wristwatch*
Armee f (-n) *army*
Ärmelkanal m *the English Channel*
Armut f *poverty*
Art f (-en) *kind, sort, type*
artig adj *well-behaved*
Arzt/Ärztin m/f (¨e/-nen) *doctor*
Asien n *Asia*
atmen v *to breathe*
Atmosphäre f (-n) *atmosphere*
attraktiv adj *attractive*
auch adv *also*
auf prep + acc/dat *up, on*
auf dem Lande *in the country*
auf die Nerven gehen *to get on one's nerves*
auf diese Weise *in this way*
Auf Wiederhören! *Goodbye! (phone)*
Auf Wiedersehen! *Goodbye!*
Aufenthalt m (-e) *stay*
Aufenthaltsraum m (¨e) *games room*
Aufgabe f (-n) *exercise / task*
aufgeben v sep ir *to give up*
aufhören v sep *to stop (doing something)*
aufmachen v sep *to open*
aufnehmen v sep ir *to pick up / to receive / to record*
aufpassen v sep *to pay attention, watch out*
aufpassen auf v sep *to look after*
aufräumen v sep *to tidy up / clear away*
aufregend adj *exciting*
aufs Land *to the country*
Aufschnitt m (-e) *cold cut meat*
aufstehen v sep ir *to get up*
aufwachen v sep *to wake up*
Aufzug m (¨e) *lift (elevator)*
Auge n (-n) *eye*
Augenblick m (-e) *moment*
August m *August*
Aula f (Aulen) *school hall*
aus prep + dat *out of*
ausbilden v sep *to train*
Ausbildung f (-en) *training*
Ausfahrt f (-en) *departure / exit*
Ausflug m (¨e) *trip, excursion*
ausführen v sep *to take out*
ausfüllen v sep *to fill in (form)*
Ausgang m (¨e) *exit*
ausgeben v sep ir *to spend (money), to give out*
ausgehen v sep ir *to go outside*
ausgezeichnet adj *excellent*
auskommen mit v sep ir *to get on with*
Auskunft f (¨e) *information*
Ausland n *abroad*
Ausländer/in m/f (-/-nen) *foreigner*
ausländisch adj *foreign*
ausleihen v sep ir *to lend*
ausmachen v sep *to turn off*
auspacken v sep *unpack*
ausrichten v sep *pass on (message)*
ausruhen sich v sep *to have a rest*
Ausrüstung f (-en) *equipment*
aussehen v sep ir *to look (appearance)*
außen adv *outside*
außer prep + dat *except for*
außerdem adv *moreover, as well*
außerhalb prep + gen *outside*
aussetzen v sep *to abandon*
Aussicht f (-en) *view, prospect*
aussteigen v sep ir *to get out/off*
Ausstellung f (-en) *exhibition*
Austausch m (-e) *exchange*
Australien n *Australia*
Ausverkauf m (¨e) *sale*
ausverkaufen v sep *to sell out*
ausverkauft adj *sold out*
Auswahl f (-en) *choice, selection*
Ausweis m (-e) *ID card*
ausziehen sich v sep ir *to get undressed*
Auto n (-s) *car*
Autobahn f (-en) *motorway*
Autofähre f (-n) *car ferry*
Automat m (-en) *machine*
Autovermietung f (-en) *car rental firm*

## B

babysitten v *to baby sit*
Bach m (¨e) *stream*
backen v ir *to bake*
Bäcker/in m/f (-/-nen) *baker*
Bäckerei f (-en) *bakery*
Backofen m (¨) *oven*
Backstein m (-e) *brick*
Bad n (¨er) *bath*
Badeanzug m (¨e) *swimming costume*
Badehose f (-n) *swimming trunks*
baden v *to have a bath, to bathe / swim*
Badeort m (-e) *seaside resort*
Badetuch n (¨er) *bath towel*
Badewanne f (-n) *bathtub*
Badezimmer n (-) *bathroom*
Badminton n *badminton*
Bahn f (-en) *railway*
Bahnhof m (¨e) *station*
Bahnsteig m (-e) *platform*
bald adv *soon*
Balkon m (-e or -s) *balcony*
Ball m (¨e) *ball*
Banane f (-n) *banana*
Band f (-s) *band, group*
Bank f (-en) *bank*
Bankkarte f (-n) *bank card*
Bär m (-en) *bear*
Bargeld n *cash*
Bart m (¨e) *beard*
basteln v *to make (craft)*
Batterie f (-n) *battery*
Bauarbeiter/in m/f (-/-nen) *building worker/labourer*
Bauch m (¨e) *stomach / tummy*
bauen v *to build*
Bauer/Bäuerin m/f (-n/-nen) *farmer*
Bauernhaus n (¨er) *farmhouse*
Bauernhof m (¨e) *farm*
Baum m (¨e) *tree*
Baumwolle f *cotton*
Bayern n *Bavaria*
Beamte(r) *official, civil servant*
beantworten v *answer*
bedecken v *to cover*
bedeckt adj *covered, overcast*
bedienen v *to serve*
Bedienung f (-en) *service*
bedrohen v *to threaten / endanger*
bedürftig adj *needy*
beeilen sich v *to hurry up*
beenden v *to end*
befehlen v ir *to order / command*
befinden sich v ir *to be located / situated*
befriedigend adj *satisfactory*
begegnen v *to meet*
Begeisterung f (-) *enthusiasm*
Beginn m *beginning*
beginnen v ir *to begin*
begleiten v *to accompany*
begrüßen v *to greet*
behalten v ir *to keep*
behandeln v *to treat*
Behandlung f (-en) *treatment*
bei prep + dat *near, with, next to*
beide pron *both*
beiliegend adj *enclosed*
Bein n (-e) *leg*
Beispiel n (-e) *example*
beitragen (zu) v sep ir *contribute (to)*
bekommen v ir *to receive*
beleidigen v *to insult / offend*
Belgien n *Belgium*
Belgier/in m/f (-/-nen) *Belgian*
belgisch adj *Belgian*
beliebt adj *popular*
bemerken v *to notice, observe*
benachteiligen v *to put at a disadvantage, to discriminate against*
benutzen v *to use*
Benutzer/in m/f (-/-nen) *user*
Benzin n *petrol*
bequem adj *comfortable*
beraten v ir *to advise*
bereit adj *ready*
Berg m (-e) *mountain*
Bericht m (-e) *report*
Beruf m (-e) *job, occupation*
Berufsausbildung f *vocational training*

Berufsberater/in m/f (-/-nen) *careers advisor*
Berufsschule f (-n) *vocational school, technical college*
berufstätig adj *working*
berühmt adj *famous*
berühren v *to touch*
beschäftigt adj *busy*
beschließen v ir *to decide / resolve*
beschreiben v ir *to describe*
beschweren sich v *to complain*
besetzt adj *occupied, engaged*
besichtigen v *to visit, to see (sights)*
besitzen v ir *to own*
Besitzer/in m/f (-/-nen) *owner*
besonders adv *especially*
besprechen v ir *to discuss*
besser adj/adv *better*
Besteck n (-e) *cutlery*
bestehen v ir *pass (exam)*
bestehen aus v ir *to consist of*
bestellen v *to order*
bestimmt adv *definitely*
bestrafen v *to punish*
Besuch m (-e) *visit*
besuchen v *to visit*
Betreff m (-e) *subject (of letter/e-mail)*
betreten v ir *to enter, to step/walk on*
Betrieb m (-e) *firm, company*
Betriebspraktikum n (-praktika) *work experience*
betrunken adj *drunk*
Bett n (-en) *bed*
Betttuch n (¨er) *sheet*
Bettwäsche f *bed linen*
bevor conj *before, while*
bevorzugen v *to prefer*
bewegen v *to move*
bewerben sich um v ir *to apply for*
Bewerbung f (-en) *application*
bewölkt adj *cloudy*
Bewusstsein n *consciousness*
bezahlen v *to pay (for)*
Bezahlung f (-en) *payment*
Bezug m (¨e) *reference* (in Bezug auf = *with regard to, concerning*)
BH (= Büstenhalter) m *bra*
Bibliothek f (-en) *library*
Bibliothekar/in m/f (-e/-nen) *librarian*
Biene f (-n) *bee*
Bier n (-e) *beer*
bieten v ir *offer*
Bild n (-er) *picture*
Bildschirm m (-e) *screen*
billig adj *cheap*
Biologie f *biology*
biologisch adj *biological, organic*
Biomüll m *organic waste*
Birne f (-n) *pear, light bulb*
bis prep + acc *until*
bis bald/morgen/später *see you soon / tomorrow / later*
bisschen (ein) adj/adv *a little bit*
bitte *here you are, please*
bitte schön *you're welcome*
bitten v ir *to ask*
bitten um v ir *to ask for*
Blatt n (¨er) *leaf, sheet of paper*
blau adj *blue*
Blei n (-e) *lead (metal)*
bleiben v ir *to stay, to remain*
bleifrei adj *unleaded*
Bleistift m (-e) *pencil*
Blick m (-e) *look, glance, view*
Blitz m (-e) *lightning*
blitzen v *to flash with lightning*
Blockflöte f (-n) *recorder*
blöd adj *silly, stupid*
Blödsinn m *stupidity, rubbish*
Blume f (-n) *flower*
Blumenhändler/in m/f (-e/-nen) *florist*
Blumenkohl m *cauliflower*
Blumenladen m (¨) *florist's shop*
Bluse f (-n) *blouse*
Blut n *blood*
Bockwurst f (¨e) *boiled sausage*
Boden m (¨) *ground, floor*
Bodensee m *Lake Constance*
Bohne f (-n) *bean*
Bonbon n or m (-s) *sweet*
Boot n (-e) *boat*
böse adj *nasty, angry*

nouns — **m**: *masculine* **f**: *feminine* **n**: *neuter* **pl**: *plural* **v**: *verb* **v sep**: *separable verb* **v ir**: *irregular verb* **adj**: *adjective* **adv**: *adverb*

Bowling n (ten-pin) bowling
Brand m (-¨e) fire
Braten m (-) joint, roast meat
braten v ir to roast
Bratkartoffeln f pl fried potatoes
Bratpfanne f (-n) frying pan
Bratwurst f (-¨e) fried sausage
Brauch m (-¨e) custom
brauchen v need
braun adj brown
BRD (= Bundesrepublik Deutschland) f (Federal Republic of) Germany
brechen v ir to break
breit adj broad, wide
Bremse f (-n) brake
bremsen v to brake
Brennstoff m (-e) fuel
Brief m (-e) letter
Brieffreund/in m/f (-e/-nen) pen friend
Briefkasten m (-¨) postbox
Briefmarke f (-n) stamp
Brieftasche f (-n) wallet
Briefträger/in m/f (-/-nen) postman/woman
Briefumschlag m (-¨e) envelope
Brille f (-n) glasses
bringen v ir to bring
Brite/Britin m/f (-n/-nen) Briton
britisch adj British
Broschüre f (-n) brochure/leaflet
Brot n (-e) bread, loaf of bread
Brötchen n (-) bread roll
Brücke f (-n) bridge
Bruder m (-¨) brother
Brunnen m (-) well, fountain
Buch n (-¨er) book
buchen v to book
Bücherei f (-en) library
Bücherregal n (-e) bookcase
Buchhandlung f (-en) bookshop
Büchse f (-n) tin, can
Buchstabe m (-n) letter (of alphabet)
buchstabieren v to spell
Bude f (-n) stall, booth
Bügeleisen n (-) iron
bügeln v to iron
Bühne f (-n) stage
Bundesstraße f (-n) Federal road (= A-road)
bunt adj bright, multi-coloured
Burg f (-en) castle, fort
Bürgersteig m (-e) pavement
Büro n (-s) office
bürsten v to brush (e.g. hair)
Bus m (-se) bus
Busbahnhof m (-¨e) coach station
Bushaltestelle f (-n) bus stop
Büstenhalter m (-) bra
Butterbrot n (-e) sandwich

## C

Café n (-s) café
Campingplatz m (-¨e) campsite
Cent m (- or -s) cent
Champignon m (-s) mushroom
Charakter m (-e) character
chatten v to chat (online)
Chef/in m/f (-s/-nen) boss
Chemie f chemistry
chemisch adj/adv chemical(ly)
Chips m pl crisps
Chor m (-¨e) choir
Cola f (-s) cola
Computer m (-) computer
Computerprogrammierer/in m/f (-/-nen) computer programmer
Computerspiel n (-e) computer game
Couch f (-s/-en) couch
Cousin(e) m/f (-s,-n) cousin
Currywurst f (-¨e) curried sausage

## D

da adv there
da drüben over there
Dach n (-¨er) roof
dafür adv instead
dagegen adv against it/that
damals adv then (at that time)
Dame f (-n) lady
damit adv so that, with that
Dampfer m (-) steamer, steamship
danach adv after that
Däne/Dänin m/f (-n/-nen) Dane
Dänemark n Denmark
dänisch adj Danish
dankbar adj grateful
danke (schön) thank you (very much)
danken v to thank
dann adv then
das heißt (d.h.) that is (i.e.)
das pron that
das stimmt that's right
dass conj that
Datum n (Daten) date
dauern v to last
DB (= Deutsche Bundesbahn) German railway company
Decke f (-n) roof, ceiling, blanket
decken v to lay (e.g. table), to cover
Delikatessengeschäft n (-e) delicatessen
denken v ir to think
Denkmal n (-¨er) monument, memorial
denn conj then, than, because
dennoch adv nevertheless
deshalb adv therefore
deswegen adv therefore
Detail n (-s) detail
deutsch adj German
Deutsch n German (language)
Deutsche(r)/Deutsche m/f German (person)
Deutschland n Germany
Dezember m December
d.h. (= das heißt) i.e.
Diät f (-en) diet
dicht adj dense, thick
dick adj fat, thick
Dieb m (-e) thief
Diebstahl m (-¨e) theft
Diele f (-n) hallway
Dienstag m Tuesday
diese/r/s pron this
Diesel m diesel
Ding n (-e) thing
Diplom n (-e) degree, diploma
direkt adj/adv direct(ly)
Direktor/in m/f (-en/-nen) headteacher, director
Disko f (-s) disco
Diskothek f (-en) disco
Diskriminierung f (-en) discrimination
diskutieren v to discuss
Disziplin f (-en) discipline
doch conj yes (in opposition to what has been said before)
Dokumentarfilm m (-e) documentary
Dom m (-e) cathedral
Donau f the Danube
Donner m (-) thunder
donnern v to thunder
Donnerstag m Thursday
doof adj stupid
Doppelbett n (-en) double bed
Doppelhaus n (-¨er) semi-detached house
Doppelstunde f (-n) double period
Doppelzimmer n (-) double room
Dorf n (-¨er) village
dort adv there, in that place
dort drüben adv over there
dorthin adv there (to there)
Dose f (-n) tin, can
Dosenöffner m (-) tin opener
Drama n (Dramen) drama
draußen adv outside
dreckig adj dirty
Dreieck n (-e) triangle
dreieckig adj triangular
drinnen adv inside
Drittel n (-) a third
drittens adv thirdly
Droge f (-n) drug
Drogenhändler m (-) drug dealer
Drogensüchtige(r) m/f drug addict
Drogerie f (-n) chemist's
drüben adv over there
Druck m (-¨e) pressure
drucken v to print
drücken v to press/push
Drucker m (-) printer
dumm adj stupid
dunkel adj dark
dünn adj thin
durch prep + acc through, by
durchfallen v sep ir to fail (exam)
dürfen v ir to be allowed to ("may")
Durst m thirst
durstig adj thirsty
Dusche f (-n) shower
duschen v to shower
Dutzend n (-e) dozen
dynamisch adj dynamic
D-Zug m (-¨e) express train

## E

eben adj/adv smooth; just, precisely
ebenso adv (+ wie) just as
echt adj real, genuine
Ecke f (-n) corner
egal adj/adv all the same (Das ist mir egal = I don't mind)
egoistisch adj selfish
Ehefrau f (-en) wife
ehemalig adj former, previous
Ehemann m (-¨er) husband
Ehepaar n (-e) married couple
ehrlich adj honest, sincere
Ehrlichkeit f honesty
Ei n (-er) egg
eigene/r/s adj own
eigentlich adj/adv actual(ly)
eilen v to hurry
eilig adj in a hurry, hurried
einander pron each other, one another
einatmen v sep breathe in
Einbahnstraße f (-n) one-way street
einfach adj easy, single (ticket)
Einfahrt f (-en) entry, arrival (of train)
Einfamilienhaus n (-¨er) detached house
Eingang m (-¨e) entrance
eingehen v sep ir to enter
einige pron a few, some
Einkäufe m pl shopping (purchases)
einkaufen v sep to shop
einkaufen gehen v sep to go shopping
Einkaufskorb m (-¨e) shopping basket
Einkaufsliste f (-n) shopping list
Einkaufstasche f (-n) shopping bag
Einkaufswagen m (-) shopping trolley
Einkaufszentrum n (-zentren) shopping centre
einladen v sep ir invite
Einladung f (-en) invitation
einmal adv once
einnehmen v sep ir to take, to earn, to take up (space)
einpacken v sep to pack
einrichten v sep to furnish, to fit out
einsam adj lonely
einschlafen v sep ir to go to sleep
einschalten v sep to switch on
einsteigen v sep ir get on/in (vehicle)
einstellen v sep to put in, to hire, to stop, to adjust
Eintopf m (-¨e) stew
eintreten v sep ir to enter
Eintritt m (-e) entrance, admission charge
Eintrittsgeld n (-er) admission charge
Eintrittskarte f (-n) entrance ticket
einverstanden adj in agreement
Einwanderer/Einwanderin m/f (-/-nen) immigrant
einwerfen v sep ir break (window), post (letter)
Einwohner/in m/f (-/-nen) resident, inhabitant
Einzelbett n (-en) single bed
Einzelkind n (-er) only child
einzeln adj single
Einzelzimmer n (-) single room
einzig adj only, sole
Eis n ice, ice cream
Eisbecher m (-) ice cream sundae
Eisbahn f (-en) ice rink
Eisdiele f (-n) ice cream parlour
Eisen n (-) iron
Eisenbahnlinie f (-n) railway line
Eishalle f (-n) ice rink
Eis laufen n ice skating
ekelhaft adj disgusting
Elektriker/in m/f (-/-nen) electrician
elektrisch adj electric(al)
Elektrogeschäft n (-e) electrical shop
Elektroherd m (-e) electric cooker
Eltern pl parents
E-Mail f (-s) email
Empfang m (-¨e) reception
Empfänger/in m/f (-/-nen) recipient
Empfangschef/in m/f (-s/-nen) head porter
Empfangsdame f (-n) receptionist
empfehlen v ir to recommend
Ende n (-n) end
enden v to end
endlich adv at last, finally
Endspiel n (-e) final (e.g. sport)
Energie f (-n) energy
eng adj narrow, tight
England n England
Engländer/in m/f (-/-nen) English person
englisch adj English
Enkel/in m/f (-/-nen) grandson/granddaughter
Enkelkind n (-er) grandchild
enorm adj/adv enormous(ly)
Ente f (-n) duck
entfernt adj distant
entlang prep + acc/dat along
entscheiden sich v ir to decide
entschuldigen sich v to apologise
entschuldigen Sie! excuse me!
Entschuldigung f (-en) apology, Excuse me!
entsetzlich adj horrible, terrible
entsorgen v to dispose of
entspannen sich v to relax
entweder…oder either… or
entwerten v to invalidate (a ticket)
Erbse f (-n) pea
Erdbeere f (-n) strawberry
Erde f (-n) earth
Erdgeschoss n (-e) ground floor
Erdkunde f geography
Erdnuss f (-¨e) peanut
erfahren adj experienced
Erfahrung f (-en) experience
Erfolg m (-e) success
erfolgreich adj successful
Erfrischungen f pl refreshments
erfüllen v to fill/to fulfil
erhalten v ir to receive
erinnern (sich) v to remind of (to remember)
erkälten sich v to catch a cold
Erkältung f (-en) a cold
erkennen v ir to recognise
erklären v to explain, to declare
erlauben v to allow
erleben v to experience
Ermäßigung f (-en) reduction
ermüdend adj tiring
Ernährung f (-) food, nutrition
ernst adj serious
erreichen v reach, achieve
erschöpft adj exhausted
erst adv first, not before, only then
erstaunt adj astonished
Erste Hilfe f first aid
erstens adv firstly
erster Klasse first class
Erwachsene(r) adult
erwarten v to expect
erzählen v to tell
Erzählung f (-en) story
Essecke f (-n) eating area
Essen n (-) food, meal
essen v to eat
Essig m (-e) vinegar
Esszimmer n (-) dining room
Etage f (-n) floor, storey
Etagenbett n (-en) bunk bed
Etui n (-s) case
etwa adv about, roughly, approximately
etwas pron something
Euro m (-/-s) euro
Europa n Europe
Europäer/in m/f (-/-nen) European
europäisch adj European
Examen n (-/Examina) examination
Experiment n (-e) experiment

## F

Fabrik f (-en) factory
Fach n (-¨er) subject
Fähre f (-n) ferry
fahren v ir to go, to drive
Fahrer/in m/f (-/-nen) driver
Fahrgast m (-¨e) passenger
Fahrgeld n (-er) fare
Fahrkarte f (-n) ticket
Fahrkartenautomat m (-en) ticket machine
Fahrkartenschalter m (-) ticket offic
Fahrplan m (-¨e) timetable
Fahrpreis m (-e) fare
Fahrrad n (-¨er) bicycle
Fahrradverleih m (-e) cycle hire firm
Fahrradweg m (-e) cycle path
Fahrschein m (-e) ticket
Fahrstuhl m (-¨e) lift (elevator)
Fahrt f (-en) journey, drive
fallen v ir to fall
fallen lassen v ir to drop
falsch adj wrong, false
Familie f (-n) family
Familienmitglied n (-er) member of the family
Familienname m (-n) surname
fantastisch adj fantastic
Farbe f (-n) colour
Fasching m (-e/-s) (pre-Lent) carniv
fast adv almost
faszinierend adj fascinating
faul adj lazy
Fax n (-e) fax
FCKWs m pl CFCs
Februar m February
fehlen v to go wrong, to fail, to miss
Fehler m (-) mistake, fault
Feier f (-n) party, celebration
Feierabend m (-e) evening (leisure time)
feiern v to celebrate
Feiertag m (-e) holiday
Feld n (-er) field
Fenster n (-) window
Ferien pl holidays
Ferienhaus n (-¨er) holiday house
Ferienwohnung f (-en) holiday flat
Fernsehapparat m (-e) TV set
Fernsehen n TV
fernsehen v ir sep to watch TV
Fernseher m (-) TV set
Fernsehgerät n (-e) TV set
Fernsehraum m (-¨e) TV room
fertig adj ready, finished
fest adj solid, firm
Fest n (-e) festival, party
Fett n (-e) fat
fettig adj greasy
feucht adj damp
Feuer n (-) fire
Feuerwehr f (-en) fire brigade
Feuerwehrmann/frau m/f (-¨er/-en) firefighter
Feuerwerk pl fireworks
Fieber n (-) fever, temperature
Film m (-e) film
filtern v to filter
Filzstift m (-e) felt-tip pen
finden v ir to find
Finger m (-) finger
Firma f (Firmen) firm, company
Firmenchef/in m/f (-s/-nen) company head
Fisch m (-e) fish
Fischgeschäft n (-e) fishmonger's
Fitnesszentrum n (-zentren) fitness centre
flach adj flat
Flamme f (-n) flame
Flasche f (-n) bottle
Fleisch n meat
Fleischer/in m/f (-/-nen) butcher
Fleischerei f (-n) butcher's
fleißig adj hard-working
flexibel adj flexible
Fliege f (-n) fly
fliegen v ir to fly
fliehen v ir to escape/flee
Flöte f (-n) flute
Flug m (-¨e) flight
Flughafen m (-¨) airport
Flugzeug n (-e) aeroplane
Flur m (-e) corridor, hallway
Fluss m (-¨e) river
Flussufer n (-) riverbank
folgen v to follow
Forelle f (-n) trout
Form f (-en) form, shape
Formular n (-e) form (to fill in)

**prep**: preposition **pron: pronoun** **conj**: conjunction **bits in brackets**: plural ending **(¨)**: plural — add umlaut

chen v to research
tschritt m progress
sil adj fossil(ised)
o n (-s) photo
bapparat m (-e) camera
ograf/in m/f (-en/-nen) photographer
grafieren v take a photo
ge f (-n) question
ren v to ask
nkreich n France
nzose/Französin m/f (-n/-nen) French person
nzösisch n French (language)
zösisch adj French
u f (-en) Mrs, woman
ulein(!) n (-) Miss, young lady (waitress!)
ch adj cheeky
frei adj free
ibad n (-er) (open air) swimming pool
heit f (-en) freedom
itag m Friday
willig adj voluntary, optional
iwillige(r) m/f volunteer
izeit f free time
izeitaktivität f (-en) leisure activity
izeitbeschäftigung f (-en) free time/leisure activity
izeitpark m (-s) amusement park
izeitzentrum n (-zentren) leisure centre
mdsprache f (-n) foreign language
ssen v ir (of animals) to eat
ude f (-n) joy
uen sich v to be pleased/happy
uen sich auf v + acc to look forward to
uen sich über v + acc to be pleased about
und/in m/f (-e/-nen) friend
undlich adj friendly
undschaft f (-en) friendship
ieren v ir to freeze
kadelle f (-n) meatball, rissole
ch adj fresh
seur/Friseuse m/f (-e/-n) hairdresser
seursalon m (-s) hairdresser's salon
h adj happy
he/Fröhliche Weihnachten! Happy Christmas!
chtsaft m (-e) fruit juice
h adj early
her adj/adv former(ly)
hling m (-e) spring
hstück n (-e) breakfast
hstücken v to have breakfast
len sich v to feel
ren v to lead
rerschein m (-e) driving licence
en v to fill
ler m (-) (fountain) pen
ndbüro n (-s) lost property office
ktionieren v to function, work
prep + acc for
jetzt for the moment
chtbar adj/adv terrible/terribly
m (-e) foot
ball m (-e) football
boden m (-) floor
gänger m (-) pedestrian
gängerzone f (-n) pedestrian zone
weg m (-e) footpath
tern v to feed (animals)
bel f (-n) fork
ng m (-e) corridor
ns f (-e) goose
z adv completely, quite
ztags adj all day
ztagsjob m (-e) full-time job
ztagsstelle f (-n) full-time job
nicht adv not at all
rage f (-n) garage
antieren v to guarantee
rdine f (-n) curtain
rten m (-) garden
rtner/in m/f (-/-nen) gardener
sherd m (-e) gas cooker
st m (-e) guest
stfreundschaft f hospitality
stgeber/in m/f (-/-nen) host(ess)

Gasthaus n (-"er) guest house, pub
Gasthof m (-"e) inn
Gaststätte f (-n) restaurant, pub
Gebäude n (-) building
geben v ir to give
Gebiet n (-e) region, area
Gebirge n (-) mountain range
geboren born, née
gebraten adj roast
Gebrauch m (-"e) use, custom
gebrochen adj broken
Geburt f (-en) birth
Geburtsdatum n (-daten) date of birth
Geburtsort m (-e) place of birth
Geburtstag m (-e) birthday
geduldig adj/adv patient(ly)
Gefahr f (-en) danger
gefährlich adj dangerous
gefallen v to like, to please
Gefühl n (-e) feeling
gegen prep + acc against, towards
Gegend f (-en) region
Gegenstand m (-"e) object
Gegenteil n the opposite
gegenüber prep + dat opposite
Gegenwart f present (time)
Gehalt n (-"er) salary
gehen v ir to go (by foot)
Gehirn n (-e) brain
gehören v to belong to
Geige f (-n) violin
gekocht adj cooked
gekochtes Ei n boiled egg
gelb adj yellow
Geld n (-er) money
Geldschein m (-e) banknote
Geldstück n (-e) coin
Geldtasche f (-n) money purse, wallet
Gelegenheit f (-en) opportunity
gelingen v ir to succeed
gemein adj nasty, common
gemischt adj mixed
Gemüse n (-) vegetable
Gemüsehändler/in m/f (-/-nen) greengrocer
gemütlich adj comfortable, cosy
genau adj/adv exact(ly)
Genf n Geneva
genießen v ir to enjoy
genug adj enough
geöffnet adj open(ed)
Geografie f geography
Gepäck n luggage
Gepäckaufbewahrung f (-en) left luggage
geplant adj planned
gerade adj/adv straight, precisely / just
geradeaus adv straight ahead
Gerät n (-e) piece of equipment / apparatus
gerecht adj/adv just(ly), fair(ly)
Gericht n (-e) dish, law-court
gern adv with pleasure, willingly
gern geschehen! you're welcome, don't mention it
gern haben v ir to like
Geruch m (-"e) smell
Gesamtschule f (-n) comprehensive school
gesandt von sent by
Geschäft n (-e) business, shop
Geschäftsmann/frau m/f (-"er/-en) businessman/woman
geschehen v ir happen
Geschenk n (-e) present (gift)
Geschichte f (-n) history, story
geschieden adj divorced
Geschirr n (-e) dishes, crockery
Geschirrtuch n (-"er) tea towel
geschlossen adj closed
Geschmack m (-"e) taste
Geschwister pl siblings
Gesellschaft f (-en) society
Gesicht n (-er) face
Gespräch n (-e) conversation, discussion
gestern adv yesterday
gestreift adj striped
gesund adj/adv healthy/ healthily
Gesundheit f health
Getränk n (-e) drink
getrennt adj/adv separate(ly), separated

Gewalt f (-en) power
gewaltig adj huge
gewinnen v ir to win
Gewitter n (-) thunder storm
gewöhnen sich an v +acc to get used to
Gewohnheit f (-en) habit
gewöhnlich adj/adv usual(ly)
Gewürz n (-e) spice
Gitarre f (-n) guitar
Glas n (-"er) glass, jar
glatt adj smooth, straight (e.g. hair)
Glatteis n black ice
glauben v to believe/think
gleich adv immediately, in a moment
gleich adj same, similar, equal
Gleichheit f (-en) similarity
Gleis n (-e) platform, track
global adj global
Glück n happiness, luck
glücklich adj happy
GmbH (= Gesellschaft mit beschränkter Haftung) Ltd.
Goldfisch m (-e) goldfish
goldig adj sweet, cute
Gott m (-"er) God
Grad m (-e) degree, extent
Gramm n (-/-e) gram
Gras n (-"er) grass
gratis adv free (of charge)
gratulieren v to congratulate
grau adj grey
Grenze f (-n) border
Grieche/Griechin m/f (-n/-nen) Greek
Griechenland n Greece
griechisch adj Greek
Grill m (-s) grill, barbecue
grillen v to grill, to barbecue
Grippe f (-n) flu
groß adj big, tall
großartig adj magnificent
Großbritannien n Great Britain
Größe f (-n) size, height
Großeltern pl grandparents
Großmutter f (-) grandmother
Großstadt f (-"e) city
Großvater m (-") grandfather
grün adj green
Grund m (-"e) ground, reason
Grundschule f (-n) primary school
Gruppe f (-n) group
Gruß m (-"e) greeting
Grüß Gott hello
gültig adj valid
günstig adj favourable
Gürtel m (-) belt
Gummi n or m (-s) rubber
Gurke f (-n) cucumber
gut adj/adv good/ well
gut bezahlt well paid
gut gelaunt in a good mood
gute Nacht goodnight
gute Reise have a good journey
guten Abend good evening
guten Appetit! enjoy your meal!
guten Aufenthalt enjoy your stay
guten Tag hello, good day
Gymnasium n (Gymnasien) secondary school for more academic pupils
Gymnastik f exercises, gymnastics

## H

Haar n (-e) hair
Haarbürste f (-n) hairbrush
haben v ir to have
Hafen m (-) harbour, port
Hafenstadt f (-"e) port
Haferflocken f pl porridge oats
Hagel m hail
hageln v to hail
Hähnchen n (-) chicken
halb adj/adv half
Halbpension f half board (at hotel)
Hälfte f (-n) half
Halle f (-n) hall
Hallenbad n (-"er) indoor swimming pool
Hallo! Hello
Hals m (-"e) throat, neck
Halskette f (-n) necklace
Halsschmerzen m pl sore throat
halten v ir to hold, to stop
Haltestelle f (-n) stop (e.g. bus)

Hamburger m (-) hamburger
Hand f (-"e) hand
Handball m handball
Händler/in m/f (-/-nen) trader, dealer, shopkeeper
Handschuh m (-e) glove
Handtasche f (-n) handbag
Handtuch n (-"er) hand towel
Handy n (-s) mobile phone
Hansaplast n 'Elastoplast ®'
hart adj hard, harsh, severe, unkind
Hase m (-n) hare
hassen v to hate
hässlich adj ugly
Hauptbahnhof m (-"e) main station
Hauptgericht n (-e) main course
Hauptschule f (-n) secondary school for vocational/practical training
Hauptstadt f (-"e) capital city
Hauptstraße f (-n) major road, main street
Haus n (-"er) house
Hausarbeit f (-en) housework, homework
Hausaufgabe f (-n) homework
Hausfrau f (-en) housewife
Haushalt m (-e) household
Hausmann m (-"er) househusband
Hausmeister/in m/f (-/-nen) caretaker
Hausnummer f (-n) house number
Hausschuh m (-e) slipper
Haustier n (-e) pet
Haustür f (-en) front door
Hauswirtschaftslehre f home economics
Hautfarbe f (-n) skin colour
Hecke f (-n) hedge
Heft n (-e) exercise book
heftig adj violent, heavy (rain etc.)
Heftpflaster n (-) sticking plaster
Heiligabend m (-e) Christmas Eve
Heim n (-e) home
Heimat f (-en) home, homeland
Heimfahrt f (-en) home journey
Heimleiter/in m/f (-/-nen) warden of home/hostel
Heimleitung f (-en) person in charge of home/ hostel
Heimweg m (-e) way home
heiraten v marry
heiß adj hot
heißen v ir to be called (named)
heiter adj bright (weather)
heizen v to have the heating on
Heizkörper m (-) radiator
Heizung f (-en) heating
helfen v ir to help
hell adj light, pale (colour)
Helm m (-e) helmet
Hemd n (-en) shirt
her adv (to) here
heraus adv out
Herbergseltern pl wardens (of youth hostel)
Herbst m (-e) autumn
Herd m (-e) cooker
herein! come in!
hereinkommen v sep ir to come in
Herr m (-en) Mr, gentleman
Herr Ober! waiter!
herrlich adj splendid, wonderful
herrschend adj ruling, dominant, prevailing
herum adv around
herumfahren v sep ir to travel/drive around
herunterladen v sep ir to download
hervorragend adj outstanding, excellent
Herz n (-en) heart
herzlich willkommen! welcome!
herzlichen Glückwunsch! congratulations!
heute adv today
heutzutage adv nowadays
hier adv here
Hilfe f (-n) help
hilfreich adj helpful
hilfsbereit adj helpful
Himbeere f (-n) raspberry
Himmel m (-) sky, heaven
hin und zurück adv return (ticket)
hinaus adv out

hinein adv in
hinlegen sich v sep to lie down
hinsetzen sich v sep to sit down
hinten adv behind, at the back
hinter prep + acc/dat behind
historisch adj/adv historic(al)
Hitze f (-n) heat
HIV-positiv adj HIV positive
hoch adv high
hochachtungsvoll adv yours faithfully, yours sincerely
Hochhaus n (-"er) skyscraper
hochladen v sep ir to upload
Hochschule f (-n) college, university
Hochzeit f (-en) wedding
Hockey n hockey
hoffen v to hope
höflich adj/adv polite
holen v to fetch
Holland n Holland
Holländer/in m/f (-/-nen) Dutch person
holländisch adj Dutch
Holz n (-"er) wood
Honig m (-e) honey
hören v to hear
Hörer m (-) receiver (telephone), headphone
Horrorfilm m (-e) horror film
Hose f (-n) trousers
Hotel n (-s) hotel
Hotelverzeichnis n (-se) list of hotels
hübsch adj pretty
Hubschrauber m (-) helicopter
Hügel m (-) hill
hügelig adj hilly
humorlos adj humourless
humorvoll adj humorous
Hund m (-e) dog
Hunger m hunger
hungrig adj hungry
Husten m cough
husten v to cough
Hut m (-"e) hat

## I

ICE-Zug m (-"e) intercity express train
ideal adj/adv ideal(ly)
Idee f (-n) idea
illegal adj/adv illegal(ly)
Illustrierte f (-n) magazine
im Freien in the open air
Image n (-s) image
Imbiss m (-e) snack
Imbissstube f (-n) café
immer adv always
immer noch adv still
in prep + acc/dat in, into
in Ordnung OK
inbegriffen adj included
Indien n India
Industrie f (-n) industry
industriell adj industrial
Informatik f ICT, computing
Informatiker/in m/f (-/-nen) computer scientist
Informationsbüro n (-s) information office
informativ adj informative
Ingenieur/in m/f (-e/-nen) engineer
inkl. (= inklusive) adj inclusive
Insektizid n (-e) insecticide
Insel f (-n) island
intelligent adj intelligent
interessant adj interesting
Interesse n (-n) interest
interessieren sich für v to be interested in
Internat n (-e) boarding school
Internet n internet
Internetseite f (-n) web page
Interview n (-s) interview
inzwischen adv in the meantime, meanwhile
Ire/Irin m/f (-n/-nen) Irish person
irgend- some-
irgendetwas pron something
irgendwo adv somewhere (or other)
irisch adj Irish
Irland n Ireland
Italien n Italy
Italiener/in m/f (-/-nen) Italian person
italienisch adj Italian

*nouns — m: masculine f: feminine n: neuter pl: plural v: verb v sep: separable verb v ir: irregular verb adj: adjective adv: adverb*

GERMAN—ENGLISH DICTIONARY

# J

ja *yes*
Jacke f (-n) *(casual) jacket*
Jahr n (-e) *year*
Jahreszeit f (-en) *season*
Jahrhundert n (-e) *century*
jährlich adj/adv *annual(ly)*
Januar m *January*
je prep + acc *per*
jede/r/s pron *each, every, everybody*
jedoch conj/adv *however*
jemand pron *someone, somebody*
jene/r/s pron *that*
jetzt adv *now*
jobben v *to do a job/jobs*
joggen v *to jog*
Joghurt m or n (-s) *yoghurt*
Journalist/in m/f (-en/-nen) *journalist*
Jugendherberge f (-n) *youth hostel*
Jugendklub m (-s) *youth club*
Jugendliche m/f (-n) *young person*
Juli m *July*
jung adj *young*
Junge m (-n) *boy*
jünger adj *younger*
Juni m *June*
Juwelier/in m/f (-e/-nen) *jeweller*
Juweliergeschäft n (-e) *jeweller's shop*

# K

Kaffee m (-s) *coffee*
Kaffeekanne f (-n) *coffee pot*
Käfig m (-e) *cage*
Kakao m (-s) *cocoa*
Kalbfleisch n *veal*
Kalender m (-) *calendar, diary*
kalt adj *cold*
Kamera f (-s) *camera*
Kamm m (-e) *comb*
kämmen v *to comb*
Kanal m (-e) *canal, channel*
Kandidat/in m/f (-en/-nen) *candidate*
Kaninchen n (-) *rabbit*
Kännchen n (-) *jug, pot*
Kantine f (-n) *canteen*
Kanufahren n *canoeing*
Kapelle f (-n) *chapel*
kaputt adj *broken*
Karneval m (-e or -s) *carnival*
Karotte f (-n) *carrot*
Karriere f (-n) *career*
Karte f (-n) *map, ticket, card*
Kartoffel f (-n) *potato*
Kartoffelbrei m *mashed potatoes*
Kartoffelchips pl *crisps*
Kartoffelpüree m (-s) *mashed potatoes*
Kartoffelsalat m (-e) *potato salad*
Karton m (-s) *cardboard box*
Käse m (-) *cheese*
Kasse f (-n) *checkout*
Kassette f (-n) *cassette*
Kassettenrekorder m (-) *cassette recorder*
Kassierer/in m/f (-/-nen) *cashier*
Katze f (-n) *cat*
kaufen v *to buy*
Kaufhaus n (-er) *department store*
Kaugummi m *chewing gum*
kaum adv *hardly*
kegeln v *to bowl, to play skittles*
kehren v *to turn*
kein pron *no (= not any)*
Keks m (-e) *biscuit*
Keller m (-) *cellar*
Kellner/in m/f (-/-nen) *waiter/waitress*
kennen v ir *know (a person)*
kennen lernen v *to get to know*
Kenntnis f (-se) *knowledge*
Kennwort n (-er) *password*
Kfz (= Kraftfahrzeug) n *motor vehicle*
Kilometer m (-) *kilometre*
Kind n (-er) *child*
Kindheit f *childhood*
Kindergarten m (-) *nursery school*
Kinn n (-e) *chin*
Kino n (-s) *cinema*
Kiosk m (-e) *kiosk*
Kirche f (-n) *church*
Kirchturm m (-) *steeple, church tower*
Kirsche f (-n) *cherry*
Kissen n (-) *cushion*
Klamotten pl *clothes, clobber*
klar adj *clear*

Klarinette f (-n) *clarinet*
Klasse f (-n) *class*
klasse adj *great*
Klassenarbeit f (-en) *test*
Klassenfahrt f (-en) *school trip*
Klassenkamerad/in m/f (-en/-nen) *classmate*
Klassenzimmer n (-) *classroom*
klassisch adj/adv *classic(al)*
Klavier n (-e) *piano*
kleben v *to stick*
Klebstoff m (-e) *glue*
Kleid n (-er) *dress*
Kleider n pl *clothes*
Kleiderschrank m (-e) *wardrobe*
Kleidung f *clothing*
Kleidungsgeschäft n (-e) *clothes shop*
klein adj *small, short*
Kleingeld n *(small) change*
Klempner/in m/f (-/-nen) *plumber*
klettern v *to climb*
klicken v *to click*
Klima n (-s) *climate*
Klingel f (-n) *bell*
klingeln v *to ring (doorbell)*
Klo n (-s) *loo*
klopfen v *to knock*
Klub m (-s) *club*
klug adj *clever*
Kneipe f (-n) *pub*
Knie n (-) *knee*
Knopf m (-e) *button*
Koch/Köchin m/f (-e/-nen) *cook*
Kochen n *cooking*
kochen v *to cook*
Koffer m (-) *suitcase, trunk*
Kohl m (-e) *cabbage*
Kohle f (-n) *coal*
Kollege/in m/f (-n/-nen) *colleague*
Köln n *Cologne*
komisch adj *funny*
kommen v ir *to come*
Kommode f (-n) *chest of drawers*
Komödie f (-n) *comedy*
kompliziert adj *complicated*
können v ir *to be able to*
Kontakt m (-e) *contact*
Konto n (Konten) *(bank) account*
Kontrolleur/in m/f (-e/-nen) *(ticket) inspector*
kontrollieren v *to check, to supervise, to control*
Konzert n (-e) *concert*
Kopf m (-e) *head*
Kopfhörer m (-) *headphones*
Kopfkissen n (-) *pillow*
Kopfsalat m (-e) *lettuce*
Kopfschmerzen pl *headache*
kopieren v *to copy*
Korb m (-e) *basket*
Körper m (-) *body*
Korridor m (-e) *corridor*
korrigieren v *to correct, to mark*
kosten v *to cost*
kostenlos adj *free*
köstlich adj *delicious*
Kostüm n (-e) *(women's) suit, costume*
Kotelett n (-e) *cutlet, chop*
krank adj *ill*
Krankenhaus n (-er) *hospital*
Krankenpfleger m (-) *(male) nurse*
Krankenschwester f (-n) *(female) nurse*
Krankenwagen m (-) *ambulance*
Krankheit f (-en) *illness*
Krawatte f (-n) *tie*
Krebs m (-e) *cancer*
Kreditkarte f (-n) *credit card*
Kreide f (-n) *chalk*
Kreis m (-e) *circle*
Kreisverkehr m (-e) *roundabout*
Kreuzung f (-en) *crossroads*
kriegen v *to get*
Krimi m (-s) *crime story, thriller*
Kriminalität f *crime*
kritisieren v *to criticise*
Küche f (-n) *kitchen*
Kuchen m (-) *cake*
Kugelschreiber m (-) *biro, ballpoint pen*
Kuh f (-e) *cow*
kühl adj *cool*
Kühlschrank m (-e) *fridge*

Kuli m (-s) *biro*
kümmern sich um v *to take care of*
Kunde/Kundin m/f (-n/-nen) *customer*
kündigen v *to cancel, to hand in notice*
Kündigung f (-en) *cancellation, notice (to quit)*
Kunst f (-e) *art*
Kunstgalerie f (-n) *art gallery*
Künstler/in m/f (-/-nen) *artist*
Kunststoff m (-e) *plastic, synthetic material*
Kunstwerk n (-e) *work of art*
Kurs m (-e) *course*
Kurve f (-n) *bend, curve*
kurz adj *short*
kürzlich adv *recently*
Kusine f (-n) *cousin (f)*
Kuss m (-e) *kiss*
küssen v *to kiss*
Küste f (-n) *coast*

# L

Labor n (-s/-e) *laboratory*
lächeln v *to smile*
lachen v *to laugh*
Lachs m (-e) *salmon*
Laden m (-) *shop*
laden v ir *to load, to charge*
Ladenbesitzer/in m/f (-/-nen) *shopkeeper*
Lagerfeuer n (-) *campfire*
Lamm n (-er) *lamb*
Lammfleisch n *lamb (meat)*
Lampe f (-n) *lamp*
Land n (-er) *country, administrative district*
landen v *to land*
Landkarte f (-n) *map*
Landschaft f (-en) *landscape*
lang adj *long*
langsam adj/adv *slow(ly)*
langweilen sich v *to be bored*
langweilig adj *boring*
Lärm m *noise*
lästig adj *annoying (person)*
lassen v ir *to leave*
Lastwagen m (-) *lorry, truck*
Latein n *Latin*
laufen v ir *to go, to walk, to run*
Laune f (-n) *mood*
launisch adj *moody*
laut adj/adv *loud(ly), noisy*
lautlos adj/adv *silent(ly)*
Leben n (-) *life*
leben v *to live*
lebendig adj *living, lively*
Lebenslauf m (-e) *CV*
Lebensmittel n pl *food, groceries*
Lebensmittelgeschäft n (-e) *grocer's shop*
Leber f (-n) *liver*
lebhaft adj *lively, busy*
lecker adj *delicious*
Leder n (-n) *leather*
ledig adj *single (unmarried)*
leer adj *empty*
leeren v *to empty*
legal adj/adv *legal(ly)*
legen v *to put, to lie something down*
Lehre f (-n) *apprenticeship, teaching*
lehren v *to teach*
Lehrer/in m/f (-/-nen) *teacher*
Lehrerzimmer n (-) *staff room*
Lehrling m (-e) *apprentice*
lehrreich adj *educational*
leicht adj *easy, light (weight)*
Leichtathletik f *athletics*
Leid tun v ir *to regret, be sorry (es tut mir Leid = I'm sorry)*
leiden können v ir *to like*
leider adv *unfortunately*
leihen v ir *to lend*
leihen sich v ir *to borrow*
leise adj/adv *quiet(ly)*
Leistung f (-en) *performance, achievement*
Leiter/in m/f (-/-nen) *manager, leader*
Leiter f (-n) *ladder*
lernen v *to learn*
Lesen n *reading*
lesen v ir *to read*
letzte/r/s adj *last*
Leute pl *people*

Licht n (-er) *light*
lieb adj/adv *kind(ly), likeable, nice(ly)*
Liebe f (-n) *love*
lieben v *to love*
lieber adv *rather*
Lieber/Liebe *Dear (in a letter)*
Liebesfilm m (-e) *romantic film*
Lieblings- *favourite*
Lied n (-er) *song*
liefern v *to deliver*
Lieferwagen m (-) *(delivery) van*
liegen v ir *to lie*
Liga f (Ligen) *league*
lila adj *purple*
Limo(nade) f (-s/-n) *lemonade*
Lineal n (-e) *ruler*
Linie f (-n) *line, route*
linke/r/s adj *left*
links adv *left*
Lippe f (-n) *lip*
Lippenstift m (-e) *lipstick*
Liste f (-n) *list*
Liter m or n (-) *litre*
Lkw (= Lastkraftwagen) m (-) *lorry*
Loch n (-er) *hole*
lockig adj *curly*
Löffel m (-) *spoon*
Lohn m (-e) *wage*
Lokal n (-e) *pub*
löschen v *to erase, to delete, to switch off (light), to extinguish*
Lotto n (-s) *national lottery*
Löwe m (-n) *lion*
lügen v *to tell a lie*
Luft f *air*
Luftverschmutzung f *air pollution*
Lunge f (-n) *lungs*
Lust (f) haben v ir *to feel like (doing something)*
lustig adj *funny*
Luxus m *luxury*

# M

machen v *to make, to do*
Mädchen n (-) *girl*
Magen m (-) *stomach*
Magenschmerzen m pl *stomach ache*
mähen v *to mow*
Mahl n (-e/-er) *meal*
Mahlzeit f (-en) *meal*
Mai m *May*
Mal n (-e) *time*
malen v *to paint*
Maler/in m/f (-/-nen) *painter*
malerisch adj *picturesque*
Manager/in m/f (-/-nen) *manager*
manchmal adv *sometimes*
Mann m (-er) *man, husband*
männlich adj *male*
Mannschaft f (-en) *team*
Mantel m (-) *coat*
Margarine f (-n) *margarine*
Marke f (-n) *brand, make*
Marketing n *marketing*
Markt(platz) m (-e) *market (place)*
Marmelade f (-n) *jam, marmalade*
März m *March*
Maß n (-e) *measure, measurement*
mäßig adj/adv *moderate(ly)*
Mathe(matik) f *maths*
Mauer f (-n) *wall*
Maurer/in m/f (-/-nen) *builder*
Maus f (-e) *mouse*
Maximum n (Maxima) *maximum*
Mechaniker/in m/f (-/-nen) *mechanic*
Medienwissenschaft f *media studies*
Medikament n (-e) *medicine*
Meer n (-e) *sea*
Meerschweinchen n (-) *guinea pig*
mehr pron/adv *more*
Mehrbettzimmer n (-) *shared room*
mehrere pron *several*
Mehrfamilienhaus n (-er) *house for several families*
Mehrzweckraum m (-e) *multi-purpose room*
Meile f (-n) *mile*
mein/e/r pron *my*
meinen v *to think, to mean*
Meinung f (-en) *opinion*
meistens adv *mostly*
Meisterschaft f (-en) *championship*
Melodie f (-n) *melody*

Melone f (-n) *melon*
Menge f (-n) *quantity, load, crowd*
Mensch m (-en) *person*
merkwürdig adj/adv *strange(ly), odd*
Messe f (-n) *mass*
messen v ir *to measure*
Messer n (-) *knife*
Metall n (-e) *metal*
Meter m or n (-) *metre*
Metzger/in m/f (-/-nen) *butcher*
Metzgerei f (-en) *butcher's*
mies adj *lousy*
Miete f (-n) *rent*
mieten v *to rent*
Mikrowelle f (-n) *microwave*
Mikrowellenherd m (-e) *microwave oven*
Milch f *milk*
Million f (-en) *million*
Mindest- *minimum*
mindestens adv *at least*
Mineralwasser n *mineral water*
Minimum n (Minima) *minimum*
Minute f (-n) *minute*
mit prep + dat *with*
mit freundlichen Grüßen *yours sincerely*
mit Vergnügen! *with pleasure!*
mitgehen v sep ir *to go with*
Mitglied n (-er) *member*
mitkommen v sep ir *come (along)*
mitmachen v sep *to join in*
mitnehmen v sep ir *take (with you)*
Mittag m *midday*
mittags adv *at midday*
Mittagessen n (-) *lunch*
Mittagspause f (-n) *lunch break*
Mitte f (-n) *middle*
mitteilen v sep *to inform*
Mitteilung f (-en) *(text) message*
Mittel n (-) *means, method*
mittelgroß adj *medium/average heig...*
mittellang adj *medium/average leng...*
Mittelmeer n *Mediterranean Sea*
mitten adv *in the middle*
Mitternacht f *midnight*
Mittwoch m *Wednesday*
Mobbing n *workplace bullying*
Möbel n (-) *furniture*
Möbelstück n (-e) *piece of furniture*
möbliert adj *furnished*
Mode f (-n) *fashion*
Modegeschäft n (-e) *clothes shop*
modern adj *modern*
modisch adj *fashionable*
Mofa n (-s) *moped*
mögen v ir *to like*
möglich adj *possible*
Möglichkeit f (-en) *possibility*
Moment m (-e) *moment*
Monat m (-e) *month*
monatlich adj/adv *monthly*
Mond m (-e) *moon*
Montag m *Monday*
Morgen m (-) *morning*
morgen adv *tomorrow*
morgen früh *tomorrow morning*
morgens adv *in the morning(s)*
Mosel f *the Moselle (river)*
Motor m (-en) *engine*
Motorrad n (-er) *motorbike*
Motorradfahrer/in m/f (-/-nen) *motorbike rider*
müde adj *tired*
mühsam adj *laborious*
Müll m *rubbish*
Mülltonne f (-n) *dustbin*
multikulturell adj *multicultural*
München n *Munich*
Mund m (-er) *mouth*
mündlich adj/adv *oral(ly)*
Münze f (-n) *coin*
Museum n (Museen) *museum*
Musik f *music*
Musiker/in m/f (-/-nen) *musician*
musizieren v *to play a musical instrument*
müssen v ir *to have to*
Mutter f (-) *mother*
Mutti f (-s) *mum, mummy*
Mütze f (-n) *cap, hat*
MwSt. (= Mehrwertsteuer) f *VAT*

---

**prep:** preposition **pron:** pronoun **conj:** conjunction **bits in brackets:** plural ending (-): plural — add umlaut

GERMAN—ENGLISH DICTIONARY

# N

nach prep + dat *after, to*
nach Hause *home*
nach oben *upwards, upstairs*
nach unten *downwards, downstairs*
Nachbar/in m/f (-n/-nen) *neighbour*
nachdem conj *after*
nachgehen v sep ir *to follow*
nachher adv *afterwards*
Nachmittag m (-e) *afternoon*
nachmittags adv *in the afternoon(s)*
Nachrichten f pl *news*
nachsehen v sep ir *to check, to look up, to watch*
Nachspeise f (-n) *dessert*
nächste/r/s adj *next*
Nacht f (-̈e) *night*
Nachteil m (-e) *disadvantage*
Nachthemd n (-en) *nightshirt*
Nachtisch m (-e) *dessert*
nachts adv *at night*
Nachttisch m (-e) *bedside table*
nahe adj *near*
Nähe f *nearness, vicinity*
Nahrung f *food*
Nase f (-n) *nose*
nass adj *wet*
Natur f (-en) *nature*
natürlich adj/adv *of course, naturally*
Naturwissenschaft f (-en) *science*
Nebel m (-) *fog, mist*
nebelig adj *foggy*
neben prep + acc/dat *next to*
Nebenjob m (-s) *side job*
Neffe m (-n) *nephew*
nehmen v ir *to take*
nein *no*
nennen v ir *to name, to call*
nerven v *to get on someone's nerves*
nervös adj/adv *nervous(ly)*
nett adj *nice, kind*
Netz n (-e) *net*
neu adj *new*
neulich adv *recently*
nicht adv *not*
nicht einmal *not even*
nicht mehr *no longer*
nicht nur … sondern auch *not only … but also*
nicht wahr? *isn't it?*
Nichte f (-n) *niece*
nichts pron *nothing (Das macht nichts = It doesn't matter)*
nie adv *never*
Niederlande n pl *Netherlands*
Niederschlag m *precipitation*
niedrig adj/adv *low*
niemals adv *never*
niemand pron *no one*
nirgends adv *nowhere*
noch adv *still*
noch einmal *again*
noch nicht adv *not yet*
nochmal adv *again*
Nordamerika n *North America*
Norden m *north*
nördlich adj/adv *in/to the north*
Nordsee f *North Sea*
normal adj *normal*
normalerweise adv *normally*
Nostalgie f *nostalgia*
Not f (-̈e) *need, distress, trouble*
Notausgang m (-̈e) *emergency exit*
Note f (-n) *mark, grade*
notieren v *to note*
nötig adj *necessary*
Notizbuch n (-̈er) *notebook*
notwendig adj *necessary*
November m *November*
Nudeln f pl *pasta, noodles*
Nummer f (-n) *number*
nun adv *now*
nur adv *only*
Nuss f (-̈e) *nut*
Nutzen m (-) *use, usefulness*
nützlich adj *useful*
nutzlos adj/adv *useless(ly)*

# O

ob conj *whether*
obdachlos adj *homeless*
oben adv *at the top, above, upstairs*
Oberstufe f (-n) *6th form*

Obst n *fruit*
Obst- und Gemüseladen m (-̈) *fruit and veg shop*
obwohl conj *although*
oder conj *or*
Ofen m (-̈) *heater, oven*
offen adj *open*
öffentlich adj *public, municipal*
öffentliche Verkehrsmittel n pl *public transport*
öffnen v *to open*
Öffnungszeiten f pl *opening times*
oft adv *often*
ohne prep + acc *without*
ohne Zweifel *without doubt*
Ohr n (-en) *ear*
Ohrring m (-e) *earring*
Oktober m *October*
Öl n (-e) *oil*
Öltanker m (-) *oil tanker*
Oma f (-s) *granny*
Omelett n (-e/-s) *omelette*
Onkel m (-) *uncle*
Opa m (-s) *grandpa*
Oper f (-n) *opera*
Operation f (-en) *operation (medical)*
Opfer n (-) *victim, sacrifice*
optimistisch adj/adv *optimistic(ally)*
Orangenmarmelade f (n) *marmelade*
Orchester n (-) *orchestra*
ordentlich adj *tidy*
Ordnung f (-en) *order, routine*
organisch adj/adv *organic(ally)*
organisieren v *to organise*
Ort m (-e) *place*
örtlich adj/adv *local(ly)*
Osten m *east*
Ostern n *Easter*
Österreich n *Austria*
Österreicher/in m/f (-/-nen) *Austrian*
österreichisch adj *Austrian*
östlich adj/adv *in/to the east*
Ostsee f *Baltic Sea*
Ozonloch n *hole in the ozone layer*
Ozonschicht f *ozone layer*

# P

Paar n (-e) *pair*
paar (ein) adj *a few/couple*
Päckchen n (-) *packet, small parcel*
Packung f (-en) *packet*
Paket n (-e) *package, packet*
Palast m (-̈e) *palace*
Pampelmuse f (-n) *grapefruit*
Panne f (-n) *breakdown, flat tyre*
Papier n (-e) *paper*
Papiere n pl *papers, (official) documents*
Pappe f (-n) *cardboard*
Parfüm n (-e/-s) *perfume*
Parfümerie f (-en) *perfumery*
Park m (-s) *park*
parken v *to park*
Parkhaus n (-̈er) *multistorey car park*
Parkplatz m (-̈e) *parking place*
Partei f (-en) *(political) party*
Partnerstadt f (-̈e) *twin town*
Pass m (-̈e) *passport*
Passagier m (-e) *passenger*
passen v *to fit, to be suitable*
passieren v *to happen*
Passkontrolle f (-n) *passport control*
Patient/in m/f (-en/-nen) *patient*
Pause f (-n) *break*
Pech n *bad luck*
Pension f (-en) *guest house*
perfekt adj/adv *perfect(ly)*
Person f (-en) *person*
Personalausweis m (-e) *identity card*
Persönlichkeit f (-en) *personality*
pessimistisch adj/adv *pessimistic(ally)*
Pestizid n (-e) *pesticide*
Pfand n (-̈er) *security, deposit*
Pfarrer/in m/f (-/-nen) *pastor, vicar*
Pfeffer m (-) *pepper*
Pferd n (-e) *horse*
Pfingsten n (-) *Whitsun, Pentecost*
Pfirsich m (-e) *peach*
Pflanze f (-n) *plant*
Pflaume f (-n) *plum*
Pflichtfach n (-̈er) *(compulsory) subject*
Pfund n (-e) *pound*

Pfund Sterling n *pound sterling*
Physik f *physics*
physisch adj/adv *physical(ly)*
Picknick n (-e/-s) *picnic*
picknicken v *to (have a) picnic*
Pilz m (-e) *mushroom, toadstool*
Plakat n (-e) *poster*
Plan m (-̈e) *plan*
planen v *to plan*
Plastik n *plastic*
Platz m (-̈e) *place, room, seat, square, court*
plaudern v *to chat*
plötzlich adv *suddenly*
PLZ (= Postleitzahl) f *post code*
Polen n *Poland*
Polizei f *police*
Polizeiwache f (-n) *police station*
Polizist/in m/f (-en/-nen) *policeman/woman*
Pommes frites n pl *chips*
Popmusik f *pop music*
Portemonnaie n (-s) *wallet, purse*
Portion f (-en) *portion, helping*
Post f *post, post office*
Postamt n (-̈er) *post office*
Postbote/botin m/f (-n/-nen) *postman/woman*
Poster n (-/-s) *poster*
Postkarte f (-n) *postcard*
Postleitzahl f (-en) *post code*
praktisch adj/adv *practical(ly)*
Pralinen f pl *chocolates*
Preis m (-e) *price*
Preisliste f (-n) *price list*
preiswert adj *cheap, good value*
Priester m (-) *priest*
prima adj *great*
privat adj *private, personal*
Privatschule f (-n) *private school*
pro prep *per*
pro Stunde *per hour*
probieren v *to try out*
Problem n (-e) *problem*
produzieren v *to produce*
Programm n (-e) *program(me)*
Programmierer/in m/f (-/-nen) *computer programmer*
Projekt n (-e) *plan, project*
Projektor m (-en) *projector*
Prospekt m (-e) *leaflet*
prost! *cheers!*
Prozent n (-e) *per cent*
prüfen v *to test, to examine, to check*
Prüfung f (-en) *exam*
Pullover, Pulli m (-, -s) *pullover*
Punkt m (-e) *point, full stop*
pünktlich adj/adv *punctual, on time*
Pute f (-n) *turkey (hen)*
putzen v *to clean*

# Q

Quadrat n (-e) *square*
Qualifikation f (-en) *qualification*
Qualität f (-en) *quality*
Quantität f (-en) *quantity*
Quatsch m *rubbish (nonsense)*
Querflöte f (-n) *flute*
Quittung f (-en) *receipt*
Quizsendung f (-en) *quiz show*

# R

Rabatt m (-e) *discount*
Rad n (-̈er) *bicycle, wheel*
Radfahren n *cycling*
Radfahrer/in m/f (-/-nen) *cyclist*
Radiergummi m (-s) *rubber, eraser*
Rand m (-̈er) *edge*
Rapmusik f *rap*
Rasen m (-) *lawn*
Rasse f (-n) *race (people)*
Rassenproblem n (-e) *race problem*
Rassismus m *racism*
rassistisch adj *racist*
Raststätte f (-n) *motorway services*
raten v ir *to advise*
Rathaus n (-̈er) *town hall*
Rauch m *smoke*
rauchen v *to smoke*
Raucher(in) m/f (-/-nen) *smoker*
Realschule f (-n) *secondary school*
rechnen v *to count, to calculate*

Rechnung f (-en) *bill*
recht haben v ir *to be right*
Rechteck n (-e) *rectangle*
rechts adv *right*
Rechtsanwalt/anwältin m/f (-̈e/-nen) *lawyer*
rechtzeitig adj/adv *punctual / on time*
recyceln v *to recycle*
Rede f (-n) *speech*
reden v *to talk*
reduziert adj *reduced*
Regal n (-e) *shelves*
Regel f (-n) *rule*
regelmäßig adj/adv *regular(ly)*
Regen m (-) *rain*
Regenmantel m (-̈) *raincoat*
Regenschirm m (-e) *umbrella*
regnen v *to rain*
regnerisch adj *rainy*
reich adj *rich*
reichen v *to be enough, to reach*
reif adj *mature, ripe*
Reifen m (-) *tyre*
Reifenpanne f (-n) *puncture*
Reihe f (-n) *row (of seats etc.)*
Reihenhaus n (-̈er) *terraced house*
reinigen v *to clean*
Reinigung f *cleaning, dry cleaning*
Reis m *rice*
Reise f (-n) *journey*
Reisebüro n (-s) *travel agency*
Reisebus m (-se) *coach*
reisen v *to travel*
Reisende(r) m/f *traveller*
Reisepass m (-̈e) *passport*
Reisescheck m (-s) *traveller's cheque*
Reisetasche f (-n) *holdall, travel bag*
Reiseziel n (-e) *destination*
reiten v ir *to ride*
Reiten n *horse riding*
Reklame f (-n) *advert*
Religion f (-en) *religion, R.E.*
rennen v ir *to run*
Rennen n (-) *running, racing, race*
Rentner/in m/f (-/-nen) *pensioner*
Reparatur f (-en) *repair*
reparieren v *to repair*
reservieren v *to reserve*
Reservierung f (-en) *reservation*
Rest m (-e) *rest, remainder*
Resultat n (-e) *result*
retten v *to save*
Rezept n (-e) *prescription, recipe*
Rezeption f (-en) *reception*
Rhein m *the Rhine*
richtig adj *right, true*
Richtung f (-en) *direction*
riechen v ir *to smell*
Riegel m (-) *bar (of chocolate etc.)*
Rindfleisch n *beef*
Ring m (-e) *ring*
Risiko n (-s/Risiken) *risk*
Rock m (-̈e) *skirt*
Rockmusik f *rock music*
roh adj/adv *raw, rough(ly)*
Rollbrett n (-er) *skateboard*
Roller m (-) *scooter*
Rollschuh laufen v ir *to go roller-skating*
Rolltreppe f (-n) *escalator*
Roman m (-e) *novel*
romantisch adj *romantic(ally)*
rosa adj *pink*
Rosenkohl m (-e) *Brussels sprout*
rot adj *red*
Rücken m (-) *back*
Rückfahrkarte f (-n) *return ticket*
Rückfahrt f (-en) *return journey*
Rucksack m (-̈e) *rucksack*
rückwärts adv *backwards*
rudern v *to row*
Ruderboot n (-e) *rowing boat*
rufen v ir *to call, to shout*
Rugby n *rugby*
Ruhe f *peace, calm*
ruhig adj *peaceful, calm*
rund adj *round (shape)*
Rundfahrt f (-en) *tour (on transport)*
Rundgang m (-̈e) *tour (walking)*
Russe/Russin m/f (-n/-nen) *Russian*
russisch adj *Russian*
Russland n *Russia*

# S

Saal m (Säle) *hall, ballroom*
Sache f (-n) *thing*
Sackgasse f (-n) *cul-de-sac*
Saft m (-̈e) *juice*
sagen v *to say, to tell*
Sahne f *cream*
Salat m (-e) *salad, lettuce*
Salz n (-e) *salt*
Salzkartoffeln f pl *boiled potatoes*
sammeln v *to collect*
Sammlung f (-en) *collection*
Samstag m *Saturday*
Sand m (-e) *sand*
Sandburg f (-en) *sand castle*
Sandale f (-n) *sandal*
sanft adj/adv *soft(ly), gentle/gently*
Sänger/in m/f (-/-nen) *singer*
Satellitenfernsehen n *satellite TV*
satt adj *full (having eaten)*
satt haben v ir *to be fed up with something*
sauber adj *clean*
sauer adj *sour, angry*
Sauerkraut n *pickled cabbage*
Sauerstoff m *oxygen*
saurer Regen m (-) *acid rain*
S-Bahn f (-en) *suburban railway*
Schach n *chess*
Schachtel f (-n) *small box (e.g. of chocolates)*
schade adj *(what a) shame*
schaden v *to damage, to harm*
Schaden m (-̈) *damage*
schädlich adj *harmful*
Schaf n (-e) *sheep*
schaffen v ir *to create, to make*
Schal m (-s/-e) *scarf, shawl*
Schale f (-n) *skin, peel, shell*
Schalter m (-) *ticket office, switch*
schämen sich v *to be ashamed*
scharf adj *sharp, hot (spicy)*
Schaschlik n (-s) *kebab*
Schatten m (-) *shadow*
schattig adj *shady*
schauen v *to look*
Schauer m (-) *(rain) shower*
Schaufenster n (-) *display window*
Schauspieler/in m/f (-/-nen) *actor/actress*
Scheck m (-s) *cheque*
Scheckheft n (-e) *cheque book*
Scheibe f (-n) *slice*
scheiden (sich scheiden lassen) v ir *to get divorced*
Schein m (-e) *banknote*
scheinen v ir *to seem, to appear, to shine*
Scheinwerfer m (-) *headlight*
schenken v *to give (a present)*
Schere f (-n) *pair of scissors*
Schichtarbeit f *shift work*
schick adj/adv *stylish(ly)*
schicken v *to send*
schießen v ir *to shoot, to score*
Schiff n (-e) *ship*
Schild n (-er) *signpost*
Schildkröte f (-n) *tortoise*
Schinken m (-) *ham*
Schlafanzug m (-̈e) *pyjamas*
schlafen v ir *to sleep*
Schlafraum m (-̈e) *dormitory, bedroom*
Schlafsack m (-̈e) *sleeping bag*
Schlafwagen m (-) *sleeping car*
Schlafzimmer n (-) *bedroom*
schlagen v ir *to hit, to knock*
Schläger m (-) *racquet, stick, bat*
Schlagsahne f *whipped cream*
Schlagzeug n (-e) *drums*
Schlange f (-n) *snake, queue*
Schlange stehen v ir *to queue*
schlank adj *slim*
schlecht adj *bad*
schließen v ir *to close*
Schließfach n (-̈er) *locker*
schließlich adv *eventually, after all, finally*
schlimm adj *bad*
Schlips m (-e) *tie*
Schlittschuhlaufen n *ice skating*
Schloss n (-̈er) *castle, lock*
Schlüssel m (-) *key*

nouns — **m:** *masculine* **f:** *feminine* **n:** *neuter* **pl:** *plural* **v:** *verb* **v sep:** *separable verb* **v ir:** *irregular verb* **adj:** *adjective* **adv:** *adverb*

Schlüsselbund m or n (-e) keyring, bunch of keys
Schlussverkauf m (-¨e) (end-of-season) sale
schmal adj narrow
schmecken v to taste, to taste good
Schmerz m (-en) pain
schmerzhaft adj painful
Schmuck m (-e) jewellery
schmutzig adj dirty
Schnaps m (-¨e) schnapps, spirits
Schnee m snow
schneiden v ir to cut
schneien v to snow
schnell adj/adv quick(ly)
Schnellimbiss m (-e) snack bar
Schnitzel n (-) (veal/pork) escalope
Schnupfen m (-) a cold
Schnurrbart m (-¨e) moustache
Schokolade f (-n) chocolate
schon adv already
schön adj beautiful, fine (weather)
Schornstein m (-e) chimney
Schotte/Schottin m/f (-n/-nen) Scot
schottisch adj Scottish
Schottland n Scotland
Schrägstrich m (-e) forward slash
Schrank m (-¨e) cupboard
schrecklich adj/adv terrible/terribly
Schreibblock m (-s or -¨e) writing pad
schreiben v ir to write
Schreibpapier n writing paper
Schreibtisch m (-e) desk
Schreibwarengeschäft n (-e) stationer's
schreien v ir to scream/shout
schriftlich adj written
Schublade f (-n) drawer
schüchtern adj/adv shy(ly)
Schuh m (-e) shoe
Schulabschluss m (-¨e) school leaving certificate
Schulbildung f education
Schulbuch n (-¨er) school book
Schulbus m (-se) school bus
Schuldirektor/in m/f (-en/-nen) head teacher
Schule f (-n) school
Schüler/in m/f (-/-nen) school pupil
Schüleraustausch m (-e) school exchange
Schülerzeitung f (-en) school magazine
Schulhof m (-¨e) school playground
Schulleiter/in m/f (-/-nen) headmaster/mistress
Schulstunde f (-n) lesson
Schultag m (-e) school day
Schultasche f (-n) school bag
Schulter f (-n) shoulder
Schüssel f (-n) bowl
schützen v to protect
schwach adj weak, poor (e.g. schoolwork)
Schwager/Schwägerin m/f (¨e/-nen) brother/sister-in-law
schwänzen v to skip, to play truant
schwarz adj black
schwarze Johannisbeere f (-n) blackcurrant
Schwarzwald m the Black Forest
schwatzen v to chat
schweigen v ir to be silent, to say nothing
Schweinefleisch n pork
Schweiz f Switzerland
Schweizer/in m/f (-/-nen) Swiss person
schweizerisch adj Swiss
schwer adj/adv heavy/heavily, difficult/with difficulty, serious(ly)
Schwester f (-n) sister
schwierig adj difficult
Schwimmbad n (¨er) swimming pool
Schwimmen n swimming
schwimmen v ir to swim
See f/m (-n) sea (f); lake (m)
seekrank adj seasick
Segelboot n (-e) sailing boat
segeln v to sail
sehen v ir to see
sehenswert adj worth seeing
Sehenswürdigkeit f (-en) sight (something worth seeing)
sehr adv very
Seide f (-n) silk
Seife f (-n) soap
Seifenoper f (-n) soap opera
sein v ir to be
seit prep + dat since
seitdem conj since
Seite f (-n) side, page
Sekretär/in m/f (-e/-nen) secretary
Sekretariat n (-e) office
Sekt m (-e) (German) champagne
Sekunde f (-n) second
selbst pron/adv self/even
selbständig adj/adv independent(ly)
Selbstbedienung f self-service
selten adj/adv rare(ly), infrequent(ly), seldom
Semester n (-) term, semester
senden v to send
Sendung f (-en) (TV) programme
Senf m (-e) mustard
sensibel adj/adv sensitive(ly)
September m September
Serie f (-n) series (e.g. on TV)
servieren v to serve
Serviette f (-n) serviette, napkin
Sessel m (-) armchair
setzen sich v to sit down
sicher adj/adv certain(ly), sure(ly)
Sicherheitsgurt m (-e) seat belt
Silber n silver
Silvester n New Year's Eve
simsen v to text
singen v ir to sing
Sitz m (-e) seat
sitzen v ir to sit
sitzen bleiben v ir to repeat a (school) year
Ski fahren v ir to ski
Skifahren n skiing
Skilehrer/in m/f (-/-nen) ski instructor
Slip m (-s) briefs
SMS f text message
SMV (= Schülermitverwaltung) f school/student council
sniffen v to sniff/snort (drugs)
so ... wie as ... as
so dass so that
so viel wie as much as
sobald conj as soon as
Socke f (-n) sock
Sofa n (-s) sofa
sofort adv immediately
sogar adv even
Sohn m (-¨e) son
Soldat/in m/f (-en/-nen) soldier
sollen v ir to be supposed to
Sommer m (-) summer
Sonderangebot n (-e) special offer
Sonnabend m Saturday
Sonne f (-n) sun
sonnen sich v to sun oneself
Sonnenbrand m sunburn
Sonnenbrille f (-n) sunglasses
Sonnencreme f (-s) suncream
Sonnenschirm m (-e) sunshade
sonnig adj sunny
Sonntag m Sunday
sonst adv otherwise
sonst nichts nothing else
Sorge f (-n) worry
sorgen für v to take care of
Soße f (-n) sauce, gravy
Souvenir n (-s) souvenir
sowohl ... als (auch) both ... and
Spanien n Spain
Spanier/in m/f (-/-nen) Spaniard
Spanisch n Spanish (language)
spanisch adj Spanish
spannend adj exciting, tense
sparen v to save (up)
Sparkasse f (-n) savings bank
sparsam adj/adv thrifty, economic(al), sparing(ly)
Spaß m fun
spät adj late
später adj/adv later
spazieren v to walk
spazieren gehen v ir to go for a walk
Spaziergang m (-¨e) walk
Speck m (-e) bacon
speichern v to store
Speisekarte f (-n) menu
Speisesaal m (--säle) dining room
Speisewagen m (-) restaurant car
spenden v to donate, to give
Spezialität f (-en) speciality
Spiegel m (-) mirror
Spiegelei n (-er) fried egg
Spiel n (-e) game, match
spielen v to play
Spieler/in m/f (-/-nen) player
Spielfilm m (-e) feature film
Spielplatz m (-¨e) play area
Spielzeug n (-e) toy
Spielzimmer n (-) playroom
Spinat m (-e) spinach
Spitze! brilliant!
Spitzname m (-n) nickname
Sport m sport, PE
Sport treiben v ir to do sport
Sportausrüstung f sports equipment
Sporthalle f (-n) sports hall
sportlich adj sporty
Sportplatz m (-¨e) sports field
Sportzentrum n (-zentren) sports centre
Sprache f (-n) language
Sprachlabor n (-s or -e) language lab
Spraydose f (-n) aerosol (can)
sprechen v ir to speak
Sprechstunde f (-n) surgery/consulting hours
springen v ir to jump
Spritze f (-n) syringe, injection
spritzen v to spray, to inject
Sprudel m (-) sparkling mineral water, fizzy drink
Spülbecken n (-) sink
Spüle f (-n) sink
spülen v to wash up
Spülmaschine f (-n) dishwasher
staatlich adj state
Stadion n (Stadien) stadium
Stadt f (-¨e) town
Stadtbummel m (-) stroll around town
Stadtführer m (-) town/city guidebook
Stadtführung f (-en) guided tour of town/city
Stadtmitte f (-n) town centre
Stadtplan m (-¨e) street map
Stadtrand m (-¨er) edge of the town
Stadtrundfahrt f (-en) guided tour of the town
Stadtteil m (-e) district
Stadtviertel n (-) district
Stadtzentrum n (-zentren) town centre
Stahl m steel
Star m (-s) celebrity
stark adj strong
starten v to start, to take off (plane)
statt prep + gen instead of
stattfinden v ir sep to take place
Stau m (-e or -s) traffic jam
Staub saugen v to hoover/vacuum
stecken v to place, to insert, to stick
Stehcafé n (-s) stand-up cafe
stehen v ir to stand, to suit someone (e.g. clothing)
stehlen v ir to steal
steigen v ir to climb, to rise, to get on
steil adj/adv steep(ly)
Stein m (-e) stone
Stelle f (-n) job (position)
stellen v to put/place
Stellenangebote n pl situations vacant
Steppdecke f (-n) duvet, quilt
sterben v ir to die
Stereoanlage f (-n) stereo
Steward/ess m/f (-s/-en) air steward/stewardess
Stiefel m (-) boot
Stift m (-e) pen
still adj quiet, peaceful
stimmt! right!
Stock m (-) storey
Stockwerk n storey
Stoff m (-e) material
stolz adj proud
stoppen v to stop
Strand m (-¨e) beach
Straße f (-n) street
Straßenbahn f (-en) tram
Straßenkarte f (-n) street map
Straßenschild n (-er) roadsign
Streik m (-s) strike
Streit m (-e) argument, quarrel
streiten v ir to quarrel
streiten sich v ir to argue, to quarrel
streng adj strict
stressig adj stressful
Strom m electricity
Strumpf m (-¨e) sock, stocking
Strumpfhose f (-n) tights
Student/in m/f (-en/-nen) student
studieren v to study
Stück n (-e) piece, coin
Stückchen n (-) (little) piece, bit
Studium n (Studien) (course of) study
Stufe f (-n) stair, level
Stuhl m (-¨e) chair
Stunde f (-n) hour, lesson
Stundenplan m (-¨e) timetable
Sturm m (-¨e) storm
stürmisch adj stormy
suchen v to seek, to look for
Sucht f (-¨e) addiction
süchtig adj addicted
Südamerika n South America
Süden m the South
südlich adj/adv in/to the south
Supermarkt m (-¨e) supermarket
Suppe f (-n) soup
Surfbrett n (-er) surfboard
surfen v to surf (im Internet surfen = to surf the internet)
süß adj sweet
Süßigkeiten f pl sweets
sympathisch adj nice (person)

## T

Tabak m (-e) tobacco
Tabakwarengeschäft n (-e) tobacconist's
Tablett n (-s or -e) tray
Tablette f (-n) tablet, pill
Tafel f (-n) (black)board, bar (e.g. of chocolate)
Tag m (-e) day
Tagebuch n (¨er) diary
Tagesgericht n (-e) dish of the day
Tageskarte f (-n) menu/dish (of the day)
Tagesmenü n (-s) menu of the day
täglich adv daily
Tal n (-¨er) valley
tanken v to fill up (e.g. petrol tank)
Tankstelle f (-n) petrol station
Tannenbaum m (-¨e) fir tree, Christmas tree
Tante f (-n) aunt
Tanz m (-¨e) dance
tanzen v to dance
Tanzen n dancing
Tapete f (-n) wallpaper
Tasche f (-n) bag, pocket
Taschenbuch n (¨er) paperback
Taschengeld n (-er) pocket money
Taschenlampe f (-n) torch
Taschenmesser n (-) pocket knife, pen-knife
Taschenrechner m (-) calculator
Taschentuch n (¨er) handkerchief
Tasse f (-n) cup
Tastatur f (-en) keyboard
Taste f (-n) key (of keyboard)
Tätowierung f (-en) tattoo
Taufe f (-n) baptism, christening
Taxi n (-s) taxi
Taxifahrer/in m/f (-/-nen) taxi driver
Techniker/in m/f (-/-nen) technician
Technologie f (-n) technology
Tee m (-s) tea
Teekanne f (-n) teapot
Teelöffel m (-) teaspoon
Teil m or n (-e) part
teilen v share, split
Teilnahme f (-n) participation
Teilzeit f part-time
Telefon n (-e) telephone
Telefonanruf m (-e) telephone call
Telefonbuch n (¨er) phone book
telefonieren v to telephone
Telefonnummer f (-n) phone number
Telefonzelle f (-n) phone box
Teller m (-) plate
Tellerwäscher/in m/f (-/-nen) dishwasher
Temperatur f (-en) temperature
Tennis n tennis
Teppich m (-e) carpet
Termin m (-e) date, appointment, deadline
Terminkalender m (-) diary (for appointments)
Terrasse f (-n) terrace, patio
teuer adj expensive
Theater n (-) theatre
Theatergruppe f (-n) theatre group
Theaterstück n (-e) play
Theke f (-n) counter
Therapie f (-n) therapy
Thunfisch m (-e) tuna
tief adj deep
Tiefkühlschrank m (¨e) freezer
Tiefkühltruhe f (-n) chest freezer
Tier n (-e) animal
Tierarzt/ärztin m/f (-¨e/-nen) vet
Tierheim n (-e) animal home
tippen v to type
Tisch m (-e) table
Tischdecke f (-n) tablecloth
Tischler/in m/f (-/-nen) joiner, carper
Tischtennis n table tennis
Tischtuch n (-¨er) tablecloth
Toastbrot n bread for toasting
Tochter f (-¨) daughter
Tod m (-e) death
Toilette f (-n) toilet
Toilettenpapier n (-e) toilet paper
toll adj great
Tomate f (-n) tomato
Ton m (-¨e) tone, sound
Topf m (-¨e) pot, pan
Tor n (-e) gate, goal
Torte f (-n) gateau, cake
tot adj dead
total adj/adv total(ly)
Tour f (-en) tour
Tourismus m tourism
Tourist/in m/f (-en/-nen) tourist
Touristeninformation f (-en) tourist information (office)
tragen v ir to carry, to wear
Tragödie f (-n) tragedy
trainieren v to train, to coach
Trainingsanzug m (¨e) track suit
Trainingsschuhe m pl trainers
Traube f (-n) grape
Traum m (-¨e) dream
traurig adj sad
Trauring m (-e) wedding ring
treffen v ir to meet
Treffpunkt m (-e) meeting place
Treibhauseffekt m greenhouse effec
Treibhausgas n (-e) greenhouse gas
trennen sich v to split up
Treppe f (-n) staircase
Treppenhaus n (¨er) stairwell
treten v ir to step, to kick
Trimester n (-) term
trinken v ir drink
Trinkgeld n (-er) tip
Trinkwasser n drinking water
trocken adj dry
trocknen v to dry
Trompete f (-n) trumpet
trotz prep + gen despite
trotzdem adv nevertheless
Truthahn m (¨e) turkey
tschüss bye
Tube f (-n) tube
Tuch n (¨er) cloth
tun v ir to do
Tunnel m the Channel Tunnel
Tür f (-en) door
Türkei f Turkey
Turm m (-¨e) tower
turnen v to do gymnastics
Turnen n gymnastics, PE
Turnhalle f (-n) gym
Turnschuhe m pl trainers
Tüte f (-n) small bag
Typ m (-en) type, bloke
typisch adj/adv typical(ly)

## U

U-Bahn f (-en) underground (railwa
U-Bahnstation f (-en) underground station
übel adj nasty, ill
üben v to practise

prep: preposition pron: pronoun conj: conjunction bits in brackets: plural ending (¨): plural — add umlaut

German—English Dictionary

r prep + acc/dat  over, above
rall adv  everywhere
rbevölkert adj  overpopulated
rfahrt f (-en)  (sea) crossing
rhaupt nicht  not at all
rmorgen adv  the day after tomorrow
rnachten v  to stay the night
rnachtung f (-en)  overnight stay
rqueren v  to cross
rrascht adj  surprised
rwachen v  to supervise
gens adv  moreover, by the way
ng f (-en)  practice
n (river) bank
f (-en)  watch, clock, o'clock
aviolette Strahlen m pl  UV rays
prep + acc  around
.. zu conj  in order to
rage f (-n)  opinion poll, survey
jeben von  surrounded by
gebung f (-en)  surroundings, neighbourhood
kleidekabine f (-n)  changing cubicle
kleideraum m (-e)  changing room
eitung f (-en)  diversion, detour
schlag m (-e)  envelope
steigen v sep ir  change (trains)
welt f  environment
weltfeindlich adj  environmentally damaging
weltfreundlich adj  environmentally friendly
weltproblem n (-e)  environmental problem
ziehen v sep ir  to move (house)
ziehen sich v sep ir  to get changed
conj  and
all m (-e)  accident
adj  unfit
eundlich adj  unfriendly
eduldig adj  impatient
efähr adv  about, approximately
erecht adj  unjust, unfair
esund adj  unhealthy
laublich adj  unbelievable
öflich adj  impolite
orm f (-en)  uniform
versität f (-en) (Uni)  university
möglich adj  impossible
rdentlich adj  untidy
echt haben v ir  to be wrong
icher adj  uncertain, insecure
ympathisch adj  unpleasant
en adv  at the bottom, below, downstairs
er prep + acc/dat  under
ergeschoss n  basement
erhalten sich v ir  to converse
erhaltung f  entertainment
erhaltungsmöglichkeiten f pl  entertainment, things to do
erhose f (-n)  underpants
erkunft f (-e)  accommodation
ernehmungslustig adj  enterprising, adventurous
erricht m  lessons, classes
errichten v  to teach, to inform
erschied m (-e)  difference
erschiedlich adj  different, variable
erschreiben v ir  to sign
erschrift f (-en)  signature
erstützen v  to support
ertasse f (-n)  saucer
erwäsche f  underwear
erwegs adv  on the way
orstellbar adj  unimaginable
ufrieden adj  discontented
ub m (-e)  holiday
v. (= und so weiter)  etc.

dalismus m  vandalism
ille f  vanilla
er m (-)  father
m (-s)  dad
etarier/in m/f (-/-nen)  vegetarian
antwortlich adj  responsible
antwortung f (-en)  responsibility
bal adj  verbal
bessern v  to improve
besserung f (-en)  improvement, correction


verbieten v ir  to forbid
verbinden v ir  to connect
Verbindung f (-en)  connection
verboten adj  prohibited, forbidden
Verbrauch m  use, consumption
Verbrechen n (-)  crime
verbringen v ir  spend (time)
verdienen v  to earn, to deserve
Verein m (-e)  club, organisation
Vereinigte Staaten m pl  USA
Vergangenheit f  past, past tense
vergeben v ir  to forgive, to give away
vergessen v ir  to forget
Vergleich m (-e)  comparison
Verhältnis n (-se)  relationship, ratio
verheiratet adj  married
verhindern v  to prevent
verkaufen v  to sell
Verkäufer/in m/f (-/-nen)  salesperson
Verkehr m  traffic
Verkehrsamt n (-er)  tourist information office
Verkehrsmittel n (-)  mode of transport
Verkehrsunfall m (-e)  road accident
verlassen v ir  to leave, to abandon
verletzen v  to injure
Verletzung f (-en)  injury
verlieren v ir  to lose
verloben sich v  to get engaged
verlobt adj  engaged
Verlobungsring m (-e)  engagement ring
vermeiden v ir  to avoid, to prevent, to warn
vermieten v  to rent out
verpacken v  to pack, to wrap up
Verpackung f (-en)  packing
verpassen v  to miss (bus/train etc.)
Versammlung f (-en)  meeting, assembly
verschieden adj/adv  different(ly), various(ly)
verschmutzen v  to dirty, to pollute
Verschmutzung f (-en)  pollution
verschwinden v ir  to disappear
verspäten sich v  to be late
Verspätung f (-en)  delay, lateness
versprechen v ir  to promise
verstehen v ir  to understand
verstehen sich v ir  to get on well
Versuch m (-e)  experiment, attempt
versuchen v  to try
Vertreter/in m/f (-/-nen)  representative
verursachen v  to cause
Verwandte(r)  relative
verzeihen v ir  to forgive
Verzeihung!  Sorry!
Vetter m (-)  cousin
viel/e pron/adj  lots, many
Viel Glück!  good luck
vielleicht adv  perhaps, maybe
viereckig adj  rectangular
Viertel n (-)  quarter
Virus n/m (Viren)  virus
Vitamine n pl  vitamins
Vogel m (-)  bird
Volksmusik f  folk music
voll adj  full
völlig adv  completely
Vollpension f  full board (at hotel)
von prep + dat  from, of
vor prep + acc/dat  before, in front of, outside
vor kurzem  recently
voraus adv  in front, ahead (im Voraus = in advance)
vorausgesetzt, dass  provided that
vorbei adv  past, by
vorbeifahren v sep ir  to go past
vorbeigehen v sep ir  to pass by, to go by
vorbereiten v sep  to prepare
Vorfahrt f  right of way
vorgehen v sep ir  to go forward, to go on ahead
vorgestern adv  the day before yesterday
vorhaben v sep ir  to intend, to have planned
Vorhang m (-e)  curtain
vorher adv  beforehand, previously
vorkommen v  to occur


Vorliebe f (-n)  preference
Vormittag m (-e)  morning
vormittags adv  in the morning(s)
vorn/e adv  at the front, in front
Vorname m (-n)  first name
Vorort m (-e)  suburb
vorschlagen v sep ir  to suggest, to propose
Vorspeise f (-n)  starter
vorstellen v sep  to introduce
vorstellen sich v sep  to introduce oneself, to imagine
Vorstellung f (-en)  showing, performance, idea
Vorteil m (-e)  advantage
Vorwahl f (-en)  area code
vorwärts adv  forwards
vorziehen v sep ir  prefer

## W

wachsen v ir  to grow
Wagen m (-)  car
Wahl f (-en)  choice
Wahlfach n (-er)  option subject
wählen v  to choose, to dial
wahr adj  true (nicht wahr? = isn't it?)
während conj  during, while
Wahrheit f (-en)  truth
wahrscheinlich adv  probably
Wald m (-er)  forest
Wales n  Wales
Waliser/in m/f (-/-nen)  Welsh person
walisisch adj  Welsh
Wand f (-e)  wall
wandern v  to walk, hike
Wanderung f (-en)  walk, hike
wann adv  when
Warenhaus n (-er)  (department) store
warm adj  warm
warnen v  to warn
warten v  to wait
warten auf v  to wait for
Warteraum m (-e)  waiting room
Wartesaal m (-säle)  waiting room
Wartezeit f  waiting period, wait
Wartezimmer n (-)  waiting room
warum adv  why
was pron  what
was für…  what kind of…
Waschbecken n (-)  washbasin
Wäsche f  washing, underwear
waschen (sich) v ir  to wash (oneself)
Wäscherei f (-en)  laundry
Waschküche f (-n)  laundry room
Waschmaschine f (-n)  washing machine
Waschpulver n (-)  washing powder
Waschsalon m (-s)  launderette
Wasser n  water
Wasserhahn m (-e)  tap
Wasserski n  waterskiing
Wasserskilaufen n  waterskiing
Wasserverschmutzung f (-en)  water pollution
Webseite f (-n)  web page
Website f (-s)  website
Wechselgeld n  change
Wechselkurs m (-e)  exchange rate
wechseln v  to change
Wechselstube f (-n)  bureau de change
wecken v  to wake someone
Wecker m (-)  alarm clock
weder ... noch conj.  neither ... nor
Weg m (-e)  way, path
wegen prep + gen  because of
weggehen v sep ir  to go away
wegwerfen v sep ir  to throw away
wehtun v ir sep  to hurt
weiblich adj  female
weich adj/adv  soft(ly)
Weihnachten n (-)  Christmas
Weihnachtsbaum m (-e)  Christmas tree
Weihnachtsmarkt m (-e)  Christmas market
weil conj  because
Wein m (-e)  wine
weinen v  to cry
Weintraube f (-n)  grape
Weise f (-n)  way
weiß adj  white
Weißbrot n (-e)  white bread


weit adj  far
weiterfahren v sep ir  to continue
weitermachen v sep  to continue (e.g. studies), to carry on
Welle f (-n)  wave
Wellensittich m (-e)  budgerigar
Welt f (-en)  world
weltweit adj/adv  worldwide
wem pron  who, to whom
wen pron  who, whom
wenig pron/adj  little, few
weniger adv  less
wenigstens adv  at least
wenn conj  if, when
wer pron  who
Werbung f (-en)  advertising
werden v ir  to become, to get
werfen v ir  to throw
Werken n  handicrafts, design technology
Werkstatt f (-en)  workshop, garage
Werkzeug n (-e)  tool(s)
wertvoll adj  valuable
Wespe f (-n)  wasp
wessen pron  whose
Westen m  the west
westlich adj/adv  in/to the west
Wetter n (-)  weather
Wetterbericht m (-e)  weather report
Wettervorhersage f (-n)  weather forecast
wichtig adj  important
wie adv  how, as, like
wie bitte?  pardon?
wie geht's?  how are you?
wie viel(e) adv  how much/many
wieder adv  again
wiederholen v  to repeat
wiegen v ir  to weigh
Wien n  Vienna
Wiese f (-n)  meadow
wieso adv  why
willkommen adj  welcome
Wind m (-e)  wind
windig adj  windy
windsurfen v  to windsurf
Winter m (-)  winter
wirklich adv  really
wissen v ir  to know (facts)
witzig adj  funny
wo adv  where
Woche f (-n)  week
Wochenende n (-n)  weekend
wöchentlich adj/adv  weekly
woher adv  where from
wohin adv  where to
Wohltätigkeit f  charity
Wohnblock m (-e or -s)  block of flats
wohnen v  to live
Wohnort m (-e)  place where you live
Wohnung f (-en)  flat
Wohnwagen m (-)  caravan
Wohnzimmer n (-)  living room
Wolke f (-n)  cloud
wolkenlos adj  cloudless
wolkig adj  cloudy
Wolle f (-n)  wool
wollen v ir  to want
Wort n (-e or -er)  word
Wörterbuch n (-er)  dictionary
Wunde f (-n)  wound
wunderbar adj  wonderful
wunderschön adj  really beautiful
Wunsch m (-e)  wish
wünschen v  to wish, to want
wünschen sich v  to desire, to wish for
Wurst f (-e)  sausage
Wurstbude f (-n)  sausage stand

## Z

z.B. (= zum Beispiel)  for example (e.g.)
Zahl f (-en)  figure
zahlen v  to pay
zählen v  to count
zahlreich adj  numerous
Zahn m (-e)  tooth
Zahnarzt/ärztin m/f (-e/-nen)  dentist
Zahnbürste f (-n)  toothbrush
Zahnpasta f (-pasten)  toothpaste
Zahnschmerzen m pl  toothache
ZDF  German television company


Zebrastreifen m  zebra crossing
Zeichentrickfilm m (-e)  cartoon
Zeichnen n  drawing (subject)
zeichnen v  to draw
zeigen v  to show
Zeit f (-en)  time
Zeitpunkt m (-e)  moment
Zeitschrift f (-en)  magazine
Zeitung f (-en)  newspaper
Zeitungskiosk m (-e)  newspaper stall
Zelt n (-e)  tent
zelten v  to camp
Zelten n  camping
Zentimeter n/m (-)  centimetre
Zentralheizung f (-en)  central heating
Zentrum n (Zentren)  centre
zerbrechlich adj  fragile
zerstören v  to destroy
Zettel m (-)  piece of paper, note
Zeugnis n (-se)  school report
Zeug n (-e)  stuff, things
ziehen v ir  to pull
Ziel n (-e)  aim, goal
ziemlich adv  quite
Zigarette f (-n)  cigarette
Zimmer n (-)  room
Zimmermädchen n (-)  maid
Zitrone f (-n)  lemon
Zoll m (-e)  customs, toll
Zoo m (-s)  zoo
zornig adj  angry
zu adj/adv/prep + dat  to, too (e.g. too old), closed
zu Ende  over, finished
zu Fuß  on foot
zu Händen von  for the attention of
zu Hause  at home
Zucker m  sugar
zuerst adv  at first, first of all
zufällig adj  accidental, random
zufrieden adj  satisfied
Zug m (-e)  train
Zugführer/in m/f (-/-nen)  guard (on train)
Zuhause n  home
zuhören v sep  to listen to
Zukunft f  future
zuletzt adv  at last, in the end
zum Beispiel  for example
zum Mitnehmen adj  take away (meals)
zum Wohl!  cheers!
zumachen v sep  to close, to shut
zunehmen v sep ir  to increase, to put on weight
zurück adv  back
zurückfahren v sep ir  to go back, to drive back
zurückgehen v sep ir  to return
zurückkommen v sep ir  to come back
zurückklassen v sep ir  to leave
zurückrufen v sep ir  to call back
zurückstellen v sep  to put back
zusammen adv  together
Zuschauer/in m/f (-/-nen)  spectator, audience
Zuschlag m (-e)  supplement
zusehen v sep ir  to look on, to watch
zustimmen v sep  to agree
Zweibettzimmer n (-)  twin-bed room
zweitens adv  secondly
zweiter Klasse  second class
Zwiebel f (-n)  onion
Zwilling m (-e)  twin
zwischen prep + acc/dat  between
zwo = zwei (telephone)

---

nouns — **m**: masculine  **f**: feminine  **n**: neuter  **pl**: plural  **v**: verb  **v sep**: separable verb  **v ir**: irregular verb  **adj**: adjective  **adv**: adverb

# Index